Reading Faulkner
ABSALOM, ABSALOM!

READING FAULKNER SERIES
Noel Polk, *Series Editor*

Reading Faulkner

ABSALOM, ABSALOM!

Glossary and Commentary by

JOSEPH R. URGO

and

NOEL POLK

University Press of Mississippi / Jackson

www.upress.state.ms.us

The University Press of Mississippi is a member
of the Association of American University Presses.

Copyright © 2010 by University Press of Mississippi
All rights reserved
Manufactured in the United States of America

First printing 2010

∞

Library of Congress Cataloging-in-Publication Data

Urgo, Joseph R.
Reading Faulkner. Absalom, Absalom! : glossary and commentary
/ by Joseph R. Urgo and Noel Polk.
p. cm. — (Reading Faulkner series)
Includes bibliographical references and index.
ISBN 978-1-60473-434-8 (cloth : alk. paper) 1. Faulkner,
William, 1897–1962. Absalom, Absalom! 2. Faulkner, William,
1897–1962—Language—Glossaries, etc. 3. Mississippi—In litera-
ture. 4. Plantation life in literature. 5. Race in literature. I. Polk,
Noel. II. Title.
PS3511.A86A76 2010
813'.52—dc22   2009021659

British Library Cataloging-in-Publication Data available

*Noel Polk: For my Grandchildren,
Sam, Emily, and Francie*

Joseph R. Urgo: For Lesley

CONTENTS

SERIES PREFACE
ix

INTRODUCTION
xi

HOW TO USE THIS BOOK
xv

Absalom, Absalom!
GLOSSARY AND COMMENTARY
3

WORKS CITED
201

INDEX
205

SERIES PREFACE

This volume is one of a series of glossaries of Faulkner's novels which is the brainchild of the late James Hinkle, who established its principles, selected the authors, worked long hours with each of us in various stages of planning and preparation, and then died before seeing any of the volumes in print. The series derives from Jim's hardcore commitment to the principle that readers must understand each word in Faulkner's difficult novels at its most basic, literal level before hoping to understand the works' "larger" issues. In pursuit of this principle, Jim, a non-Southerner, spent years of his scholarly life reading about the South and things Southern, in order to learn all he could about sharecropping, about hame strings, about mule fact and lore, about the Civil War, about blockade running, duelling, slavery and Reconstruction, Indian culture and history. When he had learned all he could from published sources, he betook himself to county and city archives to find what he could there. He was intrigued by Faulkner's names, for example, and over the years compiled a fascinating and invaluable commentary on their etymologies, their cultural and historical backgrounds, and, not least, their pronunciations: Jim is the only person I know of who listened to all of the tapes of Faulkner's readings and interviews at the University of Virginia, in order to hear how Faulkner himself pronounced the names and words he wrote. In short, for Jim, there was no detail too fine, no fact or supposition too arcane to be of interest or potential significance for readers of Faulkner: he took great pleasure in opening up the atoms of Faulkner's world, and in exploring the cosmos he found there.

It was my great fortune and pleasure to be Jim's friend and colleague for slightly more than a decade. In the late seventies, I managed to tell him something he didn't know; he smiled and we were friends for life. Our friendship involved an ongoing competition to discover and pass on something the other didn't know. I was mostly on the losing end of this competition, though of course ultimately the winner because of what I learned from him. It was extremely agreeable to me to supply him with some arcana or other because of the sheer delight he took in learning something—anything, no matter how large or small.

On numerous occasions before and after the inception of this series, we spent hours with each other and with other Faulkner scholars reading the novels aloud, pausing to parse out a difficult passage, to look up a word we didn't understand, to discuss historical and mythological allusions, to work through the visual details of a scene to make sure we understood exactly what was happening, to complete Faulkner's interruptions, to fill in his gaps, and to be certain that we paid as much attention to the unfamiliar passages as we did to the better-known ones, not to let a single word escape our scrutiny; we also paused quite frequently, to savor what we had just read. These readings were a significant part of my education in Faulkner, and I'm forever grateful to Jim for his friendship and his guidance.

This series, Reading Faulkner, grows out of these experiences in reading Faulkner aloud, the effort to understand every nuance of meaning contained in the words. The volumes in the series will try to provide, for new readers and for old hands, a handy guide not just to the novel's allusions, chronologies, Southernisms, and difficult words, but also to its more difficult passages.

Jim's death in December 1990 was a great loss to Faulkner studies; it was especially grievous to those of us embarked with him on this series. Absent his guidance, the University Press of Mississippi asked me to assume editorship of the series; I am happy to continue the work he started. The volumes in the series will not be what they would have been had Jim lived, but they all will bear his stamp and his spirit, and they all will try to be worthy of his high standards. And they will all be lovingly dedicated to his memory.

Noel Polk

INTRODUCTION

> Although those who concern themselves with details are regarded as folk of limited intelligence, it seems to me that this part is essential, because it is the foundation, and it is impossible to erect any building or establish any method without understanding its principles. It is not enough to have a liking for architecture. One must also know stone-cutting.
> —Saxe, quoted in Foucault, *Discipline & Punish*

When he completed *Absalom, Absalom!* in May 1936, Faulkner said, "I think it's the best novel yet written by an American" (Blotner 364). That assessment remains valid. It is also among the most demanding of American novels, one which, as one critic said in 1954, "should have no casual readers" (Scott 219). What we found in applying the methods of the Reading Faulkner series to *Absalom, Absalom!* is that the novel has in fact had generations of casual readers (including both of us) who have understandably been drawn to a handful of critical, powerfully meaningful passages, while too often leaving unremarked the particulars of the novel's less arresting, perhaps more difficult, ones. A discerning reader in 1974 described what a close reading of *Absalom, Absalom!* in its entirety demands: "Faulkner presents a novel as if the reader was not going to read it consecutively page by page but rather was going to be able to perceive the entire work simultaneously like a painting, and no doubt the closer the reader is able to approach this impossible ideal the closer he will come to a perfect understanding of the novel" (William Brown 219).

What we attempt in this volume is simultaneity: to create a resource capable of providing the reader a holistic rendering of the novel by attending, paradoxically, to its parts—individual words, phrases, and sentences. In a novel concerned so intimately with what is ultimately knowable in history and in human affairs, we have sought throughout the text to separate what is documentable fact from speculation and to provide as reliable as possible an accounting of what Faulkner's language actually says. Making such a claim would be fatuous were it not for the text's explicit demonstration of the function of speculation in human truth claims. *Absalom*'s critical tradition is marked by the novel's implicit encouragement, taken up by readers for over seventy years, to "play" with its meanings as do its primary characters, for whom play is serious business. In reading *Absalom, Absalom!* in the Reading Faulkner series, we intend not to forestall speculative responses to the text, but to distinguish such play from the playing field.

The Reading Faulkner series is not intended as an encyclopedia of criticism. Nonetheless, we have consulted the rich record of commentary on the novel, especially instances where particular attention to textual detail enriches the results of our inquiry. We do not read the text to test or expand upon an *a priori* claim or hypothesis or to impose any overarching thematic reading of the novel. Instead, we begin and remain at the level of the words on the page, glossing whenever the words are not self-evident or where an allusion or reference to inter- or extra-textual sources might clarify potential meaning. Although no mind works in an ideological vacuum, our purpose is continuously to ask the same, doggedly basic questions: What do these words mean? What else might they mean, in the context of what precedes and follows their appearance on the page? How might we usefully connect them to other parts of the novel?

The method employed in the Reading Faulkner series reverses the industry standard. We have not undertaken to engage the vast body of critical commentary on *Absalom*; to do so would be impossible given the space available in this volume. We have tried, however, to make use of that commentary when it was useful in helping us unpack the meaning of Faulkner's language. We have tried to avoid advancing any single reading of *Absalom* in this volume, but of course we could not help being influenced by our prejudices and predilections and, thankfully, by what we have learned as we worked together on this book. Appended to the volume is a Works Cited list, not intended to be exhaustive, but containing the commentary we have referred to and some we think will be most useful to readers who share our interest in a close, detailed reading of this novel. We especially invite readers to explore Richard Godden's *Fictions of Labor*, whose readings of *Absalom*'s textual complications are amenable to our methods but are so elaborate and intricate that we simply could not find a way to incorporate his explications into our text without copying them wholesale.

Likewise, we have not undertaken to give complete identifications of historical personages like Lee and Sherman, of Civil War battles, of historical periods (Reconstruction), or of scientific names of flora and fauna, except where such information is essential to the passage. For this sort of gloss, we happily refer readers to volumes by Calvin Brown and both books by Paul David Ragan. Elisabeth Muhlenfeld's introduction to her casebook provides the best account of Faulkner's writing of *Absalom, Absalom!*

Finally, though we have tried to identify important sites where we think it crucial to remember that all parts of *Absalom* are constructs of one or more narrators, we would like to remind readers to be *always* suspicious of any narrator's claim on fictive "truth": readers should always test each narrator's story against all other narrators'; we should also always be sensitive to what any narration tells us about the narrator (see Kartiganer).

Also true to *Absalom, Absalom!*, our method has been consistently collaborative, conjoined in this case not by a geological umbilical but by the interstate and internet highway systems connecting north Mississippi to upstate New York. We've read the entire novel to each other at least once and more than once in numerous instances; we've written and revised electronically, in pencil, and by email correspondence. In many instances we gloss a passage with multiple possible readings, recording our own disagreements and uncertainties, and, we hope, fully acknowledging that contending, debated, and even tentative meaning is a vital part of the novel's effect on a careful reader. We can no longer say who said what first or in what form—having experienced what Faulkner meant when he equated immersion with understanding. By the time we'd exchanged the second and third and later drafts, we'd forgotten who led on which entries, and there is now not two but one author, and we jointly take responsibility for its faults and omissions.

We would like to thank Kara Hobson in Oxford, Mississippi, and Karen Brown in Clinton, New York, for their assistance. At Mississippi State University we are indebted to Dr. Rich Raymond, Head of the English Department; Dr. Gary Myers, Dean of Arts and Sciences; Dr. Peter Rabideau, Provost, for their support of such activities and their friendship. We'd also especially like to thank Laura West, Julie Harman, and Seth Dawson for their more immediate work on the manuscript itself. Finally, we want to thank all those scholars whose work on *Absalom, Absalom!* has preceded and deeply influenced our own.

Joseph R. Urgo
Noel Polk

HOW TO USE THIS BOOK

The line-by-line entries are keyed to the page and line numbers of the Library of America text in *William Faulkner Novels 1936–1940*, edited by Joseph Blotner and Noel Polk. Running heads in bold type will locate passages in this text and, following the abbreviation VI, in the Vintage International text (New York, 1991). All line counts start with the top line of text on each page and do not include line spaces. Readers may make a reliable locating guide by preparing a numbered slip of paper that fits the text in hand.

Finally, we insist that you *not* attempt to use this guide during your first encounters with *Absalom, Absalom!*. We would not deny, or in any way intervene in, your own original reactions to the deliberate complexities and confusions of one of Faulkner's, and therefore literature's, most magnificent achievements. Please do not compromise your own engagement with *Absalom* with our commentary; come here after you are comfortable in your own sense of the novel so that you can judge our commentary by what you know of *Absalom*: we believe our commentary will be more valuable to you if you know the novel well enough to argue with us, to disagree on large and small points, rather than allowing this commentary, or any other criticism, to dominate your understanding of *Absalom*.

ABSALOM, ABSALOM!
Glossary and Commentary

Title ***Absalom, Absalom!*** Numerous critics have discussed the meaning of the title. Faulkner took it from 2 Samuel 18:33, which records King David's reaction to the death of his rebellious son: "O my son Absalom, my son, my son Absalom! would God I had died for thee, O Absalom, my son, my son!" While the biblical reference affirms the son, it is not apparent in Faulkner's title alone who that son is—Henry, Bon, Quentin, or Sutpen himself. Nor is it apparent how David's plaint that he wants to die for his son applies to the novel's presumptive king, Thomas Sutpen. Bernice Schrank calls the novel's title the first "authorial contribution" to the text, "distinct from the four narrators" (651). What is apparent is that there is a narrator working in the novel who is not one of the novel's principal characters. The fourth narrator is apparent from the novel's opening but may be recognized as intrusive for the first time at 7:4. See Irwin 148ff.

CHAPTER I

5:4 **a dim hot airless room with the blinds all closed and fastened for forty-three summers because when she was a girl someone had believed that light and moving air carried heat and that dark was always cooler** Someone may indeed have told Rosa this, but at the beginning of the Civil War Rosa's father sealed himself and his family inside their home by locking the front door, keeping "the front shutters closed and fastened" (67:14) and refusing to allow her "to look out the window at passing soldiers" (67:10). He himself then spent his days "behind one of the slightly opened blinds like a picquet on post, armed not with a musket but with the big family bible" (67:15) and would "declaim" to passing troops "in a harsh loud voice . . . the passages of the old violent vindictive mysticism which he had already marked as the actual picquet would have ranged his row of cartridges along the window sill" (67:25). The Coldfield house thus would seem to have always been, and continues to be, a prison for Rosa in which her father tried to protect her from whatever "reality," as he would conceive reality, exists outside the house, especially from the procreative urge of sexual desire represented by the twice-blooming wistaria just outside the window (see entry for 5:13). Her aunt, her father's sister, escaped from Coldfield's repression apparently by climbing through one of these windows and eloping with a horse trader (147:2). Throughout Faulkner's work closed windows represent sexual repression, as here but also as in "A Rose for Emily," but they also provide access to an outside world of sexual freedom—Caddy Compson in *The Sound and the Fury* and Lena Grove in *Light in August*—for those courageous enough to climb through to escape repression at home. Thus though most of the narrators vilify the problematic mansion at Sutpen's Hundred, Mr. Coldfield creates a "house" as dark and formidable as the "house" at Sutpen's Hundred.

5:12 **wistaria vine blooming for the second time that summer** an extraordinarily fruitful wistaria, marking an over-fecund world just outside Rosa Coldfield's dark, dry, dusty indoor world.

5:18 **nothusband** Thomas Sutpen, the man Rosa didn't marry, but whom she, in Quentin's reckoning, thinks of in ways that keep him and his affront close but negate him. Also possibly Charles Bon, similarly a nothusband to Judith.

5:18 **sitting so bolt upright in the straight hard chair that was so tall for her that her legs hung straight and rigid as if she had iron shinbones and ankles** Rosa never manages to convert her own house, inherited from her father, to her own needs. She thus continues to live as a child in her childhood home: the "iron shinbones and ankles" suggest a sort of physical and emotional ossification that has permanently crippled her. The "straight hard chair" must be her father's; her continuing to sit in it long after he has died may suggest his continuing dominating influence over her, her continuing self-infantalization, her inability to become an adult. Kinney proposes that Rosa's "hatred of Sutpen" is based in his "resemblance to her father, whose blindness to her was not only repressive but robbed her as well of self-respect and even of self-pity" (200).

5:23 **listening would renege and hearing-sense self-confound and the long-dead object of her impotent yet indomitable frustration would appear** As Quentin listens to Rosa—that is, as he actively engages with the words she is saying—that very act of listening reneges, refuses to do what it promises, to keep active, to understand, and even the sound of her voice, the "hearing-sense," confuses, frustrates, or ruins itself, disappearing completely, allowing Sutpen, the "long-dead object," to appear in place of the words and the sounds. A similar occurrence happens in chapter VIII (289:28) when Quentin and Shreve abandon words and visualize the climactic scene on the battlefield in which Sutpen tells Henry that Bon is part Negro. Throughout the novel when listening yields to seeing, the aural to the visual, we are on the verge of creative insight. Deeper understanding is linked to imaginative, not archival, activity.

5:25 **her impotent yet indomitable frustration** Rosa's frustration over Sutpen's insult dominates her life (138:14): it's thus indomitable because it overpowers her, but it's impotent to change things, no matter how she obsesses over it. The impotence and indomitability, resisting each other but not canceling each other out, leave Rosa helplessly yoked to her memories and her spinsterhood. But see the entry for 5:26. At 10:21 Quentin thinks that she can "neither forgive nor revenge herself upon" Sutpen.

5:26 **as though by outraged recapitulation evoked, quiet inattentive and harmless, out of the biding and dreamy and victorious dust** Sutpen lies quiet in his grave until Rosa tells her story. The word "recapitulation" suggests that for reasons of her own Rosa repeats her narrative periodically precisely to keep Sutpen alive (see entry for 141:7). The phrase "Nevermore. Nevermore. Nevermore" (307:5) and the generally gothic surround of the novel may allow us to connect Rosa's constant recreation of Sutpen—"by outraged recapitulation evoked"—to Poe's "The Raven," in which the bereaved lover of the deceased Lenore asks the visiting raven a series of questions to which the bird's single-word vocabulary, "nevermore," is the most painful response, a response that pricks his emotions with pain that keeps her memory alive. We may also detect some reference to the narrator of Coleridge's "The Rime of the Ancient Mariner," who obsessively tells his story to an equally obsessive listener.

5:29 **There would be the dim coffin-smelling gloom sweet and oversweet with the twice-bloomed wistaria against the outer wall by the savage quiet September sun impacted distilled and hyperdistilled** The sentence's structure, which allows the compounded participials "impacted distilled and hyperdistilled" to modify either or both "gloom" and "wistaria," thus identifies the gloom with the odor of the wistaria. Though it's a "quiet" sun, the setting is a "long still hot weary dead September afternoon" (5:2) during which the sun has "impacted" the gloomy odor of the wistaria, causing it to fill up every available nook and cranny; "distilled and hyperdistilled," it becomes concentrated, reduced to its primal essence, the lure and problematic of the fecundity that the twice-blooming wistaria represents. In *The Sound and the Fury* Quentin Compson has similar problems with the odor of honeysuckle. In chapter V Rosa often describes herself as the sun waiting for Sutpen to emerge from his swamp.

5:35 **rank smell of female old flesh long embattled in virginity** Though the narrative is third person, this sort of locution seems clearly to emerge from Quentin's consciousness and represents his own assessment of Rosa. His hyperconsciousness of her virginity dovetails with *Absalom*'s (and *The Sound and the Fury*'s) obsession with female virginity. That it is "embattled" suggests Rosa's defensive or aggressive posture regarding her "troth which failed to plight." Faulkner's curious reversal—"female old flesh" instead of "old female flesh"—makes "female" modify "old" flesh. In its opposition to *male* old flesh, the phrase smacks of a certain repugnance toward female bodies of all ages but especially to old women that runs rife throughout Faulkner's work in the 1920s and 30s.

6:4 **the ghost** either Sutpen or Rosa, given that Mr. Compson later says that before the Civil War southern men made the women into ladies, then "the War came and made the ladies into ghosts" (9:33).

6:6 **quiet thunderclap** Robert Zoellner describes the phrase as an example of the novel's use of "syntactical ambiguity" or syntax that demands "an inordinate amount of attention and retention" (487): "Syntactical ambiguity blurs the deceptively logical distinctiveness with which we habitually regard the written word and the reality which stands behind it" (493).

6:7 **man-horse-demon** Rosa's three-part description of Sutpen moves him from human to bestial to demonic. The man-horse obviously invokes the centaur and doubtless emerges from her association of Sutpen's ungentlemanly proposal to her with his unsettling greeting from atop his horse as he looks down upon her while she gardens when he returns from the War (see entry for 138:14).

6:13 **Immobile, bearded and hand palm-lifted the horseman sat** that is, like a statue of a great man.

6:15 **bloodless paradox** Sutpen conquers the north Mississippi wilderness not by violence, as would be normal, but by more peaceful means.

6:16 **the long unamaze** The OED gives several meanings for the word "amaze" as verb and noun. As noun, it is often "identified with" "a maze" and in its earlier uses in the thirteenth and sixteenth centuries had stronger meanings than it seems to have today. Then it meant "Loss of one's wits, mental stupefaction"; "Bewilderment, mental confusion"; "Loss of presence of mind through terror, panic." As a verb, it caused such conditions: "To put out of one's wits; to stun or stupefy, as by a blow on the head; to infatuate, craze"; "To drive one to his wit's end, bewilder, perplex"; "To overcome with sudden fear or panic; to fill with consternation, terrify, alarm." The OED lists only an adjectival form of "unamazed," as meaning "without feare." It cites Eve in Milton's *Paradise Lost* as "Not unamazed" when she hears Satan's voice (ix.552). Thus "long unamaze" would seem to mean to Quentin that though Rosa narrates her (to her) terrifying tale of Sutpen's satanic advent into north Mississippi—bringing with him a "faint sulphur-reek" (6:8)—Quentin is neither terrified nor bewildered but perhaps more analytical; the constant retelling of the story has over time dulled its capacity to cause "mental stupefaction."

6:18 **tranquil and astonished earth** Obviously the earth itself is neither tranquil nor astonished; it's rather Quentin's or Rosa's perception as they consider Sutpen's "abrupting" onto and altering it and them. Faulkner personifies the landscape as an ecological force; the environment (with heat) which produces this behavior and is more than setting, more than backdrop.

6:22 *Sutpen's Hundred* See Calvin Brown 193–94.

6:22 **the *Be Sutpen's Hundred* like the oldentime *Be Light*** Genesis 1:3: "And God said, Let there be light: and there was light." Rosa here, and elsewhere through the first few pages of *Absalom*, depicts Sutpen not just as demon but also as creator. He is God before Satan, before the forces of good and evil became distinct, when God contained both.

6:23 **Then hearing would reconcile** "reconcile" itself with his "listening" (see 5:23) so that Quentin once again hears and understands Rosa's words. But listening and hearing trigger in him a doubleness that both resists and clings to the words, the story.

6:24 **two separate Quentins** Quentin is a young man preparing to leave the South for a Harvard education; he is also one of the "ghosts" that southern history has created. His doubleness is reflected in the "other" voices with which he is twinned in dialogues throughout the novel, with Rosa, Father, Shreve, and himself. The doubleness becomes full-fledged as in the second half of the novel he and Shreve become twinned in the telling and retelling of the Sutpen story, until the final pages of chapter VIII (beginning 289:28) dissolve the separateness as Quentin and Shreve merge into a single unified narrator, whereupon they resolve the crucial question why Henry killed Bon.

6:27 **having to listen** There is something compulsive about Quentin's attentiveness to the story that neither we nor he can yet understand. That he "has to listen" suggests that there is more at stake in the Sutpen story than simply an understanding of his past, though neither we nor perhaps he knows yet what is or might be at stake. Quentin is as compulsive a listener as Rosa is a narrator, and perhaps for the same reason: see the entry for 5:25.

6:34 **in notlanguage, like this** Francine Ringold identifies Quentin's "notlanguage" as an instance of "the narrator speaking through Quentin as *not* the language of Quentin's idiom" (231). The novel's title is a similar example of what to Quentin is *notlanguage*.

6:34 ***It seems that this demon. . . . And by Quentin Compson*** Such lengthy italic passages in *Absalom* seem to suggest various registers of Quentin's unconscious. Kinney calls Shreve's demand that Quentin "tell about the South" the "novel's impersonal incipit" (196). If chapter I is a distillation of the entire novel, this passage is a hyper-distillation of one of the novel's techniques. It may be consciousness itself articulated. At another level it is Quentin's reconstruction of a conversation, or part of a conversation, he has had or is having with Rosa about Sutpen: he begins to repeat the story and she interrupts him, to make sure he gets the details, *her* details, correct. The conversation may also condense several conversations he has had with her about Sutpen. At yet a deeper level, Quentin may also be making up the conversation entirely, creating a sort of narrative matrix that serves the rest of the novel: the dialogical narration upon which the novel proceeds, especially in the Harvard sections, wherein Quentin and his Harvard roommate Shreve share the narration almost equally. Note the "strophe and antistrophe" by which Jefferson narrates Sutpen's appearance at 26:1.

6:35 ***Who came out of nowhere*** a signature mode of Sutpen's appearance in the novel, to "abrupt" upon the scene "*without warning.*" Alan Holder suggests that "this mode of appearance has a strong aesthetic appeal for Faulkner, and is an example of his fondness for abrupt effects" (61), which is then followed by a process of recovering the character's history—a process which for Faulkner "figures as an act of the imagination that is at the same time a moral act" (62).

7:4 ***Without regret, Miss Rosa Coldfield says—(Save by her) Yes, save by her. (And by Quentin Compson) Yes. And by Quentin Compson.*** See entry for 6:34. The closing lines of this italic passage seem to shift gears, somehow, by introducing a third, unidentified, narrator and perhaps a fourth, which unsettle the easy dialogue between Quentin and Rosa. Rosa claims that Sutpen died "Without regret," apparently meaning that nobody (i.e., Rosa) cared that he died; the parenthetical voice, hitherto Rosa's, which seems almost an aside to her or to the fourth voice, the same "voice" that utters the novel's title, disagrees, perhaps a bit archly pointing to Rosa's denial—*"(Save by her)"*—and the principal voice agrees. Then those two voices go through the same routine about Quentin who likewise, they also perhaps a bit archly agree, "regrets" Sutpen's dying.

The entire italic passage (6:34–7:6) raises several questions. First, who are the voices in the last four lines? Quentin and Rosa referring to themselves in the third person? Second, what can it mean that Quentin and Rosa "regret" that Sutpen died? The only reasonable answer to the second question is that if he had lived into the twentieth century, Sutpen might have lived to resolve many of the issues he creates for Rosa and Quentin, might not have been so vivid to their imaginations that they return to him so compulsively. The intruding voice here may be the narrator, could even be Shreve. If Kinney is correct in proposing that this passage suggests that Quentin is "listening to a strange story that must be corrected constantly by one who knows the tale" (194), perhaps the passage casts us forward to a moment in Quentin and Shreve's dormitory room at Harvard. At very least, the passage forecasts a narrative instability that the reader must tolerate to be able to read the novel with any understanding. That is, this passage, with its parenthetical questioning and correcting of the direct narrative, warns against looking for and finding a stable narrative voice. It sets a narrative style and establishes epistemological principles; truth is subjective, facts are secondary, insight is imaginative, not penetrative, and that narrative, the story itself, whatever its "truth" content, is fundamental. The narrators here, whoever they are, as throughout the novel, are obsessed with the Sutpen story because it has so centrally determined their own, and so they "regret" the legacy he leaves to the twentieth century—not just the legacy of slavery and racism, but the epistemological legacy which undermines all things stable and renders history unrecoverable. Even the demon, by the time Quentin and Shreve finish with him, is an object of pity.

7:23 **Only she dont mean that** he thought. *It's because she wants it told.* Quentin, like his father, nearly always distrusts Rosa; they are both as quick to assign motives to the living as to the dead. This passage introduces the novel's crucial structural device of presenting and then discarding information, motive, and explanation. The novel undermines everything offered as fact, sometimes instantly, sometimes over time. None of the narrators can be trusted: all mostly speculate, trying to force together into a seamless, coherent narrative a few disparate and putative "facts" which the Sutpen legend has bequeathed to them; each narrator is driven to construct a narrative amenable to his or her own needs and interests.

8:10 *so that people whom she will never see and whose names she will never hear and who have never heard her name nor seen her face will read it* Rosa's writing thus seems analogous to Quentin's description of Sutpen's desire to pass on his own legacy, "so that he would be able to look in the face not only the old dead ones but all the living ones that would come after him when he would be one of the dead" (182:29).

8:13 *that only through the blood of our men and the tears of our women could He stay this demon and efface his name and lineage from the earth* Quentin may be wrong. Rosa's telling is precisely to preserve, not to efface, Sutpen's memory, as when she suggests that Quentin might become a writer some day who will "remember this and write about it" (7:14).

8:24 **implacable reserve of undefeat** Poirier suggests that Rosa means the "undefeat" of Sutpen's "essentially unregenerate personality" (17).

8:29 **Confederate provost marshals' men** "The provost marshal would be charged with police functions and maintenance of order. Presumably, Mr. Coldfield hides to avoid conscription into the Confederate Army" (Ragan, *Absalom* 9).

9:17 **recovering ... from the fever which had cured the disease, waking from the fever without even knowing that it had been the fever itself which they had fought against and not the sickness, looking with stubborn recalcitrance backward beyond the fever and into the disease with actual regret, weak from the fever yet free of the disease and not even aware that the freedom was that of impotence.** Fever = the Civil War. Disease = the slave-based antebellum South. That the freedom is "that of impotence" may suggest that the post-war South was rendered economically and socially powerless when the war forced it to give up slavery, upon which its economy was based.

10:6 **that engagement which did not engage, that troth which failed to plight** Rosa's brief engagement to Sutpen.

10:7 **Might even have told your grandfather the reason why at the last she refused to marry him.** Variations on "might have" in this passage and throughout indicate the speculative nature of the novel's narration. Here and in the following lines Mr. Compson tries to explain why Rosa chooses Quentin to tell her story to, arguing that she is primarily interested in learning from Quentin how much of her own part in the story Quentin has learned, specifically whether he has learned from his grandfather, through his father, why she refused to marry Sutpen; but he doesn't even know whether she told General Compson the reason in the first place.

10:20 **as though in inverse ratio to the vanishing voice, the invoked ghost of the man ... began to assume a quality almost of solidity, permanence.** Voices "vanish" throughout *Absalom*, as Quentin glides freely between "listening" and "hearing."

10:24 **it mused (mused, thought, seemed to possess sentience, as if, though dispossessed of the peace ... which she declined to give it, it was still irrevocably outside the scope of her hurt or harm).** In losing her voice, Quentin detaches Sutpen from Rosa's actual narrative; Sutpen becomes for him something physical, actually present, not a historical person kept alive by narrative.

10:30 **as Miss Coldfield's voice went on, resolved out of itself before Quentin's eyes the two half-ogre children** See entry for 10:24.

11:26 **He wasn't a gentleman** Rosa could mean that he was not a nice person, a "gentle man," and/or that he was not a person with a known history or lineage which would identify him as somehow substantive. That he is not a "gentle man" is evident, as she sees him. According to her, the whole community resents his advent into Jefferson with no identifiable antecedents. But her strictures against him for not having known antecedents are curious indeed, since her own father likewise seems to have come to Jefferson out of unknown origins. By 1909, Rosa's forty-three years of continuity in Jefferson have apparently bestowed upon her, at least in her own reckoning, a sort of "aristocracy" of past that allows her to condemn Sutpen for not having one. See entry for 62:24

11:29 **seeking some place to hide himself** Rosa and, as she would have it, the community believe that Sutpen comes to Jefferson running to escape the law.

11:39 **Ellen: blind romantic fool** Rosa's sister Ellen is one of the novel's truly unexplained mysteries. She marries Sutpen and bears him two children, then descends, according to the different narrators, into a sort of madness that eventually kills her. There's little evidence that she is a "blind romantic fool" and her "madness" seems more likely to have come from the fact that her father more or less traded her to Sutpen, doubtless against her will, in exchange for his silence in regard to some shady or misbegotten business relationship in which he and Sutpen may have been involved together. Given Mr. Coldfield's repression of the women in his household (he makes of his house a "cold field"), it is possible that Ellen, like Rosa, is completely unprepared for a sexual relationship, especially of the sort that Sutpen would likely want. Rosa's sense of Sutpen's sexual nature is here driven by the incident in which he proposes crudely to her.

12:10 **a murderer and almost a fratricide** Henry Sutpen. Rosa's "almost" stops one. Henry is a murderer whether a fratricide or not and a good deal of the novel is based on an assumption (which it does not prove) that Henry and Bon are at least half brothers. Does Rosa mean that she knows they were not brothers but that Henry thought he was killing a brother? If so, and perhaps more important, *how* does she know this? The novel does not explain.

12:20 **notion of slaves underfoot day and night which reconciled, I wont say moved, her aunt** Ellen's aunt would be Rosa's aunt who escaped the Coldfield household to elope with a horse trader. Rosa's distancing herself from that aunt is curious, to say the least. Apparently a person with some aristocratic pretensions, the aunt seems finally to have approved of Ellen's marriage to Sutpen because Sutpen had slaves.

12:27 **wild beasts** Sutpen's Haitian slaves. Thadious Davis points out the absence of any objective confirmation that the slaves Sutpen brought to Jefferson were "wild," although "every appearance of Sutpen in Jefferson is colored by Rosa's association of him with his 'wild' slaves and land" ("Be Sutpen's Hundred" 10).

13.9 **patent of respectability** a document, perhaps, or some other visible sign that guaranteed that Sutpen was a gentleman and therefore acceptable as a husband for Ellen.

13:17 **anyone could have looked at him once and known that he would be lying about who and where and why he came from by the very fact that apparently he had to refuse to say at all.** According to Mr. Compson, the Jefferson townspeople take Sutpen's reticence to talk about his past as evidence that he has something to hide.

13:31 **not with this just one night's hard ride away** the Mississippi River, not New Orleans.

13:34 **no younger son sent out from some old quiet country like Virginia or Carolina with the surplus negroes to take up new land** Quite frequently planters on the East Coast did indeed send sons and slaves to Missis-

14:10 sippi, where land was abundant and relatively inexpensive, to establish new plantations (Ragan, *Absalom* 13–14).

14:13 **raree show** a street show, sometimes a peepshow, i.e., a show with sexual connotations.

14:24 **the price which she had paid for that house and that pride; I saw the notes of hand on pride and contentment and peace and all to which she had put her signature** Rosa resents Ellen for having married her, Rosa's, demon.

14:30 **I saw Henry repudiate his home and birthright and then return and practically fling the bloody corpse of his sister's sweetheart at the hem of her wedding gown** But Rosa admits at 121.2 that she did not actually observe these events, since the first occurred in a closed room and she was at home in town when the latter happened. Perhaps her vivid imagination convinces her that she was on site to witness these events; she probably means that she was alive during those times and was close enough to the principals to know what happened. In chapter IX, it is worth noting, Quentin, in Cambridge, "sees" and recreates the powerful scene during which Rosa goes out to Sutpen's Hundred with the sheriff and the ambulance, the conflagration that destroys the house, and Rosa's descent in to madness: "he had not been there but he could see her, struggling and fighting like a doll in a nightmare, making no sound, foaming a little at the mouth" (309:12).

15:11 **to vindicate the honor of a family the good name of whose women has never been impugned** In her rush to justification, Rosa seems to forget her aunt, who eloped with the horse trader to escape from her brother Mr. Coldfield. Clearly, he "impugns" her good name when he refuses to let her return to the house when her husband goes to war.

15:31 **his defeated Commander-in-Chief** Robert E. Lee, Commander of the Army of Northern Virginia.

15:38 **Nome** No ma'am.

16:20 **a man that anyone could look at and see that, even if he apparently had none now, he was accustomed to having money and intended to have it again** Rosa's anger at Sutpen may lead her to make mistakes in recounting his life and motives in Jefferson. If we are to believe any part of the story that Sutpen tells General Compson, he would be far from "accustomed to having" money. But Sutpen may be accustomed to having and losing money; we do not know with certainty.

17:3 **what our father or his father could have done before he married our mother that Ellen and I would have to expiate and neither of us alone be sufficient; what crime committed that would leave our family cursed** Passages such as this one, not just from Rosa, that voice the characters' sense of doom and the "gloom" that lingers, "distilled and hyperdistilled" (5:32), combine the puritan-Presbyterian notion of Original Sin with the tragic sense of history of Greek drama, of families cursed with a history of disaster. Specifically this passage rephrases the biblical belief that the sins of the fathers shall be passed on to the sons (Exodus 20:5).

17:19 **Cassandralike** Cassandra was the daughter of Priam, king of Troy. Her lover Apollo gave her the gift of prophecy then, when she spurned his love, turned her ability to prophesy into a curse by decreeing that no one would ever believe her. She went to Greece as part of Agamemnon's spoils of the Trojan war and was murdered by Aegisthus as Clytemnestra murdered Agamemnon. Such references from Mr. Compson's and Rosa's classical education provide a context for their interpretations of the Sutpen history. But Mr. Compson's education leaves a good bit to be desired, since though giving him the classical history it fails to give him the proper tools to process the events of his own family's time. His classical references and analogies are frequently wrongheaded, or at least misapplied.

17:22 **I was born too late** Presumably Rosa means that if she had been born earlier she would have been an adult along with her sister and so older than her niece and nephew and therefore a part of the conversations that as a child she only half understood and which frightened her. Born after certain defining events, she lives in the echoes that determine her life without ever being asked or consulted about the events or their meaning.

17:25 **ogre-tale** An ogre is a hideous man-eating monster in lore and folktales (OED). Rosa's image suggests the nightmare quality of her sense of the Sutpen family. We cannot tell from the novel whether the nightmare vision is one she had contemporaneously with her childhood visits to Sutpen's Hundred or one she imposes on her young self as an older narrator thinking back about her total experience with Thomas Sutpen. To read properly, readers must keep both contingencies active because both are equally plausible and worth considering.

17:30 **'Protect her, at least. At least save Judith.' A child, yet whose child's vouchsafed instinct could make that reply which the mature wisdom of her elders apparently could not make: 'Protect her? From whom and** from what? He has already given them life: he does not need to harm them further. It is from themselves that they need protection.' Rosa's sense of the Sutpen family's doom. Judith and Henry need protection from themselves presumably because that doom will eventually cause them to do things not in their own self-interest; that is, that they will be self-destructive. Again, although Rosa here attributes this reply to her child self, she has doubtless imposed on her younger self the knowledge of their fates that she subsequently came to know. To some extent, Rosa misunderstands Ellen's wish that Rosa *at least* save Judith and responds that Sutpen has doomed them both. But in Rosa's account Ellen seems to suggest that Henry, in the war and in rebellion against his father, is already, by the time of her death in 1863, beyond any protection that anybody, much less Rosa, can give him.

18:18 **djinn** a rare form of *genie*, a spirit or goblin of Arabian mythology.

18:35 **the vision of my first sight of them which I shall carry to my grave: a glimpse like the forefront of a tornado, of the carriage and Ellen's high white face within it and the two replicas of his face in miniature flanking her, and on the front seat the face and teeth of the wild negro who was driving, and he, his face exactly like the negro's save for the teeth . . . all in a thunder and a fury of wildeyed horses and of galloping and of dust** The Sutpens' notorious races to church and elsewhere may have their source in one of Sutpen's experiences, recounted in chapter VII, when he and his sister, walking down a dusty road, encounter a similar carriage carrying "two parasols" and driven by a Negro coachman who nearly runs them down. See 191:15.

20:3 **And this time it was not even the minister. It was Ellen.** not the minister who, as at 19:18, remonstrates with Sutpen about the dangers he creates by allowing his driver to drive at such reckless speeds from Sutpen's Hundred to church. Ellen somehow manages to wrest control of the ride to church from Sutpen; she and the children henceforward ride to church in the phaeton, a buggy not made for fast speeds and reckless management. See entry for 20:12.

20:4 **Our aunt** Coldfield's unnamed sister, who escapes her brother's house, according to Shreve, by climbing through a window, like many of Faulkner's escapees, and running off with a horse trader (147:2).

20:12 **phaeton** a light, four-wheeled open carriage, usually pulled by two horses.

20:14 **And Judith looked once at the phaeton and realised what it meant and began to scream, screaming and kicking while they carried her back**

into the house and put her to bed. Judith obviously likes the wild rides to church and, according to Rosa, is the one who "instigated and authorized that Negro to make the team run away" (20:23), not Sutpen. Still, it is not immediately clear what makes Judith begin screaming, especially given such scenes as the final scene of chapter I, which presents her as emotionless and stonefaced as she watches her father fight his slaves in the mud in the barn, while her brother Henry vomits. Her screaming here is problematic, since it is so unlike the serene Judith constructed later in the novel, the Judith who buys the headstones, takes the octoroon wife to the cemetery, cares for Jim Bond.

20:17 **he was not present** he = Sutpen. That is, even though Rosa notes his physical absence—not even his "lurking triumphant face behind a window curtain" (20:17)—he is there in presiding spirit, in the person of Judith. See entry for 22:14.

21:8 **what she had missed when she saw the phaeton and began to scream** See entry for 20:14.

22:7 **"'Do you love this——' papa said.**
"'Papa,' Ellen said.** Ellen refuses to discuss her husband and her marriage with her father.

22:12 **From themselves. Not from him, not from anybody, just as nobody could have saved them, even himself.** Thomas Sutpen's children need saving from themselves, since with her refusal to accept the offered help of her father Ellen sets in motion the doom that will eventually overtake them. See entry for 17:30.

22:14 **that triumph had been beneath his notice** Rosa depicts Sutpen as having conquered his family so completely that he doesn't need to be present when Ellen refuses her father's aid.

22:15 **He showed Ellen, that is: not I.** Rosa's overcorrection of her grammar creates a mild grammatical ambiguity, perhaps deliberate. She means that Sutpen showed Ellen, not Rosa, that his "triumph had been beneath his notice." She does not mean that Sutpen, instead of she herself, showed Ellen.

22:20 **Not he** Sutpen would not come in to town with his family to have dinner with his wife's family.

22:34 **it had . . . been going on** Sutpen's fighting in the barn with his slaves.

23:19 **Ellen seeing not the two black beasts she had expected to see but instead a white one and a black one, both naked to the waist and gouging**

at one another's eyes as if their skins should not only have been the same color but should have been covered with fur too. Yes. It seems that on certain occasions, perhaps at the end of the evening, the spectacle, as a grand finale or perhaps as a matter of sheer deadly forethought toward the retention of supremacy, domination, he would enter the ring with one of the negroes himself. Yes. That is what Ellen saw: her husband and the father of her children standing there naked and panting and bloody to the waist and the negro just fallen evidently, lying at his feet and bloody too save that on the negro it merely looked like grease or sweat This is one of the more vivid and memorable scenes in *Absalom*, almost a *tableau* as Faulkner presents it. It seems to suggest something essential about Sutpen. In building his mansion in the wilderness, Sutpen has led these Haitian slaves more by example than by force; that is, they all worked naked together, covering themselves with mud to keep mosquitoes and other bugs from making them miserable. The scene here recounted occurs six years after he and his family have moved in to the mansion at Sutpen's Hundred, so that he should have had no real need to continue to demonstrate his "supremacy, domination"; one assumes that that would have long since been established. There is something ritualistic in the staging: it continues the tradition, established long before Sutpen married, by which some of the white men from Jefferson would come to Sutpen's Hundred on Saturday nights to drink and to watch the fighting. The bouts between the Negroes are elimination rounds, after which Sutpen himself steps in to fight the finally victorious Negro, as if to prove domination not just over the Negroes but over the men of Jefferson, the spectators too (see 26:35, where he demonstrates his skill with a pistol by shooting through a playing card attached to a tree while riding his horse), and so over Jefferson itself and, almost certainly, to prove domination over himself. Such scenes could also be for Sutpen a sort of ritual reenactment, a Freudian *fort-da*, by which he continually repeats his experience in overthrowing the rebellion in Haiti. In chapter VII Sutpen recounts to General Compson some such experience in the Haitian struggle which he, Compson, relates to the Sutpen he has seen fighting in the barn (209). It may also reflect Sutpen's class background. He was not born to privilege but had to work (and, Jefferson thinks, maybe steal) his way into the planter class—a kind of rags-to-riches paradigm early critics remarked upon. As with any self-made man, his class authenticity is always questionable. Hence, he repeatedly and ritualistically "proves" what a man of breeding would not need to prove but would possess as the very essence of his authenticity. Sutpen must perform his authenticity in this admittedly curious way. At 191:7, Quentin notes that when Sutpen was a child, in visits after supper, "some man, usually his father in drink, [would] break out into harsh recapitulation of his own worth, the respect which his own physical prowess commanded from his fellows." The episode might well provide Sutpen an example, even a pathology, for his need to demonstrate his own physical prowess, and thus his masculinity, in the ways that the passage being glossed in this entry describes.

23:38 the spectators falling back to permit her to see Henry plunge out from among the negroes who had been holding him, screaming and vomiting The dramatic climax to the fighting scene contrasts Henry's and Judith's reactions to the violence: Henry vomits, Judith watches quietly from the loft. Henry is the "grim humorless yokel" (according to Mr. Compson [90:14]) who does not possess Judith's grim stoicism. He vomits because he faces, perhaps discovering, his father's violent nature; Judith, on the other hand, watches quietly, her serenity seemingly enabled by her father's violence. Compare 20:9 where the sight of her father's capitulation to her mother's sense of decorum causes her to scream. Judith's serenity may depend on her father's authority, as she lives in service to his values.

24:21 "'I dont expect you to understand it,' he said. 'Because you are a woman. But I didn't bring Judith down here. I would not bring her down here. I dont expect you to believe that. But I swear to it.' Sutpen's reaction to Ellen's angry accusations suggests a Sutpen in contrast to the demon that Rosa has depicted him as. It therefore may suggest a Sutpen less demonic, one if not more gentle then one at least somewhat less sure of himself than we have been led to understand. He is here apologetic, swearing to Ellen that he has not done what she accuses him of, but swearing in a way that suggests that he knows he has been caught at something he shouldn't have been doing. On the other hand, perhaps he is lying to Ellen, and did bring Judith deliberately to watch. Sutpen, the socially mobile, holds no more brief for gender roles than he has for stable class stratification. He is willing to cross either set of boundaries and allows his daughter the same liberty. But if he is lying, why would he want his daughter to see this? To shame his weak son to a more tough-minded view of the world he must live in? To assure that his daughter will not grow up to be as weak or as traditional as his wife?

CHAPTER II

25:3 time for Quentin to start to go to Rosa's.

25:10 that which he already knew since he had been born in and still breathed the same air in which the church bells had rung on that Sunday morning in 1833 Not only has Quentin been hearing Jefferson's legends of the doings at Sutpen's Hundred, he has grown up in a world not much changed from that in which Sutpen lived.

25:14 pigeons strutted and crooned or wheeled in short courses resembling soft fluid paint-smears on the soft summer sky The scene appears as a sort of tableau, like an impressionist painting.

25:20 the ladies moving in hoops among the miniature broadcloth of little boys and the pantalettes of little girls, in the skirts of the time when ladies did not walk but floated This passage also contributes to the sense of the scene as like an early impressionist painting, a street scene, perhaps. Hoops spread skirts outward from a woman's waist, so that she looked something like a bell, and they reached almost all the way to the ground to hide her legs and feet, so that women did not appear to walk but simply to float along. Pantalettes were long underpants that extended below a skirt, usually frilled at the bottom of each leg. Hoop skirts do not seem to have been a part of American *couture* until around the middle of the nineteenth century, so that Faulkner, or Mr. Compson, perhaps deliberately, perhaps out of ignorance, seems to be painting a romanticized picture of 1830s Jefferson, imposing upon it a cliché of later portraits of southern belles.

26:1 in steady strophe and antistrophe *Sutpen. Sutpen. Sutpen. Sutpen.* In Greek drama, a "strophe" was a series of poetic lines that established a system; the "antistrophe" followed as a series of lines which repeated the system's metrical structure, though with differing content. The strophe was associated with the chorus's movement from right to left on the stage, the antistrophe with its return to the right. Here the reference suggests the town of Jefferson as a chorus of voices constantly in conversation about Sutpen. The passage's repetition of Sutpen's name, of course, represents only how central he was to their consciousness, not the actual content of their discourse, like the similar italic passage recording the emotional content, not the actual content, of the conversation between Quentin and Henry in chapter IX (306). Mr. Compson, here and throughout the novel, clearly wants to associate the events he is narrating with Greek tragedy, asserting again the fatalism he voices so often in *The Sound and the Fury*. Quentin and Shreve, by contrast, spend a good bit of their own energies in chapters VI–VIII narrating instance after instance when characters make choices which determine their destinies. A classicist like Mr. Compson, not living in a world where choices create destiny and, doubtless, feeling helpless to control his own, prefers a world governed by forces outside his control.

27:9 **He did not say that he used to drink and had quit, nor that he had never used alcohol. He just said that he would not care for a drink.** General Compson may be correct in asserting that Sutpen did not drink because he didn't have the money to buy his fair share, or at least that that was what Sutpen told him. But it's at least as possible that Sutpen's refusal to drink at this point in his life is a reaction against his own father's alcoholism (chapter VII) into which he descends after the war.

28:4 **So they were certain now that he had departed to get more** more money. One of Sutpen's several mysterious trips away from Jefferson, about which the community and the narrators make some perhaps unwarranted assumptions. For example, Mr. Compson believes that one of his trips, after Henry brings Bon home from the University, is to New Orleans to discover all he can about Bon. But the novel does not otherwise reveal where Sutpen goes or what he does on any of his trips. Rosa tells Quentin many years later that Sutpen "had found some unique and practical way of hiding loot and that he had returned to the cache to replenish his pockets" (28:8) but, again, all the novel supplies by way of evidence are the narrators' speculations.

28:17 **a small, alertly resigned man with a grim, harried Latin face, in a frock coat and a flowered waistcoat and a hat which would have created no furore on a Paris boulevard** the Parisian architect, brought from somewhere by Sutpen to help him build his house. Critics have usually taken him as the novel's artist figure, the dreamer and the realist combined, who makes reality of Sutpen's dreams of magnificence. A "furore," to be distinguished from "furor," means "Enthusiastic popular admiration; a 'rage', 'craze'" (OED). Thus even if he could have been taken as being right at home in Paris, nobody claims that he is actually *from* Paris. The Jeffersonians eventually describe him as a Paris architect but these are folks who don't even recognize the "sort of French" language that the wild blacks speak. It seems more plausible to think that he is from Haiti, or Martinique, from where, the town later learns, Sutpen had recruited him away (28:25), or from New Orleans.

29:19 **absolute mud** absolute = original, "disengaged from all interrupting cause" or circumstance (OED), and, therefore, pure. Faulkner uses the word here to suggest the primal, essential, quality of the mud: mud, that is, part of the original chaos out of which Sutpen-God created Sutpen's Hundred.

29:21 **doubtless there were more than Akers who did not know that the language in which they and Sutpen communicated was a sort of French** Mr. Compson's condescending irony suggests that *nobody* in that group, perhaps even in Jefferson, knew that the Negroes spoke "some sort of French."

29:38 **some ascendancy of forbearance** some pretensions to a lineage that precedes their own. That is, he leads his slaves, according to General Compson, not by his strength, but by an assumption of aristocratic superiority over them. This image of Sutpen seems contradicted by the report at the end of chapter I of his fighting with the slaves in the barn.

30:6 **croaching and pervading mud** The OED does not recognize the word "croaching," and it may be Faulkner's coinage. It is certainly related to the word "encroach," which means to "seize or acquire wrongly" but it might have its origins in the obsolete word "croche," a form of "crochet," which means to "hook, to catch with hooks." The passage, at any rate, is clear enough: the mud, pervasive, threatens to overtake and cover everything.

30:18 **chatelaine** the mistress of a "château" or plantation or household.

30:30 **took him two years** Sutpen completes the shell of the house in 1835.

31:19 **created of Sutpen's very defeat the victory which, in conquering, Sutpen himself would have failed to gain** If the architect is the novel's artist figure, as he is often called, he is able to contain and control Sutpen's dream, as Sutpen can not, and so can make the dream reality, even if only a smaller version of the physically impossible structure they all assume Sutpen had dreamed: "the place as Sutpen planned it would have been almost as large as Jefferson itself at the time" (31:19). He may, alternatively, or additionally, be the novel's producer figure, the one who must transfer the artist's (i.e., Sutpen's) dream into material reality, thereby limit it, and be hunted down by the artist figure in chapter VI.

33:23 **unfloored wagon hood** Before moving in to the unfinished mansion, Sutpen slept on the ground under a wagonbed.

34:26 **Methodist steward** Stewardship is a biblical term referring to a person responsible for overseeing household and property: "Who then is that faithful and wise steward, whom his lord shall make ruler over his household"

(Luke 12:42). A steward is a member of an elected body charged to govern the finances and general comportment of a local Methodist church.

35:5 **matched glasses** When Sutpen arrived in Jefferson he would not drink with friends in the tavern since apparently he could not afford to buy rounds of drinks for his fair share. Now, the townsmen are under his roof and they "match glasses"—that is, drink and buy equally.

35:11 **Mr Compson told Quentin** Faulkner reminds the reader throughout how much of *Absalom* comes through oral history, from people who themselves heard the stories from somebody else.

35:18 **But I dont think so. That is, I think** Faulkner again reminds the reader how much of Mr. Compson's narrative is speculation. His preference for "thinking" certain things indicates that his interpretation is driven by a preconceived understanding of how events happen and what motivates action. Much of it may be tied to his classical education. So it's not so much Faulkner's reminder that much of this is speculation as that the peculiar form that the speculation takes is linked to Mr. Compson's idealism. He begins with principles and ideals and deductively works facts to fit them. It's a way of thinking at odds with Faulkner's fictional method, which tends to build up from specificity to multiplicity (especially when projecting human motivation), so that it becomes increasingly more difficult to say "I like to think" about one of his characters. What we come to know about Sutpen, for example, is so multifarious and so tied to specific narrators that anyone with a thorough knowledge of the novel would hesitate to say anything definitive or unqualified.

36:18 **frock coat** A frock coat is a "double-breasted coat with skirts extending almost to the knees, which are not cut away but of the same length in front as behind" (OED); Brown says the tail of a frock coat often contained capacious pockets (86).

36:19 **beaver hat** originally a hat made of beaver fur but here, in connection with the frock coat, more likely a hat made of fabric, often velvet, the color of beaver fur.

36:20 **portmanteau** a clothesbag formed to be suitable for carrying horseback. Here, it hangs on the pommel of his saddle.

37:12 **John L. Sullivan** 1858–1918. World heavyweight boxing champion (1882–92); last of the bare-knuckle champions.

37:13 **schottische** a lively dance like a Highland Fling (OED).

39:6 **faience appearance** Italian pottery, from Faenza, having a glazed appearance, like porcelain.

39:34 **It was the wedding which caused the tears: not marrying Sutpen**

Perhaps. But it's also possible that Ellen's upbringing in the Coldfield house has created in her a fear of marriage, and sexuality, that like Rosa's gives her plenty of reason to fear a union with anybody, much less Sutpen. It's also possible that she simply resents being bartered by her father to Sutpen in exchange for Sutpen's silence about whatever nefarious deals they have worked together (see entries for 41:11, 41:18, 47:30 and 146:24, and Gwin 74).

40:9 symbolical trappings and circumstances of ceremonial surrender of that which they no longer possess Women, in Mr. Compson's reckoning, long for the marriage ceremony, the public avowals, even long after they have surrendered their virginity; they are more interested, he thinks, in the ceremony of surrender than in the surrender itself.

40:10 and why not, since to them the actual and authentic surrender can only be . . . a ceremony like the breaking of a banknote to buy a ticket for the train The actual surrender of their virginity, as opposed to the symbolical and ceremonial one, the public marriage, is to women, according to Mr. Compson, of little more significance that an insignificant economic transaction. The connection between money and sexuality is more important to Mr. Compson than to women. In *The Sound and the Fury* he tells Quentin, "It's men invented virginity, not women" (936).

41:11 the business between himself and Sutpen—that affair which, when it reached a point where his conscience refused to sanction it, he had withdrawn from and let Sutpen take all the profit, refusing even to allow Sutpen to reimburse him for the loss which, in withdrawing, he had suffered No one seems to know precisely what business Coldfield and Sutpen have been engaged in, but the town's legend, as Mr. Compson relates it, assumes that it must have been something marginally legal, perhaps completely illegal. Mr. Compson emphasizes Coldfield's conscience, which won't let him actually make money from immorality of any sort.

41:18 This was the second time he did something like that. Perhaps the first time he acted against his conscience was when he engaged in business with Sutpen, the second time when he permitted his daughter to marry him.

41:23 Sutpen had brought in a half dozen of his wild negroes to wait at the door with burning pine knots to provide light as they leave the church and, if necessary, to protect Sutpen and his new wife from public indignation.

41:28 That was the other half of the reason for Ellen's tears. The first half of the reason is the empty church and/or her resentments and fear of sex; the second half the crowd outside.

41:28 **It was the aunt who persuaded or cajoled Mr Coldfield into the big wedding. Sutpen had not expressed himself. But he wanted it. In fact, Miss Rosa was righter than she knew: he did want, not the anonymous wife and the anonymous children, but the two names, the stainless wife and the unimpeachable father-in-law, on the license, the patent. Yes, patent, with a gold seal and red ribbons too if that had been practicable. But not for himself.** If it is not pure speculation, Mr. Compson's analysis of Sutpen's attitude toward the wedding draws upon information from sources he does not cite, unless we may assume his own father or Miss Rosa told him these things. Sutpen's investment in a public ceremony, and his marriage to a "stainless wife" who brings him an "unimpeachable father-in-law" obviously speak to his need to have his wife's virginity certifiable and certified, in so far as virginity can ever be certified. These are the trappings of the ceremony of the class to which Sutpen aspires; he wants these things because that is what, to him, men of this class possess. Yet when Ellen and the aunt try to "enlist him on their side to persuade Mr Coldfield to the big wedding, he refuse[s] to support them" (42:12) at least partly because he does not want to provoke the community to some sort of reaction against his marriage to Ellen. According to Mr. Compson, Sutpen recalls that two months before he had been in jail for reasons never quite made clear in the novel and that even before that, notwithstanding the numbers of men who partook of his hospitality as the mansion at Sutpen's Hundred got built, he had never "quite ever lain quiet" on the stomach of the community which had nevertheless "swallowed him" five years before (42:17). Mr. Compson also believes that the women, Ellen and the aunt, and the town mistrust him because he came from out of nowhere, with no past, no antecedents.

42:21 **two of the citizens** General Compson and Mr. Coldfield.

42:39 **Or maybe women are even less complex than that and to them any wedding is better than no wedding and a big wedding with a villain preferable to a small one with a saint.** Mr. Compson finishes his analysis of the developing wedding plans with a bad joke, which, typically for him, is misogynistic.

43:3 **So the aunt even used Ellen's tears** that is, used Ellen's tears to get Sutpen to agree to the wedding, seeing the wedding as her "one chance to thrust him back into the gullet of public opinion . . . not only to secure her niece's future as his wife but to justify the action of her brother in getting him out of jail and her own position as having apparently sanctioned and permitted the wedding which in reality she could not have prevented" (42:31).

43:24 that mistake which if he had acquiesced to it would not even have been an error and which, since he refused to accept it or be stopped by it, became his doom whatever error it was that caused him to put away his Haitian wife. Criticism has almost unanimously agreed with Quentin's and Shreve's construction at the end of chapter VIII—and with the "Chronology"—that Sutpen put her aside because she is part Negro. But see the entry for 254:18.

46:3 banquette a raised area in front of the entrance to the church. Also a military term: a raised footway, especially at the bottom of a trench, which soldiers stand upon to fire at the enemy (OED).

46:21 that aptitude and eagerness of the Anglo-Saxon for complete mystical acceptance of immolated sticks and stones To immolate means to sacrifice and is normally a transitive verb, as in "to immolate a calf," say. The OED gives a "transferred" and "figurative" use of "immolate" as "to give up to destruction," a usage not quite transitive, which could be construed to mean *to use for destruction*. Thus Anglo-Saxons have given themselves over completely to the inherited idea that violence—sticks and stones or other weapons dedicated to violence—is an acceptable way to deal with political or social problems.

47:17 the men who had composed the mob, the traders and drovers and teamsters The mob, those who came to disrupt the wedding, were not the townsfolks, but itinerants who gathered "for this one occasion like rats" and afterward "scattered, departed" (47:20).

47:24 and those who had come in the carriages and buggies to see a Roman holiday, driving out to Sutpen's Hundred to call and (the men) to hunt his game and eat his food again The villagers who had refused to accept the aunt's invitation to the wedding itself, who came and stationed themselves outside only to witness what violence might occur, after the wedding resume their relationship with Sutpen.

47:30 It blew away, though not out of memory. He did not forget that night, even though Ellen, I think, did, since she washed it out of her remembering with tears. Mr. Compson perhaps sentimentalizes here, attributing to Sutpen a long memory; he cites no source for this speculation. Likewise sentimentalizing Ellen and her tears, he is more interested in a dramatic flourish to conclude his story than in psychology. Clearly the whole episode has been traumatic for Ellen, a public humiliation from the outset—from the wedding's announcement to her aunt's insane delivery of invitations door-to-door; perhaps even the agreement between her father and Sutpen that she should marry Sutpen contributed to the trauma—a bartering she is in fact not likely to forget or to forgive. One might well speculate about the degree to which this public humiliation constitutes a trauma that caused or at least contributed to her decline into flightiness, to her retreat into her bedroom, and then to the sickness that finally took her life. In any case, Mr. Compson's account and interpretation of these events indicate a very limited insight into female consciousness. See the entry for 39:34.

CHAPTER III

48:1 **I wouldn't think she would want to tell anybody about it** *Quentin said.* John A. Hodgson suggests that chapter III "is not continuous and contemporaneous with chapter II and IV but represents instead a conversation taking place at a later date, after Quentin has returned from Sutpen's Hundred" (104). In this passage Faulkner moves the narrative act in *Absalom* into a new level of consciousness, a new epistemological register. In previous chapters, Faulkner marked the narrations of Rosa Coldfield and Mr. Compson with conventional quotation marks and speech tags. In chapter III, however, he abandons quotation marks and by putting the speech tags here and in two other places (48:3 and 50:6) in italics he problematizes the usual visual markers of speech in written narrative. In other novels Faulkner used italics to indicate varying levels of a character's conscious or unconscious thought. Here, they suggest something not so much about Mr. Compson or Quentin as about the novel's supranarrator: they suggest a narrator different from the relatively conventional narrator of chapters I and II, one somehow more distanced from the material. The lack of traditional quotation markers may actually mark soundlessness, perhaps even voicelessness; the lack may suggest that the words in roman are not actually spoken by one and heard by another but are rather being thought or imagined by someone different from Quentin, his father, and the narrator of the first two chapters. The italic speech tags may indicate a sort of fading away from attribution of the source of the narration. Thus although the three occurrences of italic speech tags noted above imply that the words, or the general outlines of what is actually said, are Quentin's and that Mr. Compson hears them, the fact that there are no other such speech tags in the chapter and, indeed, only two short passages of quoted material; and although at 63:35 the "narrator" says "I believe," the chapter slips away from a definite narrator and moves toward a narrative that becomes more and more distanced from a particular narrator and from a definite source that would give the narrator real authority to tell, to explain, the Sutpen family history. Faulkner continues to play with such typographical features in chapter V, which, almost entirely in italics, is ostensibly Rosa Coldfield's monologue to Quentin as they sit in Rosa's "office" in advance of their visit to Sutpen's Hundred. The italics throughout the chapter, however, suggest a kind of silence and, indeed, the chapter's final paragraphs revert to roman type to suggest that Quentin wasn't listening but was rather stopped at the dramatic moment in Rosa's narrative when Henry bursts into Judith's bedroom to tell her he has shot Bon. Faulkner's technique raises several questions: Are the words in italics Rosa's actual words, or are they rather some distillation by Quentin of all the conversations he has had with his father, doubtless with other townspeople, all his life about the events of that dramatic day? Does he himself manufacture "Rosa's" monologue out of his own narrative whole cloth to dramatize, to explain, perhaps by reconfiguring her explanation of the relationship between Henry and his sister for his own needs? Or is it Quentin's response to the Rosa that his father tells him about in chapter III?

The opening pages of the novel may provide an explanation. There while Quentin sits listening to Rosa his "listening . . . renege[s] and [his] hearing-sense self-confound[s] and the long-dead object of her impotent yet indomitable frustration would appear" (5:23). That is, narrative words disappear and the narrated object appears to take the words' places. The same thing happens in chapter VIII when Quentin and Shreve all of a sudden *become* Henry and Bon; that transformation occurs in italics, a long passage in which Quentin and Shreve are reconciled not even into one voice but into a vision beyond and not needing words, in which the events unfold in a kind of silent vision which they share: there, as in the first chapter, the "long-dead objects" simply appear, "in the long silence of notpeople in notlanguage" (6:33).

48:17 **born, at the price of her mother's life and never to be permitted to forget it** Rosa's mother died birthing her. Her father blames Rosa for that death and never lets her forget that her birth resulted in her mother's death, while she remains unforgiving of a father who would impregnate a woman "at least forty" (48:12).

48:21 **that closed masonry of females** not an official or ceremonial secrecy like that of men in the Masons, but a secret effected by women's experience of childbirth.

48:25 **breathing indictment ubiquitous and even transferable of the entire male principle (that principle which had left the aunt a virgin at thirty-five)** To the women of Jefferson, Rosa's existence constitutes an accusation not just against her father as the particular cause of her mother's death but also a general indictment of all males who exercise their sexual relations without regard to their wives' health or well-being. The "male principle," apparently, is a principle of power which allows them such sexual activity; that that principle "had left the aunt a virgin at thirty-five" argues that its power grants men exclusive rights not only to select their own sexual partners but also to select the sexual partners of all women whose lives, and therefore sexualities, they control; they also, of course, assume the right to *not* select a partner for such women in their control, and thus exclude them from fully realized sexuality.

48:28 **grim tight little house** the house in which Rosa grew up, as contrasted to the large and overlarge mansion at Sutpen's Hundred.

49:5 **Bluebeard** character in popular European mythologies who murdered his wives and hung them in a turret of his castle.

49:5 **transmogrified into a mask looking back with passive and hopeless grief upon the irrevocable world** To "transmogrify" is to change into something horrid or ugly; for the narrator, assumed here to be Mr. Compson, Ellen begins her descent into mental illness, sickness, and death when she moves to Sutpen's Hundred and thus becomes one of "Bluebeard's" wives who will die at his hand. In the first progression she turns into, or hides behind, an ugly mask, from which she looks out at the "irrevocable" world of her new, inescapable life at Sutpen's Hundred. The manuscript reads: "grief upon the world which she had quitted" (Langford 87), a phrase suggesting her sorrow at leaving her childhood home; Faulkner's revision makes her grief at being unable to leave the world into which she has married. That she looks "back" may also indicate that what she looks *at* from behind that mask is her childhood in the Coldfield house, her life there that created the conditions that allowed her current life with Sutpen and that she is "passively" and "hopelessly" unable to change. The "mask" is thus a stoical exterior behind which she does what she can to protect herself from the conditions of her entire life. Judith seems to wear a similar mask.

49:7 **held there not in durance but in a kind of jeering suspension by a man** Ellen is not held in an actual prison ("durance" here means forcible constraint) but in "jeering suspension," a curious phrase the meaning of which is not completely clear. "Jeering" suggests some sense of mockery and "suspension" recalls Bluebeard, who killed his wives and hung their corpses in the turret, that is, "suspended" their bodies; but "suspension" also means a condition in which change, motion, occurs slowly or not at all. It thus also conveys Mr. Compson's sense that Ellen removes herself from earthly reality in to a dream world which makes her daily life possible.

49:10 **ostensible yokemate but actually whip** Mr. Coldfield had thought of Sutpen as an equal partner in their dubious enterprise but in fact Sutpen had turned out to be the "whip," the driving force behind whatever they did.

49:16 **a grim mausoleum air of puritan righteousness and outraged female vindictiveness** the two conflicting forces which dominate the Coldfield household Rosa grows up in.

49:17 **Miss Rosa's childhood (that aged and ancient and timeless absence of youth which consisted of a Cassandra-like listening beyond closed doors, of lurking in dim halls filled with that presbyterian effluvium of lugubrious and vindictive anticipation while she waited for the infancy and childhood with which nature had confounded and betrayed her to overtake the precocity of convinced disapprobation . . .)** The narrator ratchets up several notches the "grim mausoleum" of 49:16; the Coldfield house is not just a mausoleum, a building of tombs, it is filled with a "presbyterian effluvium of lugubrious and vindictive anticipation." Rosa's childhood in that "grim mausoleum" was no normal childhood, but an endless "absence of youth" which she endured without friends or playmates, listening to what the adults were saying (and doing) in their own rooms, behind closed doors. The "presbyterian effluvium" is the forceful flowing of Presbyterian predestination; the "lugubrious and vindictive anticipation" is the Presbyterian's—her father's—mournful anticipation of the certain moral failure of human beings and of judgment upon the sinner. Rosa seems to exist in a sort of womb, waiting "for the infancy and childhood" which her physical body manifests and by which nature had confounded and betrayed her by not giving her the experiences of nurture and security that childhood and infancy require. Waiting "for the infancy and childhood . . . to overtake the precocity of convinced disapprobation," Rosa wants childhood experiences to bypass the disapprobation she has always been convinced was to be hers no matter what she did; the disapprobation is "precocious" because it is premature.

49:36 **at least as a kind of passive symbol of inescapable reminding to rise bloodless and without dimension from the sacrificial stone of the marriage-bed** Mr. Compson continues his speculations about Rosa's attitudes toward her father. Here, though she does not consider herself "an active instrument strong enough to cope with him," she can at least be an "inescapable reminder" to him of what he has done to her mother, constantly rising as the infant from her mother's death- and marriage-bed as "bloodless and without dimension," that is, not even human. Mr. Compson proposes the Coldfields' "marriage-bed" as "sacrificial stone" to suggest his marriage as a pagan sacrifice of a virgin.

50:1 **Clytemnestra** unfaithful wife of unfaithful King Agamemnon; she slew him, for sacrificing their daughter Iphegenia, when he returned from the Trojan wars.

50:24 **ironic fecundity of dragon's teeth** Sown by Cadmus, the dragon's teeth became armed warriors where they hit the ground. Mr. Compson claims irony in Sutpen's sowing because two of his progeny are women, though the third, Henry, is a male who becomes an armed soldier in the Civil War.

50:24 **which with the two exceptions were girls** Sutpen has named Clytie and Henry and Judith, but Mr. Compson claims "two exceptions" as sons: does he here mean Bon? If so, how does he know that Bon is Sutpen's son? Is it possible that Sutpen has other children?

50:25 **I have always liked to believe that he intended to name her Cassandra, prompted by some pure dramatic economy not only to beget but to designate the presiding augur of his own disaster, and that he just got the name wrong through a mistake natural in a man who must have almost taught himself to read** To make a Greek tragedy out of the Sutpen family saga Mr. Compson evokes Cassandra once again, the prophet who in Greek legend could foretell the future but was cursed to be believed by no one. Like any narrator, he shifts and interprets the "facts" to create his own story; but there is no reason to think that the name Clytemnestra would not also "designate the presiding augur" of Sutpen's disaster and that perhaps Sutpen did indeed know where her name came from. In naming his daughter Clytemnestra, Sutpen identifies himself with her father, Tyndareus, king of Sparta, who was banished from Sparta and later restored to power by Hercules. The

• 30 •

identification is particularly telling because Tyndareus had no children who could succeed him and as a result his throne passed to his son-in-law Menelaus. Sutpen's choice of name for his "illegitimate" daughter thus implies an early and persistent anxiety concerning his heirs. See entry for 153:34.

50:30 **When he returned home in '66** Faulkner originally typed "'65" here and at 49:40, then changed both places, in ink, to "'66," so the date here is no mistake. Neither Faulkner nor Mr. Compson can have made the mistake of thinking that the war ended in 1866; thousands of soldiers came home in the weeks and months immediately following Appomattox in April 1865. Sutpen, who had a horse, could have walked from Virginia to Mississippi in a matter of weeks, but Faulkner has him delay his homecoming until January 1866, a curious fact without comment or even acknowledgment by any of the narrators, given Sutpen's assumed haste to return home to begin to rebuild Sutpen's Hundred. The novel tells us nothing of his whereabouts during the eight months following the surrender. If the narrators of chapters VI–VIII are right, we may well speculate that he took his time to get home to give Henry time to deal with Bon, so that he, Sutpen, wouldn't have to. This speculation, if it is correct, may give us another reason to believe that Sutpen is not the confident demonic father that we initially see him as (Ragan, *Absalom* 28).

50:35 **mask in Greek tragedy** The theatre at Athens was so large that the actors had to wear huge masks indicating their character so that people in the most distant seats could know which part an actor was playing.

50:40 **the aunt had taught her to see nothing else** taught her to focus on Sutpen and his potential as a husband for Judith, as she herself does. Here and in the following half-page, Mr. Compson argues for the strong influence of Mr. Coldfield's sister on her nieces; she is "in very truth . . . not only Miss Rosa's mother but her father too" (51:13)

51:18 **picquets** *piquets*, stakes driven into the ground to mark off the angles and area of a fortification. Coldfield feels embattled and in need of defense— embattled no doubt by his own conscience, as the next couple of pages suggest, for having been involved with Sutpen in some sort of shady deal which even though he at last repudiated he still feels guilty over and morally culpable; at 52:22 he worries, according to Mr. Compson, that Sutpen will have revealed his culpability to his grandchildren. He also seems irrationally opposed to the Civil War, though none of the narrators attempts to explain why.

51:39 **he did not get to town every day and when he did he preferred to spend it (he used the bar now) with the men who gathered each noon at the Holston House** Like the married men in Faulkner's *The Hamlet*, Sutpen, when he can, retreats to the fellowship of men in a public place.

52:5 **She was ten now and following the aunt's dereliction (Miss Rosa now kept her father's house as the aunt had done . . .)** Her aunt's dereliction ends Rosa's childhood prematurely.

52:29 **old flavor of grim sortie** A sortie is an armed attack. Again Mr. Compson resorts to military metaphor.

52:31 **Because now that the aunt was gone, Ellen had reneged from that triumvirate of which Miss Rosa tried without realising it to make two** The triumvirate is obviously Ellen, the aunt, and Rosa, confederated in mutual defense against Sutpen at the dinner table. It is not clear how Rosa tried, without realizing it, to reduce the three to two, unless she somehow wanted or helped the aunt to escape with her horse-trader lover; or, perhaps, she did not want to go out there in order to be one of the three, and now she is alone.

52:35 **Ellen went through a complete metamorphosis, emerging into her next lustrum with the complete finality of actual re-birth** Mr. Compson treats Ellen's life as that of a butterfly, metamorphosing from cocoon to insubstantial and beautiful flightiness. She is now, he thinks, so far gone in decline as to make it impossible for her to go back.

52:37 **facing across the table the foe** Rosa faces Sutpen alone; she already thinks of him as an enemy.

52:38 **who was not even aware that he sat there not as host and brother-in-law but as the second party to an armistice** In Mr. Compson's telling Sutpen is completely oblivious to, and does not care about, the dynamic of the various intricate relationships in his own family and among his in-laws.

53:6 **as against** as compared with, weighed against. A comparative mode repeated, "as against" and "and against" (53:18), which offers comparisons of how intently Sutpen looked at various members of his family as compared to how he looked at Rosa.

53:13 **dewlaps** the fold of loose skin that hangs from the throat of cattle and other animals; here applied to Ellen, who is not yet fat, according to Mr. Compson, but soon will be.

53:14 **unscarified hands** hands as yet unscratched by work.

53:15 **damask** a rich fabric, often silk or wool, covered with colored designs.

53:15 **Haviland** china from Limoges, France, imported into the United States from the beginning of the nineteenth century (Ragan, *Absalom* 30).

53:21 **this creature** Rosa.

53:36 **the also-dead** the Confederate soldiers whom Rosa will memorialize in the poetry she will write when her father seals himself up in the attic. "Also" implies Rosa's kinship with them; she is also "dead."

53:39 **some intimation ... acquired or cultivated by listening beyond closed doors not to what she heard there but ... to the prefever's temperature of disaster which makes soothsayers and sometimes makes them right** Rosa watches Sutpen at the dinner table with a feeling of doom gleaned not from her "Cassandra-like listening beyond closed doors" (49:19) but from the "temperature of disaster" created by her father and his liaison with Sutpen.

54:25 **docking the two negroes** deducting from their wages for work they did not do.

54:32 **draft on his conscience had been discharged** The check he had written on his conscience had been cashed. With his grandchildren grown, Mr. Coldfield now feels safe from their vengeance; he is no longer really worried that Sutpen will reveal to them their grandfather's immoral liaison with their father.

54:40 **hoyden** someone rude or illbred, a clown or a boor (OED).

55:3 **partaking of it** partaking of the "pearly lambence" (55:2) of young girlhood.

55:6 **parasitic and potent and serene, drawing to themselves without effort the post-genitive upon and about which to shape, flow into back, breast; bosom, flank, thigh** Mr. Compson's description of female puberty. In grammar, a "post-genitive" is a possessive noun following the noun it qualifies (OED). Here Mr. Compson makes a noun of the term, a metaphorical-physical quality in maturing females, a core sexuality, toward which women's sexuality and sexual parts shape them as they grow older.

55:13 **It was not a volte face of character** volte face = about face. Rosa's decision to move to Sutpen's Hundred does not indicate a change in her character even though it involves living in the house with the "ogre" of her childhood.

55:27 **he hid from Confederate provost marshals in the attic** Coldfield removes himself to the attic of his house, whether to escape the need to enlist or whether he thinks the provost marshals represent some final retribution for his nefarious dealings with Sutpen, is not clear.

55:33 **Lee** Robert E. Lee, Commander of the Army of Northern Virginia.

55:37 **not for the reason that he was unable to forget it but because he could probably not have remembered it enough to have described it ten minutes after looking away** Mr. Compson insists that though Rosa has created Sutpen as a "demon" and "ogre," Sutpen has probably taken no heed whatsoever of her.

56:4 **Ellen was now at the full peak of what the aunt would have called her renegadery. She seemed not only to acquiesce, to be reconciled to her life and marriage, but to be actually proud of it** Growing up in the Coldfield house has ill prepared Ellen for marriage to anyone. Even though the aunt has pushed for the marriage, it was a "push" against Ellen's nature and upbringing. Her newfound "renegadery" is a rebellion against her own self: now she does not simply "acquiesce" to her marriage, she is "actually proud of it." It is not completely clear why the aunt would have called her acquiescence renegadery.

56:12 **his wife, Nature** Fate's wife.

56:25 **had immolated outrageous husband and incomprehensible children into shades** See entry for 46:21. Clearly, Faulkner uses "immolated" in a transitive sense to mean that Ellen has sacrificed her children by turning them into shadows, insubstantial (to her) creatures living in her house. She has also saved herself by doing so (see 56:4). She is so ill-suited to the role of wife and mother that doing so keeps her from self-destruction. See the entry for 56:4.

56:35 **duchess peripatetic with property soups and medicines among a soilless and uncompelled peasantry** Mr. Compson's portrait of Ellen's demeanor among Jeffersonians makes her appear slightly mad, a person of assumed aristocratic blood moving about dispensing medicine and food and good will to her people.

57:2 **asking her to protect the others** Ellen asked Rosa to protect only Judith, not "the others" (17:30).

57:8 **bitter purlieus of Styx** land close around the river which the dead crossed in to hell.

57:9 **rose like the swamp-hatched butterfly, unimpeded by weight of stomach and all the heavy organs of suffering and experience** Calvin Brown (42) says that butterflies do have stomachs, but the ambiguous syntax may allow "unimpeded" to modify Ellen, not the butterfly.

57:14 **Miss Rosa must not have been anything at all now: not the child who had been the object and victim of the vanished aunt's vindictive** unflagging care and attention, and not even the woman which her office as housekeeper would indicate, and certainly not the factual aunt herself. Rosa is, in Mr. Compson's construction, a nonentity to Ellen and Judith, her sister and niece, neither child nor woman nor, given her youth, an actual aunt. The phrase, "*the* factual aunt herself," seems to suggest that she has not become the sort of vindictive presence that Mr. Coldfield's sister was.

57:36 **and no one but your grandfather and perhaps Clytie ever to know that Sutpen had gone to New Orleans too** Apparently Mr. Compson gets his information about Sutpen's trip to New Orleans from his father.

58:7 **departing and inaccessible daughter** Judith doesn't, of course, depart physically, but rather emotionally.

58:17 **Ellen was shrieking with astonished appreciation.** When Rosa offers Judith "the only gift . . . in her power: . . . to teach Judith how to keep house and plan meals and count laundry," she gets from Judith "the blank fathomless stare, the unhearing 'What? What did you say?'" and from Ellen she gets ridicule. Rosa is so hurt by the mutual rejection that the next time Judith and Ellen come to town and stop at her house she refuses to see them.

59:8 **a nigger in the woodpile** In addition to the racial meanings of the word "nigger," the OED lists another definition that applies here: "A strong spiked timber by which logs are canted in a saw-mill." Apparently such a "nigger," strewn among the logs or other timbers, could injure a careless worker. Thus a "nigger in the woodpile" is something hidden and dangerous; it's also a secret from the past, like a skeleton in the closet which, if known, would compromise the present.

60:35 **Charles Bon of New Orleans** At this point in the narrative, apparently no one connects Bon with Sutpen's experiences in Haiti.

61:10 **a hobble-de-hoy** an awkward or rude young man.

61:33 **She postulated the elapsed years** Ellen granted that time had passed, even though Mr. Compson suggests that to her the "five faces looked with a sort of lifeless and perennial bloom like painted portraits hung in a vacuum." See entry for 61:35.

61:35 **five faces** Sutpen, Ellen, Judith, Henry, and Bon.

61:40 **very boards on which they had strutted and postured and laughed and wept** boards = the stage; "strutted" may echo Macbeth's famous soliloquy toward the end of Shakespeare's play, from which Faulkner also gleaned the title, *The Sound and the Fury*: "Life's but a walking shadow, a poor player, / That struts and frets his hour upon the stage, / And then is heard no more" (V.v.24–26).

62:2 not listening, who had got the picture from the first word Rosa understands, Mr. Compson thinks, that the union between Bon and Judith will never take place; apparently Bon's name—Charles the Good—dooms the union since, as she thinks, nothing good can happen to anybody in her family. The conclusion comes to her pictorially, as Quentin, "not listening," reaches an impasse in his listening to her in chapter V. See Godden 4, 69, 72–73, 75, 132.

62:4 bright glitter of delusion Ellen's, who continues to act as though the marriage will definitely take place.

62:5 one of those colored electric beams in cabarets The first cabaret opened in Paris in 1881, *Le Chat Noir*, and by 1900 similar establishments had opened in France and Germany. America's first cabaret opened in 1915, the *Sans Souci*, in New York City. In 1910 Mr. Compson may have known about Parisian cabarets, but the reference would have been lost on Quentin and, in terms of the novel, may well be anachronistic, particularly in its reference to "electric beams" (Kinnet).

62:15 It was probably just peaceful despair and relief at final and complete abnegation, now that Judith was about to immolate the frustration's vicarious recompense into the living fairy tale abnegate = to deny or renounce or give up. "Immolate," normally a transitive verb meaning to sacrifice, here and elsewhere in *Absalom* seems to mean also to sacrifice and to transform into. Rosa's attitude and demeanor in the Sutpen household are not caused by jealousy (62:8) or self-pity (62:9), but by "despair and relief" at her abnegation, or denial, of her own prospects for fulfillment in romance; Rosa gains a "vicarious recompense" by sacrificing, immolating her own frustration into a sympathetic participation in Judith's impending engagement and marriage, the "living fairy tale" that foolish young girls believe in. See entry for 46:21. Campbell suggests that the sentence "simply means that by marrying Charles and moving away to New Orleans Judith is going to take away from Rosa this source of 'vicarious recompense.'" Her "vicarious recompense (her admiration for Judith) is to be sacrificed."

62:18 It sounded like a fairy tale when Ellen told it later to your grandmother, only it was a fairy tale written for and acted by a fashionable ladies' club. It = Judith's impending marriage.

62:24 "We deserve him," Miss Rosa said. "Deserve? Him?" Ellen said, probably shrieked too. "Of course we deserve him—if you want to put it that way. . . ." another occasion on which Ellen ridicules Rosa. It's not completely clear whether Rosa means that they "deserve" Bon as punishment or as reward. Because Rosa does not participate in Ellen's "fairy tale" understanding of the marriage, she offers a conventional acknowledgment of the marriage's propriety. What seems to prompt the exchange is Rosa's childhood sense that the marriage is not a fairy tale but is "authentic, not only plausible but justified" (62:22). Rosa's pleasantry is an affront to Ellen's fairy tale, a shattering of the illusion. Ellen's response two lines later also implies a class dynamic: "I certainly hope and expect you to feel that the Coldfields are qualified to reciprocate whatever particular signal honor marriage with anyone might confer upon them" (62:27). Ellen significantly invokes her maiden name, Coldfield, rather than her married name, Sutpen, to justify Judith's worthiness to be courted. She thus responds specifically to Rosa's use of the first person plural pronoun, "*We* deserve him" at 62:24. Rosa's comment that Bon is "deserved" implies that the Coldfields are not secure in their class but are upwardly mobile, working their way into the aristocracy and their success *merits* Bon; Ellen bristles at the suggestion that her daughter is "marrying up." In 1910 Rosa sounds this same note. See entry for 11:26.

62:33 **saw Ellen depart** Ellen doesn't "depart." She simply withdraws, vanishes, "perhaps not out of Jefferson, but out of her sister's life anyway" (64:5).

62:34 **second only gift in her power** The first is the ability to keep house, the second her knowledge of how to fit clothes.

62:37 **this second gift developed late (you might say, repercussed)** Rosa's ability to fit clothes is "an unwarranted or unintended effect" (OED) of her aunt's elopement with her horse trader; that is, necessity forced Rosa to learn to sew.

63:19 **permitted conscience to cause him to withdraw from that old affair in which his son-in-law had involved him not only at the cost of his just profits but at the sacrifice of his original investment** This description of Coldfield's withdrawal from "that old affair" echoes Sutpen's description of his "withdrawal" from his marriage in Haiti (210–11).

64:9 **black foundation on which it had been erected** "black" here means evil, but specifically the evil of slavery.

64:21 **Sumpter** variant spelling of Sumter: The firing of Federal troops on Fort Sumter, in Charleston Harbor, in April 1861, signaled the beginning of the Civil War.

65:21 **the town knew that between Henry and Judith there had been a relationship closer than the traditional loyalty of brother and sister even**

Given Quentin's and Shreve's intense discussion of incest in chapters VII and VIII, it's difficult not to sense a foregrounding of incest here, though what follows describing the town's sense of their "relationship" carries no sexual overtones at all.

66:6 **when Mississippi seceded** January 9, 1861; Mississippi was the second state to secede, after South Carolina.

66:10 **Scott** Sir Walter Scott (1771–1832), Scottish novelist whose historical romances were enormously popular and influential.

66:21 **when she addressed him that one time when they told her that he was dead** There is no account of Rosa's addressing Sutpen after Bon's death. It is either a textual incongruity or a point not taken up by Quentin and Shreve when they recreate the scene together.

67:39 **close trading** trading at or very close to market closing. The practice minimizes the risk of prices falling after purchase or rising after selling. Mr. Coldfield succeeds either by such conservative trading or by "dishonesty" (67:40), these being the only sure ways to advance financially. The term thus connotes a trade at or near dishonesty, whereby one trader minimizes his own risk.

68:10 **keeping it in** it = the life, the activity that Rosa's existence consists of.

68:28 **was dated in the first year of her father's voluntary incarceration** the first of Rosa's "odes to Southern soldiers." Rosa's writing of poetry may be some form of resistance to her father's pathological response to the War, since she hates him for a lot of reasons.

69:6 **two negresses which he had freed as soon as he came into possession of them . . . writing out their papers of freedom which they could not read and putting them on a weekly wage which he held back in full against the discharge of the current market value at which he had assumed them on the debt—and in return for which they had been among the first Jefferson negroes to desert and follow the Yankee troops** Coldfield believes that chattel slavery is morally wrong, so he technically frees the slaves he buys, but keeps them in economic bondage by forcing them to buy that freedom with wages he doesn't give them.

69:18 **not in the money but in its representation of a balance in whatever spiritual counting-house he believed would some day pay his sight drafts on self-denial and fortitude** Coldfield's puritan nature believes that money corrupts its owner, but he can believe that his money and his worldly possessions are a measure of earthly success and a sign of God's favor. It thus represents his payment for his moral courage and his self-denial. Again, he sounds a lot like Thomas Sutpen.

69:39 **bright vacuum before the gale** the calm before the storm.

70:7 **And with the same success** with no success. That is, with the same degree of success, "as though" he could compel it.

70:9 **as though houses actually possess a sentience** Ragan attributes this idea to Poe's "The Fall of the House of Usher" (*Absalom* 37).

70:23 **the same almost plump soft (though now unringed) hands on the coverlet** For some reason Ellen no longer wears her wedding ring, whether because it no longer fits her finger comfortably or in rejection of her husband.

71:10 **living on the actual blood itself like a vampire, not with insatiability, certainly not with voracity, but with that serene and idle splendor of flowers arrogating to herself, because it fills her veins also, nourishment from the old blood that crossed uncharted seas and continents and battled wilderness hardships and lurking circumstances and fatalities, with tranquil disregard of whatever onerous carks to leisure and even peace which the preservation of it incurs upon what might be called the contemporary transmutable fountainhead who contrives to keep the crass foodbearing corpuscles sufficiently numerous and healthy in the stream** Rosa lives at Sutpen's Hundred not voraciously but taking passive advantage of the slaves—"the old blood"—who serve her as the "contemporary transmutable fountainhead," that is, as the current source of her original nourishment, of her physical health, and showing no awareness of whatever discomfort—the "onerous carks to leisure"—one might have felt in knowing of the suffering of the slaves who provide that support.

CHAPTER IV

Chapter IV and indeed the entire narrative are punctuated by phrases—*I believe, perhaps, maybe, I can imagine, he must have*—that mark the narrators' speculations about character, motive, and actions. The text constantly stresses how much of Mr. Compson's narrative is his induction from possibilities that he has created; Faulkner reminds us repeatedly how little of "fact" we and the narrators have to deal with, how much of it is a construction, a piecing together of the "rag-tag and bob-ends of old tales and telling" (250:17) that may not be related.

This narrative method reaches its zenith in Mr. Compson's well-known realization at 83:21 that the events they are describing are "just incredible. [They] just [do] not explain. Or perhaps that's it: they dont explain and we are not supposed to know." That is, after carefully sifting through the evidence, positing possible interpretations (perhaps, maybe, possibly), Mr. Compson comes to the conclusion that none of the scant available evidence "explains" the Sutpen story fully. At the University of Virginia, a student proposed that *Absalom* was like Wallace Stevens's poem "Thirteen Ways of Looking at a Blackbird," and Faulkner agreed (*FU* 273–74): none of the narrators holds the full truth about the Sutpen family, no matter how hard each tries to arrange the scant evidence into a logical, consistent, coherent pattern that will explain everything. Mr. Compson's description of his attempts to understand and tell things logically, mixing and remixing the ingredients to try to make sense, sounds a lot like Thomas Sutpen's explanation in chapter VI to General Compson of his failed attempts to put together a life that has some coherence, a design; the narrators are all trying to create a "design" that will accommodate everything they know or think they know about the Sutpen family.

74:20 **wistaria colored smoke** Wistaria blossoms come in several shades of blue that might easily be the color of the smoke from Mr. Compson's cigar; they also fade after bloom to a grayish brown.

74:22 **the hand looking almost as dark as a negro's against his linen leg** indistinguishable; "as dark as a negro's" indicates the proximity of racial difference to the consciousness of narrator and character alike. The image foregrounds the black presence throughout: Negro hands are everywhere: in the woodpile, in the shadows, all intimately involved in historical phenomena—labor, intellect, sex.

74:23 **Because Henry loved Bon** Mr. Compson's speculation based, apparently, upon inferences from the shadowy information he details in the next sentences: Henry must have loved Bon, since he "repudiated blood birthright and material security" for his sake. This chapter is replete with speculation about the homoerotic.

74:26 **intending bigamist** Mr. Compson believes that Sutpen discovered in New Orleans that Bon was already married, even if to a New Orleans quadroon woman. He is probably constructing backward to New Orleans from the appearance of the quadroon woman and Charles Etienne St.-Valery Bon at Sutpen's Hundred in chapter VII and assuming that Sutpen discovered them in New Orleans. He alters his speculation over the next pages. See entries for 76:36 and 77:28.

74:27 **on whose dead body four years later Judith was to find the photograph of the other woman and the child** There is some question about whose photograph is actually in the metal case. Rosa later claims to have seen *Judith*'s picture there (118:6; see also 295:26).

74:29 **he (Henry) could give his father the lie about a statement which he must have realised that his father could not and would not have made without foundation and proof** Mr. Compson, again deducing from Sutpen's putative trip to New Orleans where he may have learned about Bon's marriage to the quadroon, assumes a good deal about Henry's character.

74:32 **Henry himself striking the blow with his own hand** Not a literal blow with a literal hand. Mr. Compson means that Henry called his father a liar, "striking a blow" in defense of Bon.

75:28 **he must have known, as he knew that what his father had told him was true, that he was doomed and destined to kill** More of Mr. Compson's dramatic narration. We don't know what Sutpen has told Henry much less that because of it Henry knew he was "doomed" and "destined to kill" the man who wanted to marry his sister.

75:37 **It was Henry's probation; Henry holding all three of them in that durance to which even Judith acquiesced up to a certain point.** durance = forced imprisonment, but here also means "duration." Mr. Compson suggests that the period following Henry's renunciation of Sutpen and home is a period of probation Henry grants Bon in which to prove himself, an indeterminate period of waiting which "all three of them"—Henry, Judith, and Bon—must endure until he or circumstance can work out some resolution to the deadlock of Sutpen's disapproval of the union. See 80:19.

76:10 **not the male relative, the brother, but because of that relationship between them—that single personality with two bodies both of which had been seduced almost simultaneously by a man whom at the time Judith had never even seen** Mr. Compson begins to build a case for a homoerotic relationship of sorts between Henry and Bon.

76:36 **certainly not as a valid objection to marriage with a white woman** Mr. Compson believes that Sutpen's objection to Bon is his marriage to the quadroon woman in New Orleans, but posits that in the old South such a marriage would not have posed any moral or legal problem for Bon, much less a need to keep it a secret. See entries for 74:26, 77:28.

77:10 **Scythian glitter** Scythia was an ancient region in European and Asiatic Russia, populated by nomadic tribes. The reference here seems to associate some sort of wealth with Scythians; maybe so, but given Mr. Compson's interests, it seems more likely a reference to a "Scythian disease," which involves the atrophy of the male sexual organs, and of "Scythian insanity," by virtue of which one with the Scythian disease begins dressing in female dress and adopting female behaviors (OED). Throughout this chapter, Mr. Compson's interest, almost prurient, lies in what he depicts as a kind of fey bisexuality in Bon that seduces both Henry and Judith, in his luxuriant, almost effeminate manner even at the rural University of Mississippi.

77:28 **mistress and child** Now it's a mistress and child, not a wife, that Sutpen discovers during his trip to New Orleans. See entries for 74:26 and 76:36.

77:34 **troglodytes** A troglodyte is a savage cave-dweller, an ape, the reverse of a sophisticated city-dweller.

78:18 **this was not the first time he had played this part** The first time, of course, was in the ceremony uniting Bon and his octoroon woman, whatever ceremony it was.

78:23 **the letter** reproduced pp. 107–09.

78:33 **the picture of the octoroon mistress and the little boy** See entry for 74:27.

79:5 **the slightly Frenchified cloak and hat which he wore, or perhaps (I like to think this) presented formally to the man reclining in a flowered, almost feminised gown** Mr. Compson depicts Bon as sissified, dandified, almost sybaritic. His association of "Frenchness" with "feminised" is somewhat at odds with the portrait of the almost hyper-masculine, if diminutive, "French" architect who builds Sutpen's mansion.

79:10 **some tangible effluvium of knowledge, surfeit: of actions done and satiations plumbed and pleasures exhausted and even forgotten** An "effluvium" is a "flowing out." Mr. Compson continues to create a Bon so long gone in sexual and other pleasures of self-indulgence as to know and understand things that Henry has only begun to discover. He has forgotten things that Henry will never know.

79:14 **small new provincial college** The University of Mississippi was founded in 1848.

79:25 **Yes, he loved Bon, who seduced him as surely as he seduced Judith** probably not "love" in the sexual sense, but definitely eroticized. Mr. Compson has explained in the previous and the following lines the nature of Henry's unsophisticated attraction to the cosmopolitan splendor of his friend from New Orleans.

79:32 **Arabian Nights** generally, fabulous stories; specifically a reference to *A Thousand and One Nights*, the stories Scheherazade told the king to keep herself alive, one per night with a cliff-hanging ending that left him wanting more. She was the latest of 3,000 virgins to entertain the king, each of whom he beheaded after one night, in vengeance for his first wife's infidelity.

80:1 **given to instinctive and violent action rather than to thinking, ratiocination** See the end of chapter I, where Henry, watching his naked father fighting, vomits, rather than digesting the scene intellectually as his sister does.

80:3 **his fierce provincial's pride in his sister's virginity was a false quantity which must incorporate in itself an inability to endure in order to be precious, to exist, and so must depend upon its loss, absence, to have existed at all** The grammar of this passage clearly indicates that Henry's *pride* is the false quantity, but the lines immediately following make it equally clear that Mr. Compson means that Judith's *virginity* is the false quantity. In order to be valuable, he opines, virginity must be vulnerable to time and change; things are thus valuable in direct relation to their capacity to be destroyed. Perhaps this true of a "provincial's pride" too, in that the idea of provinciality emerges with the growth of cities,

80:7 **the pure and perfect incest: the brother realising that the sister's virginity must be destroyed in order to have existed at all, taking that virginity in the person of the brother-in-law, the man whom he would be if he could become, metamorphose into, the lover, the husband** Mr. Compson's reiterated speculations posit Henry's homoerotic desire for Bon as the perfect complement to his incestuous longings for Judith. Both homosexuality and incest being forbidden by his culture, Bon's marriage with Judith would be for Henry the "pure and perfect incest" because he could imaginatively substitute himself for each of them and thus fulfill both his forbidden desires.

80:22 **Henry: not Bon** 82:11 explains: "So it must have been Henry who seduced Judith, not Bon" who seduced her.

80:30 **he, the living man, was usurped** Bon the man was usurped, in Judith and Ellen's (and Henry's?), imagination by Bon the idea.

82:3 **this, mind you, in a man who had already acquired a name for prowess among women while at the University** Mr. Compson speaks as though

Bon's prowess is a fact—"this, mind you"—but the novel provides no evidence that this is the case.

82:28 **bent on marrying him to the extent of forcing her brother to the last resort of homocide** Mr. Compson speculates that the strength of her desire to marry Bon is what "forced" Henry, in reaction against her desire, to kill Bon, that Henry is himself the agent of the murder. In chapter VIII, Quentin and Shreve will have it that Sutpen "forces" him to.

82:29 **homicide, even if not murder** Mr. Compson probably means that Henry would not murder Bon in cold blood but rather, interpreting Bon's attempts to marry Judith as an assault on the Sutpen family honor, challenge him to a duel.

83:15 **morganatic ceremony** a marriage in which a person of high rank unites with another of low rank with the understanding that the lower person retains the same social rank and that none of the children from that union may inherit the higher parent's wealth (OED).

83:21 **It's just incredible. It just does not explain. Or perhaps that's it: they dont explain and we are not supposed to know** See the introduction to this chapter.

83:28 **Chocktaw** variant spelling of Choctaw.

85:9 **Lothario** a libertine, a seducer. From a character in Rowe's *Fair Penitent* (1703) (OED).

85:20 **to go to New Orleans and find what he seems to have known all the while that he would find** According to Mr. Compson earlier, Sutpen goes to New Orleans and discovers that Bon has the quadroon mistress or wife, though he doesn't earlier propose that Sutpen goes to New Orleans looking for anything specific. Here, he describes a purpose-driven Sutpen who goes to New Orleans to confirm what he already knows. But how can he suspect Bon of having a quadroon mistress or wife and son there? Does he rather propose that Sutpen recognizes in Bon some physical feature that made him fear that he might be his son? Coming after the crucial passage at 83:21, Mr. Compson now begins to question previous hypotheses and speculations: "who knows what he was thinking" (85:19). He now asks whether Sutpen knew more than he had previously assumed. He thus offers sympathy for Sutpen's predicament, who "trusted no man nor woman, who had no man's nor woman's love" (85:23) and begins to acknowledge a respect for Sutpen's strength (85:30) and intelligence.

86:14 **the body which Miss Rosa saw** Bon's body. But Rosa claims later that she never saw him, dead or alive (121).

86:28 **possible bigamy, to which Henry gave the lie** Mr. Compson speculates that during the Christmas Eve confrontation in the closed library Sutpen acquainted Henry with information he had gotten in New Orleans, that Bon was married and that his marriage with Judith would therefore possibly be bigamy. Henry called his father a liar. See entry for 89:13.

87:6 **with that complete abnegant transference, metamorphosis into the body which was to become his sister's lover** abnegant transference = by negating himself, Henry could become Bon. Mr. Compson continues his theme that Henry through Bon wittingly or unwittingly establishes the "perfect incest," that is, taking his sister's virginity through the body of the man he loves, "as though it actually were the brother who had put the spell on the sister, seduced her to his own vicarious image which walked and breathed with Bon's body" (89:3). Although according to Mr. Compson Henry has forbidden Bon to write Judith, when letters do come he intercepts them and reads them to Judith.

87:27 **Christmas gift** Traditionally at Christmas time, blacks upon meeting whites would say "Christmas gift" and be entitled to a quarter or some change the white man had in his pocket. See the episode in *The Sound and the Fury* (943).

87:35 **the Christmas eve, the explosion, and none to ever know just why or just what happened between Henry and his father** Again Faulkner emphasizes what a construct of supposition and probability Mr. Compson's version of things is.

89:6 **here is the letter** See entry for 87:6.

89:13 **Henry still in the fierce repercussive flush of vindicated loyalty** Mr. Compson dramatizes Henry and Bon's trip away from Sutpen's Hundred that Christmas eve, Henry proud of himself for having been loyal to his friend by calling his father a liar, Bon meditating how he can now tell him that his father had been right. Henry "vindicates" his loyalty to Bon by calling his father a liar and leaving Sutpen's Hundred with him. The "flush" of vindicated loyalty is "repercussive" primarily in the sense that the repudiation of father and home still reverberates in his thought and bearing; according to the OED, "repercussive" also describes a medicine designed to "repel humors or reduce swelling"; and it also means reflected light.

89:21 **Perhaps in his fatalism he loved Henry the better of the two, seeing perhaps in the sister merely the shadow, the woman vessel with which to consummate the love whose actual object was the youth** "In his fatalism" suggests a premonition that Henry will kill him and that he will desire death when it comes: his desires for Henry and for death are equal manifestations of his fatalism. Mr. Compson thus offers the possibility that Bon too is using Judith as a vicarious means whereby to have Henry, even if not necessarily in a sexual sense, though maybe that too. But see the entry for 89:25.

89:25 **cerebral Don Juan** Don Juan is known more for his physical exploits as a lover than as an intellect; Mr. Compson creates Bon as a more fey, dandified, cerebral lover perhaps more interested in the game, the seduction, than in the actual conquest, since, as Mr. Compson has suggested earlier, Bon has had access to all the physical gratifications he could want all his life, to the point of supersatiation, so that the mind games become for him more erotic and satisfying than the actual sexual conquest.

90:2 **trap** a small carriage on springs, usually two-wheeled.

91:18 **the postulation to come after the fact** A "postulation" accepts something as a fact without the need for formal proof. According to Mr. Compson, Bon here wants to teach Henry about his way of life in gradual degrees, so that he will have the proof, the fact, before Bon offers the postulation.

91:36 **But that's not it.** The sensuous, sinful, glamorous way of life of New Orleans described in the preceding lines is only the surface of what Bon introduces Henry to, is only "the foundation," which "belongs to anybody" white enough and rich enough. On pp. 92ff, Mr. Compson proposes that Bon gradually exposes Henry to what Mr. Compson calls "the supreme apotheosis of chattelry," the system which breeds beautiful quadroon women to serve the sexual and certain social needs of white men. The women occupy a place "created for and by voluptuousness, the abashless and unabashed senses" (94:35).

93:1 **the supreme apotheosis of chattelry** apotheosis = the exaltation or deification of a person or idea. See entries for 91:36 and 94:38.

93:5 **goatlike** The goat is one of the central figures of Dionysian revelry and celebration, often associated with Pan.

93:21 **a creature out of an old woodcut of the French Revolution** A woodcut was a block of wood carved with a scene or a portrait used to illustrate a text. Mr. Compson probably doesn't have a particular woodcut in mind but rather a generic one, probably from a book or magazine illustration.

94:36 **country boy with his simple and erstwhile untroubled code in which females were ladies or whores or slaves** Mr. Compson constantly contrasts Henry's rural, uncomplicated, provincial upbringing with Bon's New Orleans sophistication. Henry must adjust his simplistic worldview, Bon believes, in order to accept him as he is.

94:38 **the apotheosis of two doomed races presided over by its own victim** An "apotheosis" is an idealized form of something. Here, the octoroon is both apotheosis and victim.

95:1 **eternal Who-suffers** women.

95:21 **Not whores** Ragan points to a passage in Lyle Saxon's *Fabulous New Orleans* (1928) from which Faulkner might have derived this discussion (*Absalom* 51), though of course Faulkner may have gleaned as much from discussion with others during his time in New Orleans.

95:23 **laws which declare that one eighth of a specified kind of blood shall out-weigh seven eighths of another kind** Mr. Compson refers to the "one drop rule," which decreed that even a single drop of black blood rendered a person legally black. It was informally applied in the antebellum period as a way of insuring a larger number of slaves, but by the 1920s it was Jim Crow's law of the land.

95:25 **But that same white race would have made them slaves too, laborers, cooks, maybe even field hands, if it were not for this thousand, these few men like myself without principles or honor either. . . . We cannot, perhaps we do not even want to, save all of them; perhaps the thousand we save are not one in a thousand. But we save that one.** Bon argues that this particular form of slavery, the quadroon concubinage, is actually a blessing that sophisticated white men bestow upon certain select women: a blessing since the only alternative for them is to be laborers. This is a somewhat refined version of the self-serving argument that slaves were better off in civilized Christian America than in savage benighted Africa.

95:31 **God may mark every sparrow** In the Bible, a sparrow is generally any small, inconsequential bird, as in Matthew 10:29: "Are not two sparrows sold for a farthing? and one of them shall not fall on the ground without your Father."

96:2 **the principles of honor, decorum and gentleness applied to perfectly normal human instinct which you Anglo-Saxons insist upon calling lust and in whose service you revert in sabbaticals to the primordial caverns** Mr. Compson makes Bon's arguments for the system he is describing to

Henry logical, rational: the system allows gentlemen to indulge their physical appetites without making a moral issue out of sex as Anglo-Saxon puritans do, who like anchorites and hermits of old find ways to mortify rather than celebrate the flesh.

96:25 **the white blood to give the shape and pigment of what the white man calls female beauty, to a female principle which existed, queenly and complete, in the hot equatorial groin of the world long before that white one of ours came down from trees and lost its hair and bleached out** For Bon, as Mr. Compson would have it, the combination of white and black creates a perfect amalgam of sensuous beauty, but his argument depends upon two myths: the one that white women "flee" from sensuality "in moral and outraged horror," the other that black women, black people, are more erotic by nature, by virtue of their direct connection to something primitive.

96:28 **hot equatorial groin of the world** Africa.

96:30 **a principle apt docile and instinct with strange and ancient curious pleasures of the flesh** The "queenly and complete" "female principle" (see entry for 96:25) is "apt" because appropriate to the presumed sensual nature of black women; "docile" because though "queenly and complete" it nevertheless yields easily to the white man's sexual needs and exploitation. The OED defines "instinct with" as "impelled, excited, animated" and "imbued or inspired with."

96:34 **a principle which, where her white sister must needs try to make an economic matter of it . . . reigns, wise supine and all-powerful, from the sunless and silken bed which is her throne** an interesting image for Faulkner and for Mr. Compson, given the number of white women, including Mr. Compson's wife Caroline, in *The Sound and the Fury*, numerous others throughout Faulkner's work, and especially including Ellen Sutpen, who "reign" from sickbeds and who have real or imagined illnesses.

97:3 **For a price, of course, but a price offered and accepted or declined through a system more formal than any that white girls are sold under since they are more valuable as commodities than white girls** Mr. Compson argues that Bon operates within a system of barter for the quadroon women's favor that is more moral than that by which white women exchange sexual favors, because they operate according to a strictly negotiable system of costs and expenses and retain some power to choose to whom they give their favors. They seem to think that white women do not have that option. But the comparison is highly problematic and, for Bon and for Mr.

Compson, offered without recognition that history is replete with, in some ways even driven by, the formal barter of white women for political and economic purposes, women who, like Marie Antoinette, became queens but who nevertheless were chattel in a formal system of trade. Implicit here is a protofeminist argument that marriage is a form of prostitution.

97:7 **a woman's sole end and purpose: to love, to be beautiful, to divert** a misogynistic characterization of women, one that suits Bon's and the socioeconomic system's purposes.

97:14 **they are the only true chaste women, not to say virgins, in America** The quadroon woman is more sexually moral than a white woman because after being bought she remains faithful to the buyer not just until the man dies but also until she does. Mr. Compson here taps into the Faulknerian free-market trope of the honest whore, which by the simple economic exchange of sex for money (uncomplicated by marriage, family, and property law) produces a woman more sexually moral than one who must negotiate her sexuality within the jurisprudence of middle-class marriage. As Mr. Compson would have it, in Bon's mind, marriage corrupts women; hence, Henry's immediate middle class objection to Bon's claim that such women are "the only true chaste women in America": "But you married her" (97:18).

97:15 **they remain true and faithful to that man not merely until he dies or frees them, but until they die. And where will you find whore or lady either whom you can count on to do that?** Mr. Compson's misogyny continues to astonish and to drive his narrative, especially in what he imagines takes place in New Orleans. He assumes that *no* woman, except the quadroons, will be faithful to her husband or lover. A huge number of Faulkner's men worry about their own cuckolding, whether through their wives' insatiable appetites or their own inadequacies as lovers (Polk "Cuckold"). Mr. Compson seems to wallow vicariously in the sensuality he describes in New Orleans. Though she does not appear in *Absalom, Absalom!*, not even by implication, there is some evidence in *The Sound and the Fury* that his own wife has been unfaithful to him and that that is at least part of the cause of his drinking.

98:7 **Have you forgot that this woman, this child, are niggers?** Bon's question invokes the "trump card," the "cultural taboo ... the same one offered by Shreve and Quentin" to explain Sutpen's rejection of Bon (Ragan, *Critical Study* 65).

98:35 **Bull Run** There were two battles at Manassas Junction, Virginia, along the banks of a stream called Bull Run, during the Civil War. Both—the first on July 21, 1861, the second on August 28–30, 1862—were early Confederate successes that gave the South the heady illusion of a quick victory in the War.

98:35 **a company organising at the University** The University Grays, composed of university students, became the Eleventh Mississippi Infantry. It deployed to Corinth on May 1, 1861, participated in major battles throughout the war—including Second Manassas, Gettysburg (Pickett's Charge), Cold Harbor, and the siege at Petersburg—and surrendered at Appomattox.

99:10 **not Judith who was the object of Bon's love or of Henry's solicitude. She was just the blank shape, the empty vessel in which each of them strove to preserve, not the illusion of himself nor his illusion of the other but what each conceived the other to believe him to be—the man and the youth, seducer and seduced, who had known one another, seduced and been seduced, victimised in turn each by the other, conqueror vanquished by his own strength, vanquished conquering by his own weakness, before Judith came into their joint lives** Mr. Compson belabors his theory of the homoerotic in the Bon-Henry-Judith triangle. Judith doesn't really figure in any of this except as a slate on which the two males can articulate their passion for each other. Henry and Bon become sort of archetypal figures, or "types," whose desire for each other has existed long before a heterosexual element came in to the picture. Bon, the "conqueror," has been vanquished by the elements which made him attractive to Henry; Henry, the "vanquished," has conquered by being attractive to Bon.

99:27 **And Judith: how else to explain her. . . . No: anything but a fatalist** Because Judith is no fatalist she would have to be "corrupted" to resign herself to events. Mr. Compson is puzzled to explain Judith's motives in waiting, since she is, as he puts it, the "Sutpen with the ruthless Sutpen code of taking what it wanted" (99:31). He argues that she would have done what she wanted to do no matter what the "truth" about Bon was: "I can imagine her if necessary even murdering the other woman. But she certainly would have made no investigation and then held a moral debate between what she wanted and what she thought was right. Yet she waited" (100:5). But her "waiting" could easily be a function of the fact that she has seen Bon for a total of twelve days, that he is forty miles away at the university, three hundred miles away in New Orleans, and untold distances from her during the war. "Waiting" implies that she had a choice in the matter, and clearly she did not, even assuming that she knew about the competition from the quadroon,

• 50 •

and there's no evidence that she did. This is more of Mr. Compson's dramatizing. Compare Bon's fatalism (89:21). The knot here is "Surely Bon could not have corrupted her to fatalism in twelve days" (99:27) because if she did fall in love with him she may well have accepted his resignation to events: "how else to explain her but this way?" (99:27).

100:16 **Have you noticed how so often when we try to reconstruct the causes which lead up to the actions of men and women, how with a sort of astonishment we find ourselves now and then reduced to the belief, the only possible belief, that they stemmed from some of the old virtues?** Mr. Compson falls back on the old verities to explain Judith: love and trust, of both Bon and her father: "*I love, I will accept no substitute; something has happened between him and my father; if my father was right, I will never see him again, if wrong he will come or send for me; if happy I can be I will, if suffer I must I can*" (100:28). The phrase "stemmed from the old virtues" nonetheless does not explain anything, and what comes in italics is not an old virtue but an expression of Judith's corrupt fatalism and in fact completely miscasts her behavior after the war, behavior far from fatalistic or passive.

100:36 **Ellen took to her bed, between that Christmas day and the day when Sutpen rode away** Mr. Compson seems to suggest some connection between her husband's rift with her son, her husband's planned departure for the war, and Ellen's illness. She must take to her bed in her own darkened room at about the same time her father, Mr. Coldfield, hides in his attic. Neither ever returns from self-imposed exile.

101:1 **They were too much alike** Judith and Sutpen.

101:3 **so much alike that the power, the need, to communicate by speech atrophies from disuse and, comprehending without need of the medium of ear or intellect, they no longer understand one another's actual words** Their relationship is thus much like that later between Quentin and Shreve as they reconstruct the Sutpen story, especially in chapter VIII, when they seem to become Henry and Bon, communicating and creating beyond the need for words.

101:21 **probably the most moving mass-sight of all human mass-experience, far more so than the spectacle of so many virgins going to be sacrificed to some heathen Principle, some Priapus—the sight of young men . . . marching away to a battle** In Greek mythology, Priapus is the god of fertility, the son of Aphrodite and Dionysus. Here and at 102:5 Mr. Compson expresses an astonishing misogyny. It's not completely clear why the sacrifice of young men is more moving than the sacrifice of "so many virgins," but the comparison surely supports Mr. Compson's belief in the patriarchal ideology that values male life—and masculine heroics—more than female life. Mr. Compson is also referring to both sacrifices as a ritualistic slaughter of the young by their elders, a slaughter that both young and old find aesthetically pleasing and politically necessary—to forefend aggression by defending the homeland or to placate the gods.

102:5 **bugles, entering a hundred windows where a hundred still unbrided widows dreamed virgin unmeditant upon the locks of black or brown or yellow** Mr. Compson, in his misogynistic understanding of what he believes to be women's, virgins', inability to understand the world, repeats one of the romantic clichés of the pre-war world of the doomed and lost "cause": when the bugles sound the call to war, all the marriage-age young women—those who, "unbrided," unmarried yet, who will nevertheless be widows when their "nothusbands" (3), the men they plan or hope to marry, are killed in battle—romanticize, sentimentalize the war and the locks of hair they have as souvenirs. They dream, but are "unmeditant": as virgins and therefore innocent of the real world, they cannot think their way through to the very real possibility that their sweethearts and fiancés might not come back from the war.

102:14 **Henry and Bon ... did not join the company until after it departed, who must have emerged from whatever place it was that they lurked in, emerging as though unnoticed from the roadside brake or thicket, to fall in as the marching company passed** Though it is not clear whether or how Mr. Compson knows this or whether he simply makes it up, he would have it that Henry and Bon sneak into the University Grays after the unit has left town rather than joining in the festivities of its departure in town—perhaps, though he does not speculate why, in order not to be detected and caught by Sutpen.

102:30 **extra-academnic** a neologism that makes a Latinate noun out of the adjective "academic." Military service is something outside normal academic study.

102:32 **He received a lieutenancy before the company entered its first engagement even.** He = Bon, though this is not clear from Mr. Compson's narration.

103:4 **the private who carried that officer, shot through the shoulder, on his back while the regiment fell back under the Yankee guns at Pittsburg Landing** Henry carries Bon to safety in retreat. The Battle of Pittsburg

• 52 •

Landing or Shiloh, as it is also called, on April 6–7, 1862, was particularly bloody, in a particularly bloody war: Union casualties were 12,163, Confederate 10,699. Mr. Compson gives no source for this episode or for Bon's wounding. Later, Shreve will claim that Henry, not Bon, was the one wounded and that Henry is the source of the information (283:34).

103:17 **Ellen in bed in the shuttered room, requiring the unremitting attention of a child** Rosa waits on Ellen. This is another shuttered room, like that in her father's house, which may presage the shuttered room, the "office," in which Rosa entertains Quentin in chapter I.

104:16 **two years defunctive now** The summer is defunctive, not Ellen.

105:7 **You get born and you try this and you dont know why only you keep on trying it and you are born at the same time with a lot of other people, all mixed up with them, like trying to, having to, move your arms and legs with strings only the same strings are hitched to all the other arms and legs and the others all trying and they dont know why either except that the strings are all in one another's way** Judith, in the specific moment that Mr. Compson is describing, articulates a worldview quite at odds with his earlier declamation that the people of the past are "people too as we are and victims too as we are, but victims of a different circumstance, simpler and therefore, integer for integer, larger, more heroic and the figures therefore more heroic too, not dwarfed and involved but distinct, uncomplex" (74:7).

105:38 **No! No! Not that! Think of your——** Mrs. Compson, apparently thinking that Judith is contemplating suicide, urges her to think of her family, at least of those dependent on her, or to think of her father, who will be returning from the war.

105:40 **Oh. I? No, not that.** Not suicide. "Women dont do that for love," she explains at 106:4.

106:5 **And not now, anyway. Because there wouldn't be any room now, for them to go to, wherever it is, if it is. It would be full already. Glutted.** In the bloody days of the Civil War, men don't commit suicide for love either, because if they did there would be no place for their souls to go, hell being already overcrowded with soldiers' souls.

106:7 **Like a theatre, an opera house, if what you expect to find is forgetting, diversion, entertainment; like a bed already too full if what you want to find is a chance to lie still and sleep and sleep and sleep** War violates normal, daily expectations so completely that even so dramatic an act as suicide loses significance. If you want "forgetting, diversion, entertainment" in a theatre or peaceful sleep in bed, you won't find it in either if theatre or bed is glutted with more people than they can possibly hold.

106:25 **jackanape** an impudent or mischievous child.

106:27 **elegant and gallant and tediously contrived turns of form and metaphor** Mr. Compson doesn't allow the letter in his hand to contradict his sense of the fey Charles Bon he has been describing; the letter he has just handed to Quentin, elegant in its simple straightforwardness, its good humor, and its seriousness, is in no manner fey. The prose Mr. Compson describes is more nearly that of his own narrative than that of the letter. Evidence carries no weight against Mr. Compson's predilections.

106:29 **But keeping this one which must have reached her out of a clear sky after an interval of four years** Mr. Compson invites readers to speculate whether this was indeed the first letter Judith received in four years or whether it was one she had deliberately picked out to give to somebody to keep, for whatever reason.

107:2 **without date or salutation or signature** While giving readers this letter, one of very few actual documents to survive from the Sutpen family (the others are the tombstones), Faulkner also takes it away, by seriously qualifying it: the letter bears none of the signifying markers that would verify that Bon wrote it or, if so, when, or to whom. See entry for 107:3.

107:3 **You will notice** The letter that follows, assuming it was written by Bon, suggests a Bon quite different from the one Mr. Compson has described. The writer of this letter is by no means fey or dandyish or effeminate, but sensible, goodhumored, above all realistic about his chances of returning. Finally, though the writer is clearly in love with the recipient, its content does not connect it in any specific way with the Sutpen family or with Mississippi (Muhlenfeld).

107:8 **French watermarks** expensive hand-made paper, which Bon writes on with stove polish, a fact which bemuses him. A watermark is a device laid across the chain lines which marks a sheet of handmade paper during its manufacture; the watermark usually identifies the maker.

107:37 **loaves and the fishes** In Mark VI:30–44, Jesus blessed five loaves of bread and two fish so that they multiplied sufficiently to feed a huge crowd and had much left over.

107:37 **the incandescent Brow, the shining nimbus of the Thorny Crown** The

Brow is Jesus's, whose crown of thorns becomes a glowing halo that makes his face incandescent.

108:4 **General Sherman** William Tecumseh Sherman (1820–1891), after Grant the most powerful and successful—and, by Southerners, the most hated—of the Northern Generals. He wreaked havoc on the South with his infamous "march to the Sea" from Atlanta to Savannah, burning crops and razing buildings to feed his troops as they moved eastward.

108:15 **We have waited long enough.** This sentence and the following passage stand against a good deal of Mr. Compson's speculation about Bon and Judith in chapter IV and of Rosa Coldfield's in chapter V. It is an intimate sentence which suggests some communication, some understanding between Bon and Judith that the narrators seem not to know about and seem not to read into this letter. Certainly it tells us more about Bon than about Judith; indeed, perhaps she does not love him and perhaps she brings this particular letter to Mrs. Compson as some indication that the love was one-sided, that Bon loved her, not she him, and that that love caused all the family problems. The letter also releases Judith from the fatalistic waiting into which he had corrupted her (see entry for 99:27).

108:19 *Because what* **WAS** *is one thing, and now it is not because it is dead, it died in 1861, and therefore what* **IS** *... is something else again because it was not even alive then.* What *was* are perhaps the complications—brother and father and the plantation system—that stand in the way of their marriage; those conditions died at the beginning of the Civil War. The new circumstances of their lives, problematic though they be, have rendered the previous condition moot, and therefore they can proceed when, and if, he returns to claim her. See the entry for 216:14.

108:25 *there was that one fusillade four years ago which sounded once and then was arrested, mesmerised raised muzzle by raised muzzle, in the frozen attitude of its own aghast amazement and never repeated* A fusillade is a sustained attack or barrage, several guns firing at once or in quick succession. There have been so many continuous cannon- and pistol- and rifle-shots that there seems to have been no interval of silence in between any of them; the whole war has thus been just one single gigantic explosion lasting four years.

109:31 **It seemed to Quentin that he could actually see them, facing one another at the gate.** Quentin here anticipates the vision he and Shreve will share at the end of chapter VIII, the mental recreation of the scene in which Henry shoots Bon—the scene, the act, which the whole novel, all of its narrators, attempts to explain. Guetti emphasizes that it "only *seems* to Quentin that he can see" (76) and refers to a "paradox of vitality and decadence, of Quentin as passive seer and active sounding board" (77).

CHAPTER V

See the first entry for chapter III. Chapter V raises numerous questions about narration. Faulkner has already played with italics in chapter III, using them for speech tags—e.g., *Quentin said*—while doing away with quotation marks as the normal indicators of narrative speech as he had done in chapters I and II. Chapter V comes to us almost entirely in italics, all of it until the last couple of pages, at which point roman type interrupts just as Quentin returns to consciousness, once again hearing Rosa talk to him. The closing paragraphs suggest that on one level Rosa is narrating as she talks to him as they ride out to Sutpen's Hundred on September 9, perhaps a continuation of the monologue she had begun in chapter I. But the italics throw chapter V in to a different narrative register. The italics may be a function of what Gwin calls "the male desire (Quentin's, Mr. Compson's, Shreve's) to make Rosa disappear (or at least to make her shut up)" (64); she also suggests that Rosa's text "engages the space between consciousness and unconsciousness" (72). The italics may also suggest that the content of the monologue represents Quentin's reconstruction, conscious or unconscious, of all that he has heard from various sources from his family and from the town about Rosa. Indeed, it hardly seems likely that Rosa would use such sexually specific language about her own thwarted sexuality to anybody, much less to the much younger male, Quentin; her descriptions of her vulva as a "rending gash" (118:17), a "frenzied slash" (136:14), a "gaping wound" (136:14), the "male-furrowed meat" (120:29) are much more nearly the slangy and vulgar locutions a young male might use with his friends. Thus chapter V may partly contain Quentin's imposition of a sexual pathology on Rosa's account, his very twentieth-century attempt to understand Rosa in psychoanalytical terms perhaps borrowed, the language at least, from his father. The language thus raises the question, to what extent is any of Rosa's "monologue" a transcription of what she actually has said. At the level of common sense, we'd have to say "little," because who thinks like this? And so if little of it is transcription, the question of the graphic language is moot. Chapter V is just as much Quentin's construct of her history as all the narratives in the novel are the constructs of the narrators.

The complicated ways in which the words of this chapter call attention to themselves *as words* may argue against a suggestion that Quentin throughout is visualizing what Rosa describes rather than hearing and processing each individual word, but his awakening—"But Quentin was not listening" (142:28)—, his question to Rosa—"Ma'am? What's that? What did you say?" (143:12)—, and Rosa's response—"There's something in that house" (143:13)—argue that, at least at the end of the monologue, he is hearing something quite different from what Rosa has been saying: he is fixated on the dramatic moment when Henry bursts into his sister's room to tell her that he has killed Bon, a scene Rosa describes at the beginning of the chapter; but the italic passage which his sudden awakening interrupts contains her denial that Sutpen could have been killed by Wash Jones or anybody else. Has he listened to nothing else she has said, stopped there at that door? Chapters VI–IX, however, imply the contrary: that he has listened to and incorporated Rosa's words and experience into his knowledge of events and characters. Why, then, has listening "reneged," as happens on the novel's first page as he listens to Rosa in the "office" of her house? Does his "hearing-sense self-confound" so that the "long dead objects" have indeed been evoked, and appear, "quiet" and "attentive"? There may be no satisfactory answers to these questions. Lurie suggests that the prose of chapter V has "a narcotic, abstract, or surreal effect, such that the world of the novel appears exotic or strange and resists 'objective' representation" (104) and that because "the abstract quality of Faulkner's language causes the reader to be more aware of the language itself than of its referent, we do not engage fully with the objects of description or reference" (115).

111:1 **So they will have told you doubtless already** Rosa seems aware that she is the object of much speculation in Jefferson, though how much her awareness is justified by the facts we do not know. Although she says several times that she "holds no brief" for herself, the entire monologue is, on one level, in fact a self-defense. Marvin K. Singleton identifies in Rosa a "courtroom idiom that has entered into colloquial speech" and finds "several formal indications" that Rosa's story is "an equitable plea" and that her story is indebted to several "non-praying-relief Bills in Equity" (366–67). "Rosa's Bill, as in early equity pleading, was submitted by word of mouth, leaving it to the court to reduce to writing; but it is substantially complete as a Bill even in light of the highly formal Equity pleadings of the nineteenth century" (367).

111:6 ***garments which I had been fortunate enough to inherit from my aunt's kindness or haste or oversight*** Rosa's aunt had eloped with the horse trader and left her nothing.

111:12 ***that brute*** Wash Jones.

111:18 ***incept*** from the Latin *incipĕre*, to begin (OED). Faulkner makes a participle of the verb form.

111:32 ***And how*** They will have also told you how....

111:33 ***two years since Ellen died (or was it the four years since Henry vanished or was it the nineteen years since I saw light and breathed?)*** Rosa probes her past for a historical reference point or a point at which her account might properly be said to begin: when Ellen died, when Henry vanished, or at her birth. When did the tale begin? she asks herself.

111:37 ***two women, two young women*** Clytie and Judith.

112:17 ***bait of vittles*** food, also food used as enticement.

112:23 ***But they cannot tell you*** Rosa begins to tell the "real" story of her life at Sutpen's Hundred.

112:24 ***the house, the shell, the (so I thought) cocoon-casket marriage-bed of youth and grief*** Rosa's running metaphor not just of the Sutpen house but of the institution of marriage, which as a "cocoon-casket" combines womb and tomb, birth and death; but she compounds the metaphor to include herself, as though her youth had been wed tragically to grief—as, indeed, as she tells it, it had.

112:26 ***and found that I had come, not too late as I had thought, but come too soon*** Because Jones was driving the wagon so slowly, Rosa feared she would get to Sutpen's Hundred too late to prevent the tragedy that Jones had reported to her. Far from arriving "too late" to see the ruins, Rosa discovers she has come too soon, that the holocaust (112:31) continues to rage and she will become part of it, with her own role to play. She has, in other words, come too soon to play the part of detached witness; upon arrival, she becomes complicit, a participant in "some desolation more profound than ruin" (112:29).

112:27 ***Rotting portico and scaling walls, it stood, not ravaged, not invaded, marked by no bullet nor soldier's iron heel but rather as though reserved for something more: some desolation more profound than ruin, as if it had stood in iron juxtaposition to iron flame, to a holocaust which had*** *found itself less fierce and less implacable* Sutpen's mansion, Rosa believes, is impervious to flame, impervious even to the holocaust that is the Civil War, but not to the desolation yet to come.

113:2 **Sutpen coffee-colored face** the face of Clytie, Sutpen's half-black daughter.

113:8 **oh yes, he chose well; he bettered choosing** Apparently Rosa means that Sutpen chose a very good guard, Clytie, to protect the house's secrets; bettered choosing = beat an opponent: Sutpen's innate instincts gave him a victory over the free will of choice. He would not have had such good protection if he had thought about it and, for example, assigned one of his male slaves to guard the entrance.

113:9 **created in his own image the cold Cerberus of his private hell** Rosa calls Clytie Cerberus, the three-headed watchdog who guards the entrance to hell.

113:12 **which she still wears now at seventy-four** "Now" is 1909, the current time of the novel, since Clytie was born in 1835, according to the "Chronology." Rosa may simply be speculating that nothing could have changed Clytie's "Sutpen face," but the phrase strongly suggests that she has actually been out to Sutpen's Hundred and talked to Clytie or at least seen her. The ending of this chapter seems to suggest that she has recently discovered that something "is hidden" there. The phrase raises questions which the novel does not answer: if she knows Henry is at Sutpen's Hundred, why does she wait "four years" to go out to him? See entry for 143:15.

113:18 **Moloch's palate-paunch** Moloch was a Canaanite idol to whom children were sacrificed as burnt offerings. The "palate-paunch" would seem to combine the mouth and the belly into one organ that doesn't discriminate among tastes but simply ingests all victims.

114:2 **without moving, with no alteration of visual displacement whatever ... seemed to elongate and project upward something** Clytie doesn't move but in Rosa's hyperactive mind seems to grow into something larger than herself. The problem with this passage lies in the "visual displacement" which is not "altered," as though Clytie were already *dis*placed in Rosa's vision. Or perhaps Rosa means that Clytie's eyes displace her, Rosa, since she, Rosa, is intruding here; in the interruptive parenthesis (noted by our ellipsis), Rosa notes that "she did not even remove her gaze from mine for the reason that she was not looking at me but through me" (114:3), a phrasing which suggests that Clytie's vision displaces her, Rosa, since it doesn't even seem to recognize her presence, her existence. Clytie is drawn, visually, to something unseen in Rosa's vision and is listening, "profoundly attentive" (114:7), to something Rosa cannot hear, something which does not displace Rosa but nonetheless makes her hyperaware of what she cannot fathom.

114:9 *a brooding awareness and acceptance of the inexplicable unseen inherited from an older and a purer race than mine* Rosa accepts, as Mr. Compson does, the primitive power, sexual and instinctive, that whites associated with Negroes' ancient heritage in the jungles of Africa. Her admission that slaves are a "purer race"—that is, of purer blood—is curiously inconsistent with white racial dogmas that assumed the purity of white blood and made laws to protect "pure" white women, and therefore their own families, from diluting white blood by breeding with blacks: indeed, the famous "one-drop" rule mandated that *any* amount of black blood made a person legally black. But it's also curiously consonant with the novel's final scene, in which Shreve taunts Quentin precisely with the notion that what Southern Americans fear is precisely that the result all the intermingling and inbreeding between whites and blacks will eventually "bleach" all blackness out: all races will then be white and whites will no longer be able to claim their own all-important difference from blackness. See entry for 311:7.

114:11 *created postulated and shaped* Clytie, Rosa believes, is the harbinger of the doom, the tragedy she believes she will find at Sutpen's Hundred. Clytie, Rosa's black self, has somehow created the general tragedy, then claimed it for the present moment, and finally shaped its particulars for Rosa's moment.

114:12 *that which I believed I had come to find (nay, which I must find, else breathing and standing there, I would have denied that I was ever born)* As she explains in the next few lines, Rosa comes to Sutpen's Hundred expecting, hoping, to find a dramatic scene that will fit her romantic temperament and imagination, a "pale and bloody corpse" on the "sheetless bed," the "bowed and unwived widow kneeling beside it." She perhaps overdramatically claims that her very existence depended upon the actualization of that tragic scene, versions of which, doubtless, she has imagined for years, after the scene occurred, as the only possible conclusion to the Sutpen family history, a bloody denouement worthy of classical tragedy.

114:20 *still believed that what must be would be, could not but be* Rosa, still projecting backward, imposes on her younger self a fatalistic sense of impending doom, her attempt as a young girl to impose on experience her romantic sense of what should be.

114:23 ***his own clairvoyant will tempered to amoral evil's undeviating absolute by the black willing blood with which he had crossed it*** Clytie not only does Sutpen's bidding, she actually represents it in her blackness; Clytie's blackness is to Rosa Sutpen's evil nature in a pure form, its crystallization into an "undeviating absolute" that is, given his evil character, both pure and inevitable, the ultimate point toward which his life has led him with "undeviating" precision. Clytie, blackness, is thus an evil made more intense, more evil, by her connection with the dark mysteries of the dark skin and the dark continent.

114:31 ***not as two faces but as the two abstract contradictions which we actually were*** It is reasonably clear that Rosa makes of their meeting on the stairs a meeting of symbols, but it is not at all clear how or whether Rosa and Clytie are "contradictions" of each other—Rosa free and white, Clytie slave and black?—or whether each is within herself her own contradiction: Rosa, the free white woman enslaved in and by her own and Thomas Sutpen's family, Clytie, the chattel slave yet free to defend the house in the absence of the master.

115:2 ***Because it was not the name, the word, the fact that she had called me Rosa.*** Though racial etiquette would normally have forbidden the slave to call the white woman by her first name, the circumstances of her condition as a child when Clytie first knew her allows Clytie the right to call her Rosa. The "it" that Rosa contests is that Clytie touched her to stop her from going upstairs.

115:8 ***That was not what she meant at all*** Rosa, in 1909, now understands that Clytie did not mean to insult her by calling her "Rosa," but quite the opposite, as she explains in the following lines. But at the dramatic moment she reacts as if she has been insulted: "*Take your hand off me, nigger!*" (115:38).

115:11 ***she did me more grace and respect than anyone else I knew*** Clytie, in Rosa's reckoning, treats Rosa as a human being by calling her by her first name, thus recognizing her as a person.

115:21 ***my entire being seemed to run at blind full tilt into something monstrous and immobile*** She runs into Clytie's touch; specifically, more generally, she runs in to "the solid yet imponderable weight . . . of that will to bar me from the stairs" (115:16). It is monstrous because of Rosa's fear of it; immobile because she simply can't move it.

115:25 ***something in the touch of flesh with flesh which abrogates, cuts sharp and straight across the devious intricate channels of decorous ordering,*** *which enemies as well as lovers know because it makes them both:— touch and touch of that which is the citadel of the central I-Am's private own* Rosa introduces a spiritual sense rooted in physicality, an articulation which 118:36 defines as the "substance of remembering" in physical, muscular terms. She postulates the way in which physical touch negates or defines all social ordering, revealing to human beings their essential physical relation irrespective of their place in any social or hierarchical system. Touching thus cuts through decorum to reveal "the central I-am's private own," the spiritual essence of a human being, in the intimacy of love or hate. Ragan suggests that "This miraculous touch is what Rosa has been denied all her life" (*Critical Study* 76).

115:30 *the liquorish and ungirdled mind* the mind ecstatic and freed of the body.

115:32 *eggshell shibboleth of caste and color* "Shibboleth" is a Hebrew word used by Jephthah to distinguish fleeing Ephraimites from his own men; Ephraimites could not pronounce the sound *sh* (Judges 12:6). Hence a shibboleth is any word or code or device of armament or clothing used to distinguish one people from another, usually to mark and so protect oneself from outsiders. Rosa means that skin color is a shibboleth, which distinguishes races but does so on the flimsiest of grounds: it is as thin and vulnerable as an eggshell. All races have to do is to touch one another to see how thin is the curtain that separates human beings.

115:35 *I crying not to her, to it; speaking to it through the negro, the woman* Rosa is crying not to Clytie but rather to "it," speaking to "it." It seems clear that the "it" is Clytie's hand, "no woman's hand, no negro's hand" (115:33): that is, a hand not restricted to the identifications of race. Perhaps the "woman's hand" is for Rosa what the "balloon faces" (190:37) are to Thomas Sutpen after his first encounter with slaves, one of whom arrogantly sends him around to the back door of the mansion he presumes to visit.

116:2 *joined by that hand and arm which held us, like a fierce rigid umbilical cord, twin sistered to the fell darkness which had produced her* fell = savage, cruel. The "fell darkness which had produced her" is not just Africa but the whole appalling history of slavery. Clytie and Rosa each trace their commonality to the darkness: it is what they share, "twin sistered" to what produced Clytie and to what repulses Rosa. Robert Con Davis says that "In this momentary physical union, Rosa has the deepest recognition of a bond between them, that they are *twin sistered* in view of an '*it*' ... a male principle that Thomas Sutpen represents" (43). Thadious Davis proposes that Sutpen is "Clytie's biological father, but who also gives Rosa herself life (that is, provides her with a *raison d'être*" (215). See entry for 116:25.

116:11 *Even as a child, I would not even play with the same objects which she and Judith played with* Rosa recalls watching Judith and Henry and Clytie "scuffling in the rough games" of childhood and remarks how Clytie and Judith "even slept together" (116:7), perhaps demonstrating how "the touch of flesh with flesh . . . abrogates" (115:25) racial division. But whereas the touch of flesh makes childhood playmates of Clytie, Judith, and Henry, the same touch repulses Rosa, who would not even touch the things they touch, so deep her fear (116:16) of Clytie and of "what she was." In her childhood, Rosa prefers solitude to interracial touch and play.

116:12 *that warped and spartan solitude which I called my childhood* one of many passages in chapter V in which Rosa speaks sadly about her childhood. She is one of numerous children in Faulkner with warped and problematic childhoods caused by parental repression of natural inclinations. The solitude seems self-imposed—"But not I" (116:10). She refuses the sisterly, physical interaction enjoyed by Judith and Clytie.

116:14 *to listen before I could comprehend and to understand before I even heard* Rosa's "*warped and spartan solitude which [she] called [her] childhood*" (116:12) bequeaths to her an instinctive fear of blackness and so of Clytie, an embodiment of racial antipathy.

116:19 *some cumulative over-reach of despair itself* Rosa and Clytie stand on the stairs, Clytie's hand on Rosa to stop her from ascending. Rosa tries to explain why she yields to Clytie's force: not from outrage or terror, but from her lifelong accumulation of despair that culminates in this trip to Sutpen's Hundred. The "over-reach" seems to push her through and beyond despair.

116:20 *joined by that volitionless (yes: it too sentient victim just as she and I were)* Rosa seems to understand that Clytie, too, is under the control of social and cultural and historical forces that consume them both.

116:21 *I cried—perhaps not aloud, not with words* The text stresses the narrators' extra-verbal communication with others in the text.

116:23 *saw that face which was at once both more and less than Sutpen* "less" in the sense that it is not a duplicate of whatever identifying features a "Sutpen face" would have, more in the sense that Clytie's blackness connects Sutpen to what Rosa has earlier called evil's "undeviating absolute" (114:24).

116:25 ***what I could not, would not, must not believe*** that she had missed the dramatic moment of her romantic imagination: the dead or dying Bon lying in his blood on Judith's bed, Judith standing over him, aggrieved, Henry standing there, gun in hand. She describes this beginning 116:26.

116:25 ***I cried 'And you too? And you too, sister, sister?'*** Rosa finally articulates what lies deep in her consciousness, that she and Clytie are "twin sistered to the fell darkness" (116:3). Here she appeals to Clytie, claiming the sisterhood which until this moment she had shunned. Or, she may not in fact speak these words (116:21) but realize them consciously. By "the touch of flesh with flesh" (115:25) Rosa recalls her antipathy and senses it as well in Clytie and so asks, "And you too, sister, sister?" At once she appeals to Clytie, her twin sister, and realizes that they are enemies, revealed as such when flesh touches flesh.

116:30 ***small plain frightened creature*** Rosa.

117:1 ***time altered to fit the dream which, conjunctive with the dreamer, becomes immolated and apotheosized: 'Mother and Judith are in the nursery with the children, and Father and Charles are walking in the garden. Wake up, Aunt Rosa; wake up'*** Rosa re-imagines the scene she hoped for at Sutpen's Hundred as a nightmare from which Henry would waken her by calling her name, and she would wake to the "more than reality" (116:40) of her situation—not to the unchanging "old time," but to a time changed to fit the nightmare of her fears. The dream thus becomes "immolated" or, in Faulkner's use, sacrificed and changed not just into a bearable reality (see entry for 117:35) but into a manufactured sweet scene of marital and familial bliss: Ellen and Judith "in the nursery with the children" while Thomas Sutpen and Charles Bon, father and son-in-law, walk peacefully in the garden.

117:5 ***not even dream since dreams dont come in pairs*** "What did I expect?" Rosa laments at 116:26; here she answers, "*not even dream.*" By "dream" Rosa means not the dream of the sleeper, but the "dream" of, the hope for, an idyllic family scene such as she has described in the previous lines. Such hopes, such projections dont "*come in pairs*" but are singular, one-time possibilities: there are no second chances in Rosa's life. Whatever dream of familial bliss she held as a child is now defunct and she feels called upon to awaken from it: "*wake, Rosa, from the hoping*" (117:11).

117:6 ***had I not come twelve miles drawn not by mortal mule but by some chimaera-foal of nightmare's very self?*** In Greek mythology the chimaera was a fire-breathing monster, a horror with a lion's head, a goat's body, and a serpent's tail, that was killed by Bellerophon (OED). Something more monstrous than even nightmare, more detestable than Wash Jones's mule has brought Rosa to this point.

117:13 *believed there would be need for you to save not love perhaps, not happiness nor peace, but what was left behind by widowing* In Rosa's imagining, Henry admonishes her to wake up from illusions, especially from the illusion that by coming to Sutpen's Hundred after the killing she believes she can "save" what is left of Judith and Henry.

117:15 *and found that there was nothing there to save* Henry is gone, Bon has disappeared, and Judith seems beyond the need for help of any kind.

117:15 *who hoped to save her as you promised Ellen* hoped to save Judith.

117:16 *not Charles Bon, not Henry: not either one of these from him or even from one another* She did not promise Ellen to save either Bon or Henry.

117:18 *and now too late* Earlier she argues that she had come not too late but too soon (112:26).

117:20 *who came twelve miles and nineteen years to save what did not need the saving, and lost instead yourself* Judith does not need Rosa's help, so Rosa, unable to fulfill her dying sister's request, loses her reason for being.

117:26 *a face which was its soul's own inquisitor* An inquisitor is charged by church and state to investigate instances of heresy and to condemn heretics; thus here the Sutpen face on Clytie acts, in Rosa's mind, as a sort of punitive superego for Clytie.

117:27 *a hand which was the agent of its own crucifixion* Clytie's black hand, doing the will of the white Sutpen, acts to crucify itself. One of the novel's first images of Rosa describes her as a "crucified child" (6:1).

117:35 *fled, up the stairs and found no grieving widowed bride but Judith standing before the closed door to that chamber* The tragic scene of loss, grief, and suffering that Rosa expects, even needs, to see, does not materialize; Ellen is in complete control, seems to Rosa neither to grieve nor feel anguish.

118:4 *And how I saw* This too is among the things Rosa claims nobody but she could have told Quentin.

118:4 *that what she held in that lax and negligent hand was the photograph, the picture of herself in its metal case which she had given him* At 74:27 Mr. Compson claims the picture is not of Ellen but of Bon's octoroon mistress.

118:14 *arras-veil* An arras is a richly woven tapestry usually hung on the walls of rooms in mediæval castles. They were usually hung far enough from the wall to allow a person to stand between it and the wall, as happens most famously in Shakespeare's *Hamlet*, when Polonius positions himself there to spy on Hamlet's conversation with his mother, is discovered, and dies when Hamlet stabs him through the arras. See entry for 118:17.

118:17 **no lack of courage either: not cowardice which will not face that sickness** not cowardice which prevents one from the "rending gash" (118:17) of that arras-veil which conceals the future.

118:18 **that sickness somewhere at the prime foundation of this factual scheme** the sickness, death perhaps, that is genetic, that is part of the foundation, the very beginnings, of this "factual scheme" of our corporeal existence.

118:20 **the prisoner soul, miasmal-distillant** miasma = "infectious or noxious exhalations from putrescent organic matter" (OED). The soul, a prisoner of our corporeality, is at conception a swampy concentration of rotting matter.

118:20 **wroils ever upward sunward, tugs its tenuous prisoner arteries and veins and prisoning in its turn that spark, that dream** Death, that "prisoner soul" strives upward and outward in response to a dream of freedom or a dream of overcoming corporeality, but eventually imprisons that dream in the miasmal putrescence of its own prison; the soul cannot be victor over corporeality simply because it is already miasmal and doomed at conception.

118:22 **that dream which, as the globy and complete instant of its freedom mirrors and repeats (repeats? creates, reduces to a fragile evanescent iridescent sphere) all of space and time and massy earth** Even though doomed, the soul, striving upward out of its corporeal prison, has an instant of freedom during which it mirrors the infinity of space and time and the immensity of creation; the soul may even create that infinity as an ideal, the reverse of its own limitations.

118:25 **relicts the seething and anonymous miasmal mass which in all the years of time has taught itself no boon of death but only how to recreate, renew** "Relict" is an obsolete form of the word "relic" (OED); meaning "something left behind," it is most often applied to widows or widowers. A noun, sometimes an adjective, Faulkner uses it here as a transitive verb. Its subject, three lines up, "that dream which," thus leaves behind it all of corporeality, all of death. But as Goethe's Mephistopheles tells Faust, the earth's creative flow cannot be halted, ever, in all its seething and anonymity: one person, one body, may die, but others replace him or her, so that in the larger anonymous scheme of things, individuals do not matter.

118:27 ***and dies, is gone, vanished: nothing*** The soul aspiring toward dream vanishes with the individual.

118:28 ***but is that true wisdom which can comprehend that there is a might-have-been which is more true than truth*** Even though the aspiring, dreaming soul vanishes, it, that spark, suggesting, positing, something outside of corporeality, something that "might-have-been," operates out of a truer wisdom than that represented by the "factual scheme" of corporeality, even if it is an illusion.

118:33 ***wistaria, sun-impacted on this wall here*** The sun presses the heavy smell of wistaria against the wall.

118:38 ***there is no such thing as memory: the brain recalls just what the muscles grope for*** a familiar theme in Faulkner, adapted from Proust's famous madeleine, tasting which engenders in Marcel all the recollections he records in *À la Recherche du Temps Perdu*.

119:9 **a summer of wistaria** Rosa's consciousness of the wistaria here and of the twice-bloomed wistaria that begins the novel invokes the summer of her puberty, the awakening of her sexuality (Ragan, *Critical Study* 78).

119:12 ***the spring and summertime which is every female's who breathed above dust, beholden of all betrayed springs held over from all irrevocable time*** To be "beholden" is to owe or to be attached to, but the word is usually accompanied by the preposition "to." Faulkner's "of" reverses the direction of the attachment or the debt, so that Rosa means all those springs of her life that preceded this summer of wistaria, those that failed to bring her the love she so ardently desired, actually owe her the fulfillment of spring's promise. She is not beholden to the previous springs, they are beholden to her but do not fulfill their promise.

119:13 ***springs held over from all irrevocable time, repercussed, bloomed again*** All the springs prior to Rosa as have compacted themselves into this one spring of her adolescence, her fourteenth year, obviously the spring during which she first discovered sexual desire. See entry for 119:15.

119:15 ***that sweet conjunction of root bloom and urge and hour and weather*** The "vintage year" occurs when all the elements of sexual desire converge: when the flower's (Rosa's) root produces the bloom (Rosa's body), the urge, and the time and weather (spring in a lover's time) for sexual fulfillment all at the same time.

119:17 ***I will not insist on bloom*** Rosa claims no particular physical attractiveness for herself.

119:20 *Nor do I say leaf—warped bitter pale and crimped half-fledging intimidate of any claim to green which might have drawn to it the tender mayfly childhood sweetheart games or given pause to the male predacious wasps and bees of later lust* At 119:17 Rosa doesn't claim to be beautiful as a flower: here she is not even a green leaf that would attract the "predacious" or predatory suitors and lovers. She is only a "half-fledging" and "intimidate" to any claim on green. Faulkner uses the transitive verb "intimidate" here as a participle: she is not intimidated *by* the claim to green, but rather the agent of the intimidation. By her "warped bitter pale and crimped" appearance she intimidates the green itself, any suitor who might call.

119:24 *But root and urge I do insist and claim, for had I not heired too from all the unsistered Eves since the Snake?* Rosa insists upon her sexual nature, her desire. At 116:3 she claims to be "twin sistered" to Clytie, common products of ultimate doom or darkness. Here she locates a universal sisterhood in Eve, after whose fall all women became "unsistered Eves" in their sexual desire and in their competition for predacious males. See Godden 93–94.

119:25 *Yes, urge I do: warped chrysalis of what blind perfect seed* She insists upon her adolescent sexual urges. Ugly and malformed as she thinks of herself, she is nevertheless a "chrysalis," the shell in which caterpillar larvæ become butterflies, a womb worthy of the seed from a blind lover who does not have to look at her physically in order to impregnate her.

119:26 *for who shall say what gnarled forgotten root might not bloom yet with some globed concentrate more globed and concentrate and heady-perfect because the neglected root was planted warped and lay not dead but merely slept forgot?* Such an unattractive creature as she—a neglected root—might well produce a bloom, a child, a love even more perfect than a more beautiful creature might produce.

119:31 *That was the miscast summer of my barren youth which . . . I lived out not as a woman, a girl, but rather as the man which I perhaps should have been* A physically unattractive man can negotiate courtship and sexuality better than a physically unattractive woman, Rosa thinks.

119:36 *unpaced corridor which I called childhood which was not living but rather some projection of the lightless womb itself* "unpaced" because she seems to have been practically motionless, paused in front of closed doors trying to hear what was going on among the adults. The corridor is dark and she is as enclosed as in the womb. That is, she did not progress, or mature, but remained unchanged and childlike throughout her childhood and early maturity.

119:37 ***I gestate and complete, not aged*** Again Faulkner uses a verb as a participle: by "gestate," Rosa means she had completely gestated and should have been born into the light, but continued to live in that dark womb-corridor; she did not grow up.

119:38 ***just overdue because of some caesarean lack, some cold head-nuzzling forceps of the savage time which should have torn me free*** Nothing appeared to pull her from those dark corridor-wombs in which she continues to live—as, for example, the dark, shuttered room, the "office," in which she and Quentin sit while they talk. See entry for 120:2. Rosa feels pulled from the childhood she never experienced into a physical maturity for which she is unprepared; what "should have torn [her] free" instead thrusts her toward "doom" (119:39).

120:2 ***I like that blind subterranean fish, that insulated spark whose origin the fish no longer remembers, which pulses and beats at its crepuscular and lethargic tenement with the old unsleeping itch*** Crepuscular means "pertaining to twilight." With no experience, nor even vision, of the present world, Rosa nevertheless claims that "old unsleeping itch" to reproduce, to generate. She spends all her time in the dark shadowy hallways of her house, standing outside doors listening to adults talk. See entry for 119:38. Hönnighausen calls Rosa's description of herself as a "blind subterranean fish" a kind of fetus stuck in a "prolonged puberty . . . a dim prenatal world" (*Masks* 162).

120:5 ***old unsleeping itch which has no words to speak with other than 'This was called light', that 'smell', that 'touch'*** Rosa experiences the world second-hand, through the descriptions of others. The "old unsleeping" suggests a waking and desiring consciousness which has no physical experience to connect with the language of sensory experience she inherits.

120:7 ***that other something which has bequeathed not even name for sound of bee or bird or flower's scent or light or sun or love*** This phrase stands syntactically and grammatically parallel to her claim at 120:2 that she is "*like that blind subterranean fish*"; here she is "*like*" "*that other something*," something nameless and unidentifiable that has denied her both the experience of and language to describe all those phenomena of spring traditionally associated with burgeoning sexuality. Rosa (120:19), at fourteen years old and in the first flush of puberty, has no language to understand what is happening to her body (her aunt left her before her adolescence and her father is not likely to have helped her deal with the onset of menstruation in a healthy way, if, indeed, at all), no experience to describe desire. Rosa, as an old lady, here describes the gaps in her experience of life: she knows nothing of the trappings of courtship, nothing of the birds and bees or lovers' bouquets, though she does claim the "urge."

120:9 ***not even growing and developing, beloved by and loving light*** She is still that stunted subterranean fish that has never seen the light.

120:10 ***but equipped only with that cunning, that inverted canker-growth of solitude which substitutes the omnivorous and unrational hearing-sense for all the others*** Rosa has spent her childhood lurking in the hallways of her house, sneaking around, as she must think, with some "cunning," to avoid being discovered, listening to adults talk of the outside world, talk that inverts her solitude, which is a canker, a "gangrenous, spreading sore" (OED), makes of her solitude an omnipresence in the outside world which she has, and will have, no experience of. What she hears becomes a substitute for all the other senses. At 120:17 she says she "acquired all I knew of that light and space in which people moved and breathed" in that unlighted hallway.

120:18 ***might have gained conception of the sun from seeing it through a piece of smoky glass*** Rosa compares herself with the "blind subterranean fish" who experiences the sun only through its "crepuscular" insularity. Her conception of life, of experience, is filtered through many layers of opaque words coming at her through closed doors. See also I Corinthians 13:12: "For now we see through a glass, darkly; but then face to face: now I know in part; but then shall I know even as also I am known."

120:19 ***fourteen, four years younger than Judith, four years later than Judith's moment*** It's not clear how at fourteen Rosa is both four years younger than Judith and also four years later than Judith's "moment." She seems to be saying the same thing twice: she is four years younger than Judith, which means she reached puberty at the same age Judith did, just four years later. Or perhaps, less likely, she means that Judith reached puberty at age ten. In any case, as with everything, she follows Judith.

120:20 ***Judith's moment which only virgins know: when the entire delicate spirit's bent is one anonymous climaxless epicene and unravished nuptual . . . a world filled with living marriage like the light and air which she***

breathes For virgins, the sexual urge creates an imaginative orgy, sex with anonymous partners of either or no particular gender that is simultaneously unorgasmic, unravished, and unconsummated. Statements like this one may help us understand Rosa's tumultuous over-reaction to Sutpen's proposal that they have sex before marriage to see if she can produce for him the son and heir that he so desperately wants. For her, at that moment, sex becomes real, not imaginative, not romantic.

120:23 ***not that widowed and nightly violation by the inescapable and scornful dead which is the meed of twenty and thirty and forty*** In her romanticizing imagination, Rosa leaps ahead two or three or four decades past a woman's fruitful years to her widowhood, when her life is a lonely, "nightly violation" by her departed husband: even after her husband's death a woman is subject to masculine assault. In 1910 Rosa seems still feeding on her fear of sexuality as she talks about Sutpen; the language here and throughout suggests the terrific conflict between her desire for and her fear of sex.

120:26 ***no summer of a virgin's itching discontent; no summer's caesarian lack which should have torn me, dead flesh or even embryo, from the living: or else, by friction's ravishing of the male-furrowed meat, also weaponed and panoplied as a man instead of hollow woman*** caesarian lack = lack of progress in labor resulting in the child's being torn from the mother's body. Rosa equates this with her own lack of sexual intercourse, a lack which should have torn her from the world of the living (by which she means the world of the sexually active). "*Or else*" she might mean that since none of this happened, she might as well have been a man, "weaponed and panoplied" and inviolable. That is: because she waited for violation and never got it, she might as well have been a man, one for whom violation is impossible. See Poirier 14.

120:38 ***me, who had been born too late, born into some curious disjoint of my father's life*** Had Rosa been born earlier, she might not have caused her mother's death and so might have had a more normal childhood and adolescence.

120:39 ***his (now twice) widowed hands*** widowed once by his wife's death, a second time by his sister's abandonment of them.

121:11 ***cellar earth of mine*** her body.

121:20 ***fond dear constant violation of privacy, that stultification of the burgeoning and incorrigible I*** Rosa's definition of parental love.

121:23 ***became not mistress, not beloved, but more than even love; I became all polymath love's androgynous advocate*** Neither wife nor mistress, not sexual and not likely to be, Rosa becomes a unisexual advocate for all forms of love. Norman Jones suggests that Rosa literally refers "to her relationship to Judith and Bon" (349).

121:32 ***the way that mothers love when, punishing the child she strikes not it but through it strikes the neighbor boy whom it has just whipped or been whipped by; caresses not the rewarded child but rather the nameless man or woman who gave the palm-sweated penny*** In such passages as this, Rosa describes a relationship with a mother she never had; even so, it certainly describes her own sense of being dis- or misplaced: it is a relationship in which the child herself is substituted for some other child, becomes the agent of reward or punishment for others, receiving indirectly what was intended for others.

121:37 ***I gave him nothing, which is the sum of loving*** Rosa didn't love Bon as Judith loved him, since, as the previous lines state, she never saw him. But she claims love in a negative sense: she loved him by virtue of the fact that she gave him nothing, which is the sum of loving, so far as her own experience would indicate. She can have arrived at the notion of giving nothing as the sum of loving only through her experiences with her father and with Thomas Sutpen.

123:21 ***who ... loved with that sort beyond the compass of glib books: that love which gives up what it never had*** It is not clear whether "that love which gives up what it never had" is the love that's *in* the "glib books" or that which is beyond the books.

123:36 ***a woman more strange to me than to any grief for being so less its partner*** The woman is Clytie, more strange to Rosa than she, Clytie, is to grief itself apparently because Clytie, living in the Sutpen household, would be well-acquainted with grief; but even having lived at Sutpen's Hundred, she is much less the partner of grief than Rosa is.

124:5 ***running out of that first year*** Rosa's "running" metaphorically begins five years before Clytie's touch stops her physical running in *"midstride"* (123:38) at the top of the stairs leading to Judith's room; five years before that, of course, is when Bon first came to Jefferson and set in motion the chain of events that led to this tragic unresolvable moment.

125:22 ***fumbling ratiocination of inertia*** Wash Jones's explanation, in the following lines, of how much simpler they could make their job of putting Bon in his casket: also an example of his laziness, as Rosa would have it.

126:12 *And something walked with Judith and Clytie back across that sunset field* That "something" is Rosa, who begins identifying herself as "something," instead of as "I," at 125:37.

126:28 *the aunt, the spinster* Rosa, at eighteen.

127:10 *fee simple* In real estate, "fee simple" is the absolute ownership of property by an individual, subject only to such government claims as taxation.

127:31 *knowing that he would need us, knowing as we did (who knew him) that he would begin at once to salvage what was left of Sutpen's Hundred and restore it* Rosa seems still to believe this, in spite of his eight-month delay in returning home after Appomattox. The text does not explain his long delay and, curiously, none of the narrators speculates about it. See entries for 50:30, 131:14, 131:33, and 229:28.

129:26 *who . . . would cook twice what we could eat and three times what we could afford and give it to anyone, any stranger in a land already beginning to fill with straggling soldiers who stopped and asked for it* Rosa resents Judith's generosity to the returning soldiers; Judith, she thinks, has not "learned that that the first principle of penury . . . is to scrimp and save for the sake of scrimping and saving" (129:24). Judith's charity to the returning soldiers, her willingness to share their own meager foods, may argue for a softer, a warmer, more gracious Judith than the Judith Rosa and Mr. Compson have described to us.

131:14 *And then one afternoon in January Thomas Sutpen came home* See note for 50:30. For some reason Faulkner has Sutpen delay his return from the fighting in Virginia until 1866, when he could easily have walked home, if necessary, in a matter of weeks. The novel gives no indication where he goes or what he does during the eight months before he returns home. See the entries for 50:30, 127:31, 131:33, and 229.28.

131:33 *watched him ride up on that gaunt and jaded horse on which he did not seem to sit but rather seemed to project himself ahead like a mirage, in some fierce dynamic rigidity of impatience* more mystery surrounding Sutpen's delayed return from Virginia. To Rosa he seems impatient to get back and return to his dynasty building, but the fact of his delayed return to north Mississippi may argue that he is not in such a hurry. Rosa thinks that whatever he was doing for those eight months he was not deliberately delaying his return. The passage rather reflects the older Rosa's projection of the impending doom that she imposes upon herself out of her later knowledge of what happens. That is, Sutpen's proposal now, as she has told and re-told the episode to herself and others, seems to her more inevitable than it might have seemed at the time: his "impatience" might well be her backwards-imposed sense of his "impatient" expectation of her to agree to his proposal not just of marriage but of breeding. See entries for 131:14, 136:17.

132:11 *entire accumulation of seven months* The shooting must have occurred in April or May of 1865. See entry for 131:14.

132:35 *fabulous immeasurable Camelots and Carcassonnes* a measure of Rosa's, and perhaps the area's, sense of the size and grandeur of Sutpen's mansion. Camelot is the fabled utopian British kingdom of the Dark Ages ruled by King Arthur, which was undone by the sexual practices of his queen, Guinevere, and his most famous Knight, Sir Lancelot. Carcassonne is a very famous mediaeval walled city in the southwest of France, which Faulkner may have visited on his walking tour of France in the mid-twenties, and which figures as the metaphoric title for an early short story called "Carcassonne."

133:38 *men with pistols in their pockets gathered daily at secret meeting places in the towns* Many communities after the war formed vigilance committees ostensibly to keep carpet-baggers (133:35) and returning veterans from being nuisances or worse as they worked their way home and, more likely, to control such freed slaves as chose to stay near the plantations where they had worked and to protect the community from "negro uprisings," tales of which frightened people (133:37). Such a committee confronts Sutpen in the next lines. Perhaps such organizations were precursors the Ku Klux Klan. See entry for 137:40.

134:13 *ponderable weight of the changed new time* The "ponderable weight" of the "changed new time" necessarily invokes the "weight" of the past and the friction between the drastically altered circumstances of the old and the new dispensations.

134:14 *as though he were trying to dam a river with his bare hands and a shingle* See entry for 134:17.

134:17 *I see the analogy myself now: the accelerating circle's fatal curving course of his ruthless pride, his lust for vain magnificence* Rosa's analogy compares "the accelerating circle" of Sutpen's career to the "river" he is now trying to dam "with his bare hands and a shingle" (134:14)—a force so powerful he can no longer control it. "Shingle" is apparently a metonym for his mansion.

134:23 *unalarmed amazement* Another image which combines the static with the dynamic. Rosa describes her reaction to the "men and women" (134:24) she watched and knew during her childhood: she is experienced enough to be amazed, but not yet enough to be alarmed.

134:23 *miragy antics of men and women—my father, my sister, Thomas Sutpen, Judith, Henry, Charles Bon—called honor, principle, marriage, love, bereavement, death* antics = the socially codified behaviors called "honor, principle, marriage, love, bereavement, and death." Rosa sees the actors of these behaviors as something ludicrous or extravagant, miragy because they are both seen and unseen at the same time, fragments of the eyes' projection: she remembers them from her childhood, a time when she still lived in "that womb-like corridor where the world came not even as living echo but as dead incomprehensible shadow" (134:20). "Miragy" may also signal her detachment from any significant or meaningful participation.

134:26 *the child who watching him was not a child but one of that triumvirate mother-woman which we three, Judith Clytie and I, made* Rosa casts back to her childhood to find a pathology for her current state. But for the first time in her life she feels like an adult, forming with Judith and Clytie a single creature who functions with all the responsibilities of a woman and a mother.

134:29 *fierce vain illusion* that life is worth living.

134:40 *perhaps not even at this point or at that point but diffused (not attenuated to thinness but enlarged, magnified, encompassing as though in a prolonged and unbroken instant of tremendous effort embracing and holding intact that ten-mile square while he faced from the brink of disaster, invincible and unafraid, what he must have known would be the final defeat)* Sutpen at first seems to Rosa not to be standing at any given point on his own land but instead diffused throughout it, incorporating it into himself, holding it "intact" by sheer monstrous will. She does not think of him as attenuated to thinness, not stretched by the diffusion, but rather enlarged by it. The "final defeat" is death and sonlessness.

135:5 *but instead of that* Instead of being diffused Sutpen is "standing there in the path looking at" her.

135:14 *But it was not love* The look on Sutpen's face as he looks at Rosa is not the look of a lover upon his beloved.

135:19 *He was gone; I did not even know that either* any more than she knew when he appeared out of the swamp to stand before her.

135:19 *since there is a metabolism of the spirit as well as of the entrails, in which the stored accumulations of long time burn, generate, create and break some maidenhead of the ravening meat; ay, in a second's time;—yes, lost all the shibboleth erupting of cannot, will not, never will in one red instant's fierce obliteration. This was my instant* Not uncharacteristically,

Rosa mixes a metaphor here, as she often does when she is upset. Metabolism is the rate at which the body uses or stores the energy it derives from food; spirit has a metabolism too, which feeding upon, using, its stored fuels—her frustrated, repressed desire, need—and reaching the point of heat and consumption when it overcomes the flesh, then almost instantaneously "creates and breaks" all resistance or will, so that the flesh no longer can repress what it desires. This moment repudiates all repression and refusal, "obliterat[ing]" the "shibboleth erupting of cannot, will not, never will" in "one red instant." See the entry for 115:32. Here the "shibboleth erupting" of nots would seem to posit Rosa's negative attitude toward sexuality—"cannot, will not, never will"—as a protective shell which Sutpen's proposal, crude as it seems to be, simply obliterates, as the touch of Clytie's hand obliterates racial shibboleths.

135:30 *I might have said then, To what deluded sewer-gush of dreaming does the incorrigible flesh betray us* Rosa might have argued with herself at that first dinner with Sutpen at table, reverting to her attitudes toward sexuality as something reprehensible, awful.

136:6 *a ukase, a decree, a serene and florid boast like a sentence (ay, and delivered in the same attitude) not to be spoken and heard but to be read carved in the bland stone which pediments a forgotten and nameless effigy.* ukase = a tsar's proclamation having the power of law; sentence = not a grammatical unit but a court's decree of penal bondage. Rosa remembers Sutpen's proposal of marriage as an order, peremptory, carved in that stone which forms the base of a statue, and issued by Sutpen as if from the throne on high.

136:12 *I could have forced that niche myself if I had willed to—a niche not shaped to fit mild 'Yes' but some blind desperate female weapon's frenzied slash whose very gaping wound had cried 'No! No!' and 'Help!' and 'Save me!'* Rosa claims in the previous lines that Thomas Sutpen had not left her any time, any space, or "niche" in which to respond to his proposal of marriage, though, she also claims, she could have "forced" such a niche if she had made herself. But if she had responded, she claims, she would not have responded affirmatively but rather violently in the negative. Her language turns sexual, even vulgar, focusing on her vulva, which Sutpen's proposal, and her mute acceptance, renders vulnerable to assault. It is that very "slash," that "gaping wound" that could somehow refuse Sutpen's assault by attacking him, and at the same time by crying out for help, for Rosa to save herself from violation.

136:17 *heard him speak to Judith now, heard Judith's feet, saw Judith's hand, not Judith—that palm in which I read as from a printed chronicle the orphaning, the hardship, the bereave of love* Sutpen "proposes" marriage to Rosa without giving her much choice whether to accept or refuse; he then "speaks to Judith," obviously telling her to fetch her mother's ring to give to Rosa. As she hands the ring to Sutpen, Rosa focuses on Judith's palm, on which rests the dread symbol of matrimony that makes her sexual organ—the "frenzied slash," the "gaping wound" (136:14)—want to resist, to say '*No! No!*' and '*Help!*' and '*Save me!*' (136:15). The ring and Judith's palm become a text in which is concentrated all she has witnessed of marriage (that of her own parents and that of Sutpen and Ellen), wherein she reads a "chronicle" of "*the orphaning, the hardship, the bereave of love; the four hard barren years of scoriating loom, of axe and hoe and all the other tools decreed for men to use*" (136:19).

136:20 **bereave of love** Readers expect the noun, "bereavement," of love in such locutions. Rosa, however, uses the verb form, usually transitive, as a noun. To bereave is to deprive someone of life, hope, or love; to leave destitute, orphaned or widowed, "to snatch away (a possession); to remove or take away by violence" (OED). In the passage (see entry for 136:17) "bereave" is one of three subjects of the prepositional phrase "of love," parallel with "orphaning" and "hardship," which Rosa reads in Judith's palm that holds her mother's wedding ring. It's not precisely the simple loss of love that she reads in Judith's palm but rather the loss of other things that love causes *by being love* as Rosa understands love from her very limited experience of it. She fears that love will actually, even violently cause her further pain.

136:20 **scoriating loom** See entry for 136:17. At one level this phrase might simply refer to the damage to Judith's hands caused by their weaving at the loom. But a rare and obsolete meaning of "scoriate" is "excoriate," which means both to abrade and to denounce (OED). "Loom" is both an instrument for weaving and an apparition of the future, a "distorted and threatening appearance of something, as through fog or darkness." Thus the phrase evokes not only the damage to their bodies their work for survival causes but also the damage to their spirits of having to live with the vague, incomprehensible, impending doom that seems imminent and, for Rosa, carries with it a sense of denunciation, of implicit harsh criticism, that she has felt all of her life. See 105 and the entry for 105:7 for Mr. Compson's discussion of Judith's use of the loom metaphor as a description of the complexities of human relationships.

136:23 **Yes, analogy and paradox and madness too.** Rosa has already (134:17) compared "the accelerating circle" of Sutpen's career to the "river" he is now trying to dam "with his bare hands and a shingle" (134:14): it is a force so powerful he can no longer control it. She describes what she thinks is Sutpen's madness—and hers too—at lines 136:35ff. In each case, Sutpen was "*talking not about me or love or marriage, not even about himself... but to the very dark forces of fate which he had evoked and dared, out of that wild braggart dream where an intact Sutpen's Hundred which no more had actual being now... than it had when Ellen first heard it*" (136:28). The madness is Sutpen's, also Ellen's and potentially Rosa's, had she succumbed to marriage. The paradox is that Rosa's marriage would be no more fraudulent than Ellen's. That's why it is both analogy and paradox.

137:1 ***If I was saved that night (and I was saved; mine was to be some later, colder sacrifice when we—I—should be free of all excuse of the surprised importunate traitorous flesh)*** saved from marriage to Sutpen. The "later, colder sacrifice" is presumably the moment when Sutpen approaches her and makes their marriage contingent upon her producing him a son beforehand.

137:27 ***my presence was to him only the absence of black morass and snarled vine and creeper to that man who had struggled through a swamp with nothing to guide or drive him... and blundered at last and without warning onto dry solid ground and sun and air*** Rosa believes that to Sutpen she was not even an actual presence but a negation, merely the lack of an impediment to his ambitions.

137:40 ***who kept clear of the sheets and hoods and night-galloping horses with which men who were once his acquaintances even if not his friends discharged the canker suppuration of defeat*** Sutpen does not become one with his neighbors who join the Ku Klux Klan to reassert local power over carpetbaggers and freed slaves. Rosa's memory may be slightly anachronistic. The Klan began its nefarious work in 1866, in uniforms that prescribed head-covering masks of white but allowed body coverings of any color and design the member wanted (Trelease 53; Doyle 284).

138:11 ***there are some things for which three words are three too many, and three thousand words that many words too less*** Here, as elsewhere, Rosa's language spills over the boundaries of normal usage, as she puts "too less" into syntactical parallel with "too many." We expect to compare "many" with "few," but Faulkner upsets the parallel structure: as an adjective it compares a quality of language with a quality of discourse, since three is too many and 3,000 is not just not quantitatively enough but actually has a negative effect on quantity: it's not just "too few" words since there are more but a foreshortening of meaning amplified by so many. Edgar Whan suggests that *Absalom* "is dominated by the feeling that something has happened that cannot be explained. The narrators are never satisfied that they have communicated, so they go back and tell it again as if sheer weight would finally express the ineffable" (200).

138:14 **the bold blank naked and outrageous words** See 139:33: "the bald outrageous words exactly as if he were consulting with Jones or with some other man about a bitch dog or a cow or mare." Sutpen's "proposal" to Rosa has been much discussed, both in the novel and in the criticism. These two passages contain all she has to say on the subject. Shreve is more specific in two other passages, though he uses language that surely Sutpen did not use even if they do convey his meaning, at least as Rosa may understand it. At 147:21 Shreve has it that Sutpen approached her and suggested "that they breed together for test and sample and if it was a boy they would marry" and at 149:38 he proposes that Sutpen "suggested they breed like a couple of dogs together" —thus "inventing with fiendish cunning," Shreve says, "the thing which husbands and fiances have been trying to invent for ten million years" (149:39). Given Rosa's tendency to blow all of her outrage and her fears well out of proportion and Shreve's tendency to be laconic, flippant, and sarcastic, it cannot be clear *exactly* what Sutpen said or proposed to Rosa. Surely he said something that offended her, but given her repressive childhood and her manifest fear of sexuality, it couldn't have taken much to do that. Indeed, a perhaps drunken Sutpen—he shouts to her to come down and join him on the back gallery (139:21, 31)—clearly seems to have proposed that they have sex before they get married, but the degree to which what he actually said was as crude as that they "breed like a couple of dogs" to see if she could produce him a son is not at all certain. In the normal course of things a woman fends off numerous such advances without thinking much about them beyond, perhaps, an irritation at the unwanted attention; Rosa, however, is anything but casual in her attitudes toward the sexual realities that Sutpen represents. After all her romanticizing, rhapsodizing, about Judith and Bon and love in the previous pages, Sutpen here confronts her with the raw fact of physical sexuality—"friction's ravishing of the male-furrowed meat" (see entry for 120:26)—of which, clearly, she is terrified enough to turn a simple "pass" into a lifetime of outrage which becomes an excuse for not marrying Sutpen or anybody else, even if the war had left her anybody else to marry. It is of course possible that a drunken—or even sober—Sutpen actually used such "bald blank naked and outrageous words."

138:21 *I was that sun* that sun she described at 137:31 which greets Sutpen as he "blunders" out of the "black morass and snarled vine" of the swamp—"if there could have been such thing as sun to him." Here and in the following lines, Rosa professes to have been so shocked by Sutpen's proposal because she, the romantic, had believed that her love could redeem him, rescue him from his madness.

138:22 *that spark, that crumb in madness which is divine* At 138:6, 8 Rosa suggests that Sutpen is not really mad, since "surely there is something in madness . . . some spark, some crumb to leaven and redeem that articulated flesh." She claims to have believed that she was that sun, that spark which would "leaven and redeem" Sutpen from his madness, restore him to sanity and so make of him a good husband.

138:25 *grim ogre-bourne* Sutpen's Hundred.

138:27 *presentiment of that fateful intertwining, warned me of that fatal snarly climax before I knew the name for murder* "fateful intertwining" = the relationship between Henry and Judith; "fatal snarly climax" = Henry's killing of Bon at the gates to Sutpen's Hundred.

138:29 *and I forgave it* Rosa claims that even with the "presentiment" (138:27) she had had, even as a child, of all the misery Sutpen would cause, she forgave him all of it.

138:37 *but not the ogre; villain true enough, but a mortal fallible one less to invoke fear than pity . . . not even madness but solitary despair in titan conflict with the lonely and foredoomed and indomitable iron spirit* Rosa rationalizes her need for a husband with her image of Sutpen as the ogre-presence of her childhood: perhaps he was not an ogre, not mad, but actually a tragic hero.

139:5 *I was that sun* See entry for 138:21.

139:8 *tasting sun and light again and aware of neither but only of darkness' and morass's lack* Rosa's "swamp-freed pilgrim" (139:7), though tasting sun and light again, is not aware of their presence, but only of their lack.

139:18 *the death of pride and principle, and then the death of everything save the old outraged and aghast unbelieving which has lasted for forty-three*

- *years* Rosa has ratcheted up the intensity of Sutpen's proposition to such an extent that it has fed her outrage for forty-three years.
- 140:7 *who had buried no hopes to bugles, beneath a flag* who had lost no husband or fiancé or son to death in the war. Bugles, playing "Taps," traditionally are a part of the ceremony of military funerals.
- 140:22 *embalmed the War and its heritage of suffering and injustice and sorrow on the backsides of the pages within an old account book, embalming blotting from the breathable air the poisonous secret effluvium of lusting and hating and killing* Rosa writes her poems to lay the war to rest, to bury it, to "blot" or erase the "hating and the killing." She also writes to erase war's "lusting," a term which may apply equally to war's aggrandizers as to her own sexual feelings, which had betrayed her, made her victim to Sutpen's "courtship." Her association of "lusting" with "hating and killing" also identifies "lusting"—and love—with violence. At 136:14 Rosa describes her vulva as "a frenzied slash," "a gaping wound." She may also write the poems precisely to keep Sutpen alive—to render him "by outraged capitulation evoked" (5) and so still vulnerable to her hope for love and vengeance or simple explanation. See entries for 5:25, 136:12, 136:17, 141:7.
- 140:27 *embusque* one who avoids military service by getting a government job (OED).
- 141:5 *who would be right only right, being right, is not enough for women who had rather be wrong than just that who want the man who was wrong to admit it* would rather be wrong than just right, since being right is hollow unless the man will admit he was wrong.
- 141:7 *that's what she cant forgive him for: not for the insult, not even for having jilted her: but for being dead* Being dead, Sutpen cannot admit he was wrong (see entry for 141:5). This may well explain why Rosa continually evokes Sutpen, "by outraged recapitulation" (5:26): to keep him alive to hate, perhaps against the possibility that he may, somehow, admit he is wrong. See entries for 5:25, 140:22, and 307:4.
- 141:9 *How two months later they learned that she had packed up her belongings . . . and come back to town* The "How" reverts to earlier in chapter V, where Rosa rehearses to Quentin what the town "will have told you" about her, so that she can mount her self-defense. The phrase is slightly ambiguous. Does she mean that she stayed at Sutpen's Hundred for two months after Sutpen's "proposal" or that she left immediately and the town only found out

about her return two months later? If the latter, she must have lived there as a recluse. If the former, the passage raises the question Why did she stay there for two months? Was she considering his proposal, in all its presumptive vulgarity? Did she stay to keep herself in harm's way? Did she, finally, want the proposed violation?

141:38 *found a beau and was insulted, something heard and not forgiven, not so much for the saying of it but for having thought it about her so that when she heard it she realised like thunderclap that it must have been in his mind for a day, a week, even a month maybe, he looking at her daily with that in his mind and she not even knowing it* It would appear from this passage that Rosa is at least partially titillated by Sutpen's proposition, and perhaps she turns that titillation into outrage to erase her shame at having sexual feelings at all. In *Flags in the Dust* Narcissa Benbow has a similar reaction to the series of barely literate obscene letters Byron Snopes sends to her: she shows them to Miss Jenny to verify that they are horrible to receive, but keeps them in her underwear drawer (769).

142:14 **a walking shadow** a reference to Shakespeare's *Macbeth*, V.v.24–26, from which Faulkner took the title of *The Sound and the Fury*. See Lurie 118.

142:14 *He was the light-blinded bat-like image of his own torment cast by the fierce demoniac lantern up from beneath the earth's crust and hence in retrograde, reverse; from abysmal and chaotic dark to eternal and abysmal dark* Sutpen is a shadow, the "image of his own torment," cast by a lantern deeper in earth than he; he is thus in retrograde, in reverse, not emerging from the darkness, but returning to it, from the chaotic dark of earth's surface to the eternal dark of its hellish center. Even in her outrage, Rosa seems willing to allow that Sutpen is "tormented," a person with compulsions that he can't control. See previous entry.

142:18 *completing his descending . . . ellipsis, clinging, trying to cling with vain unsubstantial hands to what he hoped would hold him, save him, arrest him* The descending gradation is, as Rosa sees it, from Ellen to herself to Millie Jones.

142:28 **But Quentin was not listening.** See the note that begins this chapter.

143:6 *Now you cant marry him.* This and the next four lines foreshadow Faulkner's representation of the scene in chapter IX (306:24) when Quentin confronts Henry. Chapter IX takes up where chapter V leaves off.

143:15 **Something living in it. Hidden in it. It has been out there for four** years, living hidden in that house. This passage raises several questions. Does Rosa know *who* has been in the house for four years? Has she known for four years or has she just recently discovered it? In either case, *how* does she know, how did she find out? Has she talked with Clytie? If she has known for four years that Henry is there, why does it take her four years to go out there? And if she has been talking with Clytie, why does she think she will need an axe to enter the house this time? The novel supplies no answers to these questions but seems clearly to ask them.

CHAPTER VI

Throughout chapter VI, Faulkner invests the narrative with a sense of fatality. The narrative mode becomes that of free indirect discourse, whereby the narration, straddling the points of view of a putatively omniscient narrator and one or more of the characters, makes it difficult to tell which point of view the narration presents, difficult to know whether there are two or three voices or simply one, especially when they meld into one, as they frequently do. Clearly, here, though, Faulkner gives to Quentin the tragic sense of doom that pervades the book—the cause and effect at work in human chancings and mischancings, the logical "so that" that connects, or tries to, cause and effect, moving forward and backward. Fowler (112) notes the virtual disappearance of the phrase "Father said" from the text, which disappearance signals Quentin and Shreve's taking over the narration. Father's voice becomes in chapter 6 the "sloped fine hand" (144:6) of the emblematic letter.

144:1 **There was snow on Shreve's overcoat sleeve** Chapter VI moves us immediately to a different time, a different place, a different season, and a new character. Shreve McCannon, a Canadian, is Quentin's roommate at Harvard. Chapters VI–VIII take place as the two of them, sitting up late in their frigid dormitory room, retelling, re-creating, the story of Thomas Sutpen to their mutual narrative satisfaction. Why Faulkner chooses to set so much of *Absalom* in a land so alien to the land in which Sutpen lived is not completely clear, but obviously he wanted at least one non-southern narrator, one who is not in some way compromised by Sutpen and/or the racial and social history of the South: someone, that is, with some distance on the story, not so directly embroiled in it. Casting Shreve as a Canadian further removes him from the legacy of sectional antipathy characteristic of the United States; it also opens the closed Mississippi society to outside scrutiny. Shreve is thus a narrative foil who at times offers a smart-aleck counter-narrative to Quentin's story; his contributions to the narrative at first render the Sutpen saga as a comedy that wallows in the clichés of southern popular culture, then yields to its human if not precisely historical "reality." Shreve becomes, in the telling, genuinely moved and tries to contribute to the story's cohesiveness, supplying plot and motive and even character when necessary to keep the narrative moving.

We do not know how much of the story Quentin has told Shreve or in Shreve's hearing before this night: apparently at least the main outlines, since Shreve seems to know things that Quentin hasn't told before this night, or has told this night in passages that Faulkner does not give us. Certainly Quentin has had numerous chances to tell the story, since Shreve's questions on this night are not the first questions; classmates have asked since September, "nobody's first time in Cambridge": "*Tell about the South. What's it like there. What do they do there. Why do they live there. Why do they live at all*" (145:2). In one sense the narrating is a sort of ritual, so that perhaps what Quentin and Shreve do on this night is to work through some of the finer points of character, motivation, and logic that they have not worked out on previous occasions. Perhaps this is the first time they have tried to reassemble the entire story out of the fragments that Quentin has related since he arrived in Cambridge in September. Or perhaps the text may simply be dramatizing many tellings and hearings, so that what is rendered is not mimetic, not something imagined to have happened exactly as reported on the page, but rather a dramatic rendering of numerous dialogic encounters, melded into a form of representation that transcends and (to use the novel's terms) overpasses human speech to represent interlocking consciousnesses.

144:2 **vanishing** Apparently it's the snow on Shreve's sleeve that vanishes as it melts in the room's relative warmth.

144:3 **Then on the table before Quentin . . . the white oblong of envelope** The "Then" suggests that Shreve has just come from the post office with Quentin's letter from home about Rosa Coldfield's death.

144:8 **so that** more of Quentin's, and the novel's, curious logic. In a narrative built around so few "facts," the narrators must inevitably connect those few in ways that give them a cause-effect relationship. Faulkner renders cause and effect ironically, connecting two events that have no cause-effect relationship: Quentin "had prepared for Harvard so that his father's hand could lie on a strange lamplit table in Cambridge" (144:8).

144:9 **that dead summer twilight . . . attenuated up from Mississippi** the night that he and his father discussed the Sutpens on the Compson front porch, after which Quentin went with Rosa to Sutpen's Hundred and discovered Henry Sutpen there. "Attenuated," one of Faulkner's favorite words, means "Made thin in consistency, rarified, diluted" (OED); in Cambridge, that hot Mississippi evening, though evoked powerfully, is quite diluted in the Massachusetts ice and snow.

144:13 *My dear son* Mr. Compson's letter to his son begins here and concludes at 310:7, at the end of the novel. Rosa's death thus frames and provides a context for everything in between. Quentin and Shreve refer to it on occasion in the intervening pages; it lies open in front of him as Quentin sits at his desk, brooding over it throughout his interlocution with Shreve. Quentin stops reading the letter with his father's words, "*I do not know that either*" (144:30), and the boys pick up where Mr. Compson's knowledge ends, filling in the gaps in his narrative with new information and with speculation.

144:14 *Miss Rosa Coldfield was buried yesterday. She remained in the coma for almost two weeks and two days ago she died* Assuming Mr. Compson mails the letter immediately, "yesterday" would be January 9, 1910 and she would have died on January 8. We cannot deduce from these dates the date of Quentin and Shreve's conversation at Cambridge because we do not know how long it would have taken for the letter to reach them.

144:32 **needing, required, to say "No, neither aunt cousin nor uncle Rosa. Miss Rosa.** Quentin's letter from his father relating Rosa Coldfield's burial inspires Shreve's rather aggressive teasing in the following lines about the common perception that in the South everybody is kin to everybody else.

144:33 **an old lady that died young of outrage in 1866 one summer** Rosa did not, of course, literally die in 1866, but her emotional, sexual, and intellectual life did stop with the outrage she felt upon Thomas Sutpen's marriage proposal. See entry for 136:17.

144:36 **Bayard** Pierre du Terrail Bayard was a famous French knight of the fifteenth and sixteenth centuries. The name was popular in the South for its connections with heroism and gallantry. There are two Bayards among Faulkner's Sartoris family (McDaniel 6–7)

144:36 **Guinevere** wife of King Arthur, of the Round Table, and lover of one of his knights, Sir Lancelot. Their romance, their concupiscence, compromised the ideals represented by the round table and caused the eventual collapse of Camelot.

144:36 **who was no kin to you?** Shreve teases Quentin about the assumption that all southerners are kin to one another. The darker side of this "assumption" is apparently based in myths about incest as a practice common among southerners.

145:1 **then what did she die for?** Shreve's question does not follow logically from his previous statement, a question confirming that Rosa was no kin to Quentin at all (144:35). If Rosa is not a part of Quentin's family, Shreve wants to know why Quentin would care. However, the caring is both implicit in the preceding interlocution and explicit in Mr. Compson's letter. Shreve's question—then what did she die for?—really means, "what does her death mean to you?" By "death" Shreve means both deaths: the emotional one Rosa experienced in 1866 and the physical one reported in Mr. Compson's letter.

145:3 *Tell about the South. What's it like there. What do they do there. Why do they live there? Why do they live at all* a litany of questions about the South that Quentin's friends and acquaintances at Harvard have asked since September. But they are doubtless also Quentin's questions too as he tries to deal with the uncomprehending persistent questions of his northern acquaintances. Their presentation in italics here seems to connect them with the "stubborn back-looking ghosts" (9:16) that Quentin has dealt with most of his life and with the "two separate Quentins" (6:24) constantly in dialogue with each other. Indeed, the "two separate Quentins," so identified in the novel's opening pages, are precisely that one "preparing for Harvard" (6:25), where he now is, and the one "too young to deserve to be a ghost" (6:30). Faulkner describes him early as "a barracks indeed, filled with stubborn back-looking ghosts" (9:16): here, at Harvard, he is in the dormitory, a "barracks" filled, for the evening at any rate, with back-looking narrators.

145:6 **walked out of his father's talking** Apparently Mr. Compson here, as in *The Sound and the Fury*, is present in Quentin's life less as a person than as an interior voice which he can never escape.

145:9 **something which he was still unable to pass: that door, that gaunt tragic dramatic self-hypnotised youthful face** that door = the door into the decaying house at Sutpen's Hundred, where he stops before forcing his and Rosa's way in through the window and up the stairs to find Henry (see

142:29); face = Henry Sutpen's. "Self-hypnotised" suggests that at this point in Quentin's understanding he holds Henry responsible for what seems to have been an unnecessary killing; he thinks that Henry must have been deluded to murder Bon. Quentin's understanding will evolve over the course of the next three chapters, and Bon's death will become largely a desideratum of Henry's own making; he was less under Bon's influence than a victim of his own frenzy.

145:10 **like the tragedian in a college play** Henry; an amateur player.

145:11 **an academic Hamlet** the hero of Shakespeare's play who finally overcomes his reluctance to put his soul in jeopardy of hell and acts to avenge the murder that his ghost father has imposed on him. Perhaps "academic" suggests the stuffiness or the cold analytic qualities of the classroom or of an amateur performance—bad acting—though the following lines do not convey this meaning. The image continues at 145:13: that "the rest of the cast had departed last commencement" suggests that the academic Hamlet has overplayed his role, or stayed on stage to play it long past its expiration.

145:11 **waked from some trancement of the curtain's falling** The academic Hamlet moves as if in a trance out front of the falling curtain, as if to prolong his role after the play has ended, disrupting the divide between play and actuality. His dramatic revenge fantasy, or trance, intrudes on Judith's prenuptial preparations. The OED doesn't list "trancement" but does give several definitions of "trance" besides the obvious—an "unconscious or insensible condition; a swoon, a faint, a . . . prolonged suspension of consciousness and inertness to stimulation; a cataleptic or hypnotic condition"—that may apply: "trance" is from the Latin "transitus," so that it means "passage, or way through," a "passage between buildings" or "across between two streets; an entry, an alley, a close; also, a passage into, within, or through a house." It thus also carries the meaning "to die, to pass away." A "trancement," then, seems to be a condition of transition from acting to reality as the curtain falls and the stage empties of the actors and leaves the tragic hero to deal with real life. See previous entry.

145:14 **the sister facing him across the wedding dress which she was not to use** These lines evoke the scene at the end of chapter V, in which Henry runs up the stairs and into the room to tell his sister that now she can't marry Bon because he has killed him (143:6).

145:15 **the two of them slashing at one another with twelve or fourteen words** See the entry for 143:6.

145:22 **reticule** a small light purse.

145:30 **that evening, the twelve miles behind the fat mare in the moonless September dust** the dark night when Quentin and Rosa Coldfield went out to the Sutpen house, traveling the twelve miles from town by horse and buggy.

145:36 **heat-vulcanised dust** To vulcanize is to treat crude India-rubber with sulphur and then subject it to intense heat in order to make it harder, more pliable, and adaptable to many purposes. The image here suggests how hot and dense the dust is, becoming almost like a rubber coating on the "roadside undergrowth."

145:38 **perpendicular's absolute** The OED defines "absolute" as "detached in position or relation," "free from imperfection or deficiency," "perfect," "disengaged from all accidental or special circumstances." Faulkner's curious insistence describes the appearance of "roadside undergrowth" (145:35) which, rising up from the ground and "seen through the dustcloud" (145:36), appears absolutely perpendicular to the land.

145:40 **the oxygenless first principle of liquid** What muddy water remains off the roadside in this rainless summer appears so thick as to evoke a kind of primal ooze. Chemistry Professor Karen Brewer helps here: "The chapter opens with the letter about Rosa's death; the description of death (or lifelessness) continues. The context for this passage is the description of the trees along the route in which Quentin and Rosa are riding together in a buggy. 'Dead volcanic water,' containing dissolved sulfur dioxide, would be very acidic and therefore incapable of sustaining life. This water would also likely be brackish and poisonous from dissolved minerals present in the surrounding soil and clay. 'Refined' water would, at first instinct, seem to be purified water. But it is clearly not purified here in a healthful way for it is 'oxygenless' and therefore cannot sustain oxygen-breathing life (no small fish, for example). The 'first principle of liquid' might refer to the physical properties of a liquid—it has definite volume but does not have a definite shape, but rather takes the shape of the container it is in, the gulley at the side of the road."

146:8 ***Come on if you like. But I will get there first; accumulating ahead of you I will arrive first*** The dust—death (Roudiez 62)—speaks, gathering itself motionless around the moving buggy. It will always be ahead of them, waiting. Its envelopment of the buggy is a warning, advice *"to turn back now and let what is, be"* (146:14).

146:24 **this Aunt Rosa——"**

"Miss Rosa," Quentin said. Gwin suggests that Shreve "consistently distances and diminishes the authority of Rosa's narrative by misnaming her" (117).

147:1 **prove not only to themselves but to everybody else that she had been right** Shreve will have none of Rosa's claims throughout chapter V that she "holds no brief" for herself—that she is not defending her refusal to marry Sutpen. The next few lines contain Shreve's ironic litany of things she had been "right" about.

147:10 **if he hadn't made General Lee and Jeff Davis mad he wouldn't have had to nail himself up and die and if he hadn't died he wouldn't have left her an orphan and a pauper and so situated, left susceptible to a situation where she could receive this mortal affront** More of Shreve's ironic cause-and-effect recounting of events. He doesn't mean that Mr. Coldfield literally did something that made Lee and Davis angry because nobody knows exactly why he locks himself in his attic. He simply traces Rosa's "mortal affront" (see 147:21) from Sutpen back to a non-specific ultimate "cause"; the effects flowing from this cause, however, as Shreve clearly knows, are not really connected except in his comic construction of events. The irony is a clear indication of an outsider's perspective.

147:14 **this mortal affront** Sutpen's proposition that so offends Rosa (147:21).

147:17 **betrayed by the old meat** betrayed by sexual desire or, perhaps more simply, by the need for food.

147:18 **find instead of a widowed Agamemnon to her Cassandra an ancient stiff-jointed Pyramus to her eager though untried Thisbe** Agamemnon and Pyramus = Sutpen; Cassandra and Thisbe = Rosa. Agamemnon was the king who led the Greeks in the Trojan War, Cassandra the daughter of Priam, king of the Trojans. Apollo, in love with her, gave her the gift of prophecy, but when she deceived him, he changed the gift to a curse: though she could foretell the future, no one would believe her. At his victory over the Trojans, Agamemnon claimed Cassandra as his slave and lover and took her home, where his wife, Clytemnestra, and her lover, Aegisthus, murdered them both. The lovers Pyramus and Thisbe, whose story is recorded in Ovid's *The Metamorphoses*, agree to meet, against their parents' wishes, at a spring in the forest one night. Thisbe arrives first and, seeing a lion with a bloody mouth, assumes that the lion has killed Pyramus. She runs away, leaving behind a garment which the lion picks up. Pyramus arrives and, seeing Thisbe's garment in the lion's mouth, assumes that the lion has eaten Thisbe and impales himself on his sword. Thisbe then returns from her hiding place and in despair over her lost love kills herself with Pyramus's knife.

It's not clear how far to take Shreve's dual analogies as serious analyses of Rosa and Sutpen's "relationship." His comparison of Rosa with Cassandra invokes Mr. Compson's description of Rosa's childhood as an "aged and ancient and timeless absence of youth which consisted of a Cassandra-like listening beyond closed doors" (49:18), a constant activity which invests her with a prophetic sense of doom to be played out in connection to Sutpen, now widowered by Ellen's death; their relationship, like that of Agamemnon and Cassandra, spells doom for them both—as, indeed, in a real sense, her relationship with Sutpen spells both their dooms. Perhaps, too, Shreve calls Rosa Cassandra to connect her to Sutpen's Hundred's Clytemnestra, Clytie (Sutpen's daughter, not his wife), who may also in a real sense be said to cause their dooms, or at least to symbolize them in her origins in the South's, and Sutpen's, racial attitudes. At least, one might say, Agamemnon and Cassandra had a honeymoon on the ocean voyage back home. Rosa's "ancient stiff-jointed Pyramus," Sutpen, however, can't give her the sexual love that Rosa's (Thisbe's) "eager though untried" "old meat" believes it wants. Shreve's "academic" analogues also signal, in chapter V, an increasing reliance on "the best of thought" in the Harvard setting. These analogues set up the "best of thought" as ironic and informed by critical, which is to say detached, thinking.

147:21 **suggest that they breed together for test and sample and if it was a boy they would marry** See the entry for 138:14.

147:24 **gall and wormwood** A gall is an extremely painful blister or swelling, especially on a horse or mule whose trace-chains have produced it; wormwood is the plant *Artemisia absynthium*, whose leaves produce a bitter dark green oil used to make absinthe and vermouth, sometimes used to protect clothes and bedding from mosquitoes and bugs. Together, "gall and wormwood" are traditionally used to describe something particularly burdensome, vexing, and painful.

147:25 **so this was not fixed at all and forever because she couldn't even tell it because of who her successor was** more of Rosa's self-defense. At 147:3, as Shreve would have it, Rosa takes her aunt's elopement with the horse trader as evidence that she had been "right about the aunt" and so "that fixed that"; that is, the aunt's escape solved whatever problem the aunt had been for Rosa. Here, she can't be "right" about "this," her reasons for returning to

Jefferson to live: that is, she can't "fix" this problem because she can't come to terms with, much less discuss publicly, the fact that Sutpen had turned from her directly to the white trash granddaughter of Wash Jones. Her class biases are thus as strong as her moral outrage.

147:38 **that scythe, symbolic laurel of a caesar's triumph** the scythe with which Wash Jones will kill Sutpen later in this chapter. Shreve's sarcasm implies that Wash "crowns" Sutpen with this "laurel."

148:3 **how did she put it? slut wasn't all, was it?** more evidence that this is not the first time Quentin and Shreve have rehearsed the Sutpen saga. Rosa calls Milly Jones a "slut" and perhaps other epithets to claim her own moral superiority over her successor.

148:4 **scythe . . . whose symbolic shape** The crescent-shaped blade of the scythe aids in its use as a reaping tool; it is often associated with the figure of Death, or of Father Time. As a cutting tool, it is also a symbol of castration, or castration anxiety (Polk, *Children* 142; Duvall 113).

148:8 **Faustus** Legendary figure in Western culture, treated in dramas by Christopher Marlowe and Goethe, who bargains with the devil, trades or wagers his soul for success in this worldly life in exchange for eternal servitude in hell.

148:8 **Beelzebub** "Baal-Zebul," meaning "Prince Baal" was one of the titles given to the Philistine god Baal. Biblically, Beelzebub is a prince of evil spirits, and in Milton's *Paradise Lost* he is Satan's chief lieutenant.

148:9 **his Creditor's outraged face exasperated beyond all endurance** Creditor = Beelzebub or Satan, to whom Sutpen, Faustus in the analogy, has given his soul as collateral against his success in this life. In Shreve's rehearsal of Rosa's attitudes toward him, Sutpen's behavior is so morally outrageous that even Satan is appalled, so that Sutpen must hide, "scuttling into respectability like a jackal into a rockpile" (148:9).

148:16 **skuldugged** tricked.

148:19 **crystal tapestries and the Wedgwood chairs** Josiah Wedgwood (1730–1795) was known for his pottery and porcelain, but apparently not for furniture. Shreve mistakenly attributes the chairs to Wedgwood, perhaps for comic effect.

148:22 **horns and tail** appurtenances usually associated with Satan, here with Sutpen.

148:37 **the son the agent for the providing of that living bulwark between him (the demon) and the Creditor's bailiff hand** elaborates on the analogy of Sutpen's having made a bargain with the devil; his son is or should be, a "bulwark," a shelter the devil cannot successfully attack or besiege. The "bailiff hand" is the hand of the court's warden, who transports prisoners between jail and court.

149:3 **that he (the son) should do the office of the outraged father's pistol-hand when fornication threatened** Far from being a "bulwark," Henry becomes the agent of the disaster itself, although at this point Shreve thinks only that the threat of fornication was the cause of the killing. This question—why Henry shoots Bon—drives all of *Absalom*'s telling and revising: that killing is the dramatic moment toward which all the narratives point. Quentin and Shreve's resolution of all the narrators' difficulties in explaining this event—that Sutpen tells Henry to stop him because Bon is part Negro (292)—begs several larger questions about why Sutpen, if he is the powerful, demonic father Rosa and others depict him as, does not himself stop the marriage by, for example, 1) shooting Bon himself: if Bon is part Negro, no jury in the South would have convicted him of murder; or 2), less dramatically or violently, simply sending Judith away somewhere, an extended trip to Europe, perhaps, or to school somewhere in the North: the protestant equivalents of a nunnery.

149:36 **on the very day when he established definitely that he would be able to keep at least some of his land** After the Civil War, the North's plan was to break up the large plantations in the South and to divide that land among the former slaves—the famous unfulfilled promise of "40 acres and a mule." This did not happen, and many landowners were able to return to business as usual. On Reconstruction in Faulkner, see Doyle, chapter 8.

149:39 **inventing with fiendish cunning the thing which husbands and fiances have been trying to invent for ten million years** These lines drip with Shreve's sarcasm: "fiendish cunning" is a phrase from melodrama. By "the thing" Shreve obviously means a man's devious attempts to get sexual favors from a woman without marrying her. It is clear why a fiancé should try to invent such a "thing," but why should a husband have to? See next entries.

150:1 **the thing that without harming her or giving her grounds for civil or tribal action would not only blast the little dream-woman out of the dovecote but leave her irrevocably husbanded . . . with the abstract carcass of outrage and revenge** See entry for 149:39. The "thing" appears to be an occasion, or a circumstance, that will enable both the fiancé and the husband of one woman who attempts to seduce another to have sex with

• 92 •

her and then renege on the implied commitment to marry, an occasion or circumstance that will infuriate the bride-to-be or wife sufficiently that *she* will call off the wedding, and thus leave herself married ("husbanded") not to a human being but to "the abstract carcass of outrage and revenge" (150:5). Shreve thus proposes that Sutpen insults Rosa deliberately in order to get out of his engagement with her. The "grounds for . . . action" which would allow her to demand marriage, would be a claim that he made her pregnant or at very least compromised her honor. Husbands and fiancés have for ten million years been trying to invent a counter to these grounds. What is the "thing" they could invent that would remove the woman's grounds to demand marriage? Sutpen invents it in his proposal to her, and as a result, according to Shreve's sarcasm, she is irrevocably husbanded to and he cuckolded by her outrage and she is left with no grounds to demand marriage. It may also be that Sutpen's failure to invent this "thing" with his Haitian wife sets the entire catastrophe in motion: when he set her aside he set himself up to fall victim to Shreve's rule.

150:4 **and himself, husband or fiance, already safely cuckolded before she can draw breath** As Shreve sarcastically constructs it, if the intended is insulted and therefore "husbanded . . . with the abstract carcass of outrage and revenge," the husband or fiancé therefore has reason to, and is free to, leave, since the bride or bride-to-be or the other man's wife has been "unfaithful." See entry for 150:1.

150:7 **who said it and was free now** Sutpen said "the thing" that Shreve is talking about in this passage, and is now free from any obligation to marry.

150:14 **so that he didn't even need to be a demon now but just mad impotent old man** Having arranged to be free of Rosa, Sutpen no longer has to nurse his ambitions, those that made him a "demon" to Rosa; having realized that he will never fulfill his dream of magnificence, he can now retire to drinking with Wash Jones and running the small country store.

150:21 **what is it? the word? white what?—Yes, trash** perhaps a reminder that Shreve is an outsider, asking Quentin about local terminology; perhaps more of Shreve's harsh sarcasm about Sutpen's limitation in circumstances and in choices: his dream reduced to a dependence on white trash—that is, reduced to a return to the conditions of his own origins.

150:23 **what delusions of making money out of the store to rebuild the plantation** Clearly a store twelve miles from town on a ruined plantation would be no promising venture, but Shreve's imagined scene of Sutpen's "*haggling* tediously over nickels and dimes with rapacious and poverty-stricken whites and negroes" (151:40), although purely speculation, suggests a market, even if a small one. It may also suggest Shreve's ignorance of Mississippi market conditions after the War.

150:25 **the Creditor who set his children to destroying one another before he had posterity** The "Creditor," Satan, to whom Sutpen owes his soul had set in motion, long before he had children, the chain of circumstances that would cause his children, when he had them, to destroy one another.

150:28 **decided that he was wrong in being unfree and so got out of it again** Shreve imagines that Sutpen begins to believe that he can reconstruct his dream out of the puny proceeds of the little store, then takes up with Milly, Wash Jones's granddaughter.

150:33 ***He sounds just like Father. . . . Just exactly like Father if Father had known as much about it the night before I went out there as he did the day after I came back*** Several times in chapters VI–VIII, Quentin will have occasion to think that Shreve "sounds like" his own father as he has narrated the Sutpen story. It is not completely clear whether Quentin hears a resemblance in tone, in vocabulary, in interpretation. But here Quentin offers a significant qualification. Perhaps Shreve "sounds like father" in the sense that he narrates with certainty, almost with the glibness, of Mr. Compson's assumption of authority. Quentin is thus being critical here: Shreve, like Father, speaks without the knowledge that Quentin possesses. He sounds like father on that September night which comprises the time of chapters I–IV (see 150:38). *If* the elder Compson had known earlier that night what Quentin later discovered when he went to Sutpen's Hundred with Rosa and then almost certainly reported to him the next morning, although there's no evidence to suggest what, if anything, he told his father about that visit and, indeed, no evidence at all to indicate precisely what he did learn beyond the fact that Henry was still alive—and which obviously he has reported to Shreve and perhaps others in Cambridge. But nothing in Shreve's monologue of the previous pages seems based in any particular knowledge that Henry might have imparted to Quentin: his monologue is mostly his speculation, cynical and sarcastic, which he could have manufactured from the general outlines of the story.

150:35 **his naked torso pink-gleaming and baby-smooth, cherubic, almost hairless** Shreve has now taken off the coat he was wearing in the opening lines of this chapter; whether he has taken off everything else is not clear.

This curious infantalized Shreve seems somewhat at odds with his narrative cynicism. It's not clear how homoeroticized the description is.

151:2 **thinking** This word introduces a lengthy italic narration which it clearly identifies as Quentin's thinking. Yet at 153:31, a roman break in the italic narration, Quentin responds to the italicized narrator—"'Yes,' Quentin said."—which response would argue that the italics are not Quentin's thoughts at all, though the italic and roman passages could also be the two Quentins of the early pages of the novels. Faulkner has done something of the same thing in the italicized portion of chapter V, ostensibly Rosa's narration. That is, in such passages, the italicized narrations may represent what Quentin is actually thinking even while he is listening to Rosa or Shreve. A roman interruption that acknowledges an actual speaker is merely his way of being polite, of trying to stay with the conversation, no matter where his own thoughts want to take him. Indeed, at the center of page 151 Quentin is again meditating on that closed door, the door to Judith's room which Henry burst open to tell Judith she could not marry Bon because he, Henry, had killed him—the same door that he is stuck at, is thinking about, when he returns to consciousness at the end of chapter V. Perhaps the italic words are Shreve's, which Quentin subdues into the background in order to think his own thoughts. Or perhaps the italics are the *product* of the collaboration and, as suggested at 144:1, the prose here overpasses the mimetic representation of anyone's individual thought and works less to represent or account for Quentin's independent thought than to project a collaborative result, a consciousness of what is. Quentin's "yes" is then the yes of recognition, not so much of response. The entry for 151:30 may supply evidence that *thinking* is the product of collaborative contemplation.

151:18 *daughter doomed to spinsterhood who had chosen spinsterhood already before there was anyone named Charles Bon* The marriage was not something Judith wanted, but something desired by Henry; the narration never makes Judith's motivations clear. None of the male narrators attempts to penetrate beyond simplistic and often stereotypical representations of Judith and Ellen Sutpen.

151:30 *and at last forced him to use though not to cut weeds, at least not vegetable weeds* Quentin seems to believe that Sutpen has given Jones the scythe as a suicidal act, though to be sure he is imposing this after the fact, creating a dramatic foreshadowing of Sutpen's death. In thinking of Sutpen as a "weed" he seems to share Shreve's sarcastic bent.

152:4 ***the stale violently-colored candy with which even an old man can seduce a fifteen-year-old country girl, to ruin the granddaughter of his partner, this Jones*** Quentin and Shreve's speculation emphasizes Milly Jones's youthfulness by portraying her seduction with candy from Sutpen's store.

152:12 ***the very cloth from which Judith . . . helped the granddaughter to fashion a dress to walk past the lounging men in, the side-looking and the tongues, until her increasing belly taught her embarrassment*** Astonishingly, Quentin and Shreve imagine that Judith helps to dress the girl her father has impregnated, but why would she? To hide her belly as long as possible? To seduce one or more of the men so as to hide her father's behavior? To protect her father from their snickering? See entry for 20:12. See Adams 208.

152:12 ***Judith (who had not been bereaved and did not mourn)*** More of Quentin's speculation, apparently. But he's assuming something about Judith for which the novel itself does not provide evidence. We have no way of knowing that Judith actually felt bereaved or anything else. In these passages, Quentin and Shreve present her as something quite other than the victim Rosa has insisted upon.

152:16 ***Jones who before '61 had not even been allowed to approach the front of the house*** Sutpen repeats with Jones the injury he himself had received at the hands of the slave who forced him, Sutpen, to go around to the back door to take up his business with the plantation owner (189ff).

152:19 ***the seducer-to-be's wife and daughter*** Ellen and Judith.

153:16 ***when the granddaughter was only eight years old*** Milly Jones was born in 1853; the year referred to is 1861, when Sutpen went to war.

153:31 **"Yes," Quentin said.**

So that Sunday morning came If the italicized text of these pages represents Quentin's thoughts, memories, and/or constructions or distillations of all that he knows—or that he and Shreve, as collaborators, know or create— this roman-typeface interruption would seem to be Quentin's interruption of himself, a response to his own thinking. More likely, however, it's an oral response to Shreve's long convoluted question that ends at 150:32, a repetition of his own response at 150:33. See entries for 151:2 and 151:30.

153:34 ***the black stallion which he rode to Virginia and led back*** Perhaps his leading the stallion, for whatever reason, helps to explain why Sutpen takes eight months to get home after Appomattox, though many men without horses to lead or ride seem to have made it home a lot faster than that. See the entry for 50:30. The novel tells us nothing of his whereabouts during the eight months following the surrender. If the narrators of chapters VI–VIII are right, we may well speculate that he took his time to get home to give Henry time to deal with Bon, so that he, Sutpen, won't have to. This speculation, if it is correct, may give us another reason to believe that Sutpen is not the confident demonic father that we initially see him as.

153:34 *black stallion . . . had a son born on his wife Penelope* In naming his stallion's "wife" Sutpen invokes Ulysses's long-suffering wife in *The Odyssey*, who waits patiently, fighting off suitors and spinning while Ulysses is off fighting the Trojan War. Since a mare's gestation period is roughly eleven months, it would appear that Sutpen's Penelope hasn't been as faithful as her namesake. More significantly, the name becomes another part of the novel's invocations of Greek literature. Is Sutpen's name for the mare in any way an ironic genuflection to his Haitian wife? Because he does not think Sutpen is a learned man, Mr. Compson has maintained that he misnamed Clytie, believing that he "intended to name her Cassandra, prompted by some pure dramatic economy not only to beget but to designate the presiding augur of his own disaster" (see entry for 50:25). But Mr. Compson could be wrong about this, as he doubtless is about other things in the Sutpen story. Sutpen's naming the mare Penelope suggests that he might have been more of a reader than Mr. Compson allows. If Clytemnestra is the name he intended, then, perhaps it too is an ironic, perhaps bitter, gesture backward toward his Haitian wife, who was perhaps unfaithful to him, as Clytemnestra is to Agamemnon (Polk, "Cuckold").

154:4 *and the old negress squatted there and heard them, the voices, he and Jones* Clytie (b. 1834), the "old negress," is thirty-five years old when Wash kills Sutpen in 1869; so probably she gave this information to Quentin when he and Rosa went to the Sutpen house in September, 1909, when Clytie would have been seventy-five years old.

154:39 *since she ran the store herself now until she found a buyer for it* Judith runs the store once operated by Sutpen and Wash Jones.

155:6 **scuppernong** a variety of muscadine grape.

155:23 **("How** The parenthesis that opens here closes after the final word of this chapter, 179:10.

155:27 **Luster** In *The Sound and the Fury*, Luster is Dilsey Gibson's grandson and one of Benjy Compson's caretakers, barely in his early teens in 1929, the present time of that novel. *That* Luster could hardly have been born in 1909.

But he, or a character by the same name, is one of only three characters in *The Sound and the Fury* who reappears in *Absalom*, the others being Mr. Compson and, of course, Quentin. This is a curious fact, since the two novels otherwise seem so intimately related thematically. Faulkner seems both to connect the former novel with *Absalom* and to distance the two from each other, apparently to invoke the earlier novel without necessarily attaching its thematic baggage to the later, however difficult that may be for readers of both novels.

155:28 **ditch" and he** The narrative shifts at 155:22 from the collaborative italics to Quentin's singular memory of going to the graveyard with his father; here it shifts from Shreve's vocalized reminder that Quentin has indeed told him at least this much of the story before to Quentin's internalized recollection of Luster's reaction to the tombstones in the rain.

156:7 **quartered the slope** "To quarter" means here to cover all parts of an area by ranging from side to side while moving forward searching for something (OED).

156:12 **the five headstones** For Thomas Sutpen, Ellen Coldfield Sutpen, Judith Sutpen, Charles Bon, and Charles Etienne de Saint Valery Bon.

157:4 **by which system he was at the moment entitled to call himself colonel** Confederate regiments elected their officers in what were often divisive, and always reversible, contests.

157:15 **It seemed to Quentin that he could actually see them** The ability to envision signals a departure from received information to the projection of imagined, dramatic (and in the logic of the novel, the essence of truthful) knowledge.

157:25 **Gettysburg** The Battle of Gettysburg, July 1–3, 1863, was the largest battle of the Civil War; with combined combatants of nearly 200,000 men, it was and remains the largest concentration of forces ever on American soil. It was not a decisive battle, but it claimed over 51,000 casualties.

157:35 **daughter . . . whose marriage he had interdict** Sutpen hasn't yet forbidden the marriage, so far as any of the narrators suggests. In fact, if he had forbidden it immediately, there would be no novel. "Interdict" is an archaic usage.

157:37 **apparently not bereaved** further suggests that Judith does not grieve over Bon's death (see 152:12 and 160:40).

157:40 **where Miss Coldfield possibly (maybe doubtless) looked at it every day as though it were his portrait, possibly (maybe doubtless here too)** reading among the lettering more of maiden hope and virgin expectation than she ever told Quentin about The parentheses suggest an omniscient, if reticent, narrator overseeing the voices of the novel's various speakers; in this case, the authorial voice validates Quentin's imagined dramatization of the effect of the gravestone on Rosa and of her unspoken longing for Sutpen. The "maybe doubtless," twice in interruptive parentheses, ratchets up the preceding "possiblys" toward a posited narrative certainty still never attained.

158:4 since she never mentioned the stone to him at all Quentin's evidence for his thoughts at 157:40 is the fact that Rosa never mentioned the gravestone. The absence of evidence to the contrary, or absence of information generally, is used repeatedly in the novel as space for narrative speculation. Because Rosa never mentioned seeing the headstone in the hallway, she must be hiding something about it or her response to it, a concealment revealed by Quentin's phrase, "maiden hope and virgin expectation" (158:3)

158:8 *he could see it; he might even have been there. Then he thought No. If I had been there I could not have seen it this plain* emphasizes the novel's consistent privileging of imaginative projection over eye-witness accounts and the inability of such contemporary perspectives on human affairs to be objective, reliable, or informative. Quentin's statement is the most concise assertion of the novel's challenging epistemology. What Quentin sees plainly is his imagination of events; his distance from those events allows him to "see" them in an entirety not available to participants. As Quentin and Shreve begin to create facts and characters, however, the question of what "it" is that he "sees" becomes more pressing. If what Quentin sees plainly are facts and situations that never occurred, how and why is it that his sight seems privileged over that of an (even admittedly limited) eye-witness? The logic of the novel's epistemology would suggest that truth is not necessarily that which is consistent with facts or materially verifiable but rather, in a pragmatic sense, that which works best to account for events. An eye-witness, in other words, is too constrained by the preponderance of fact to see plainly what Quentin is able to project in order to get past fact to meaning.

158:18 *Charles Bon. Born in New Orleans, Louisiana.* If accurate, this is an astonishing bit of information on the epitaph. If Bon was born in New Orleans, he can't possibly be Sutpen's part-black son from the Haitian marriage. Judith, who puts the stone in place and writes the epitaph, may simply assume that he was born in New Orleans because she knows that that's where he's "from" when he first comes to Sutpen's Hundred; or, equally possible, she may have her own reasons for wanting to hide his Haitian origins. The epitaph is, at very least, yet another way in which *Absalom* first gives, or seems to give, information and then takes it away (see Schoenberg 81).

158:38 **would have been terrible for her sure enough if she had wanted to put Beloved Husband of on that first one** i.e., on the first tombstone, Bon's. It would have been terrible because Charles Etienne is evidence that Charles Bon was already married and/or had been a faithless lover.

159:6 **during that three weeks while Clytie was in New Orleans finding the boy to fetch him back** Fetching Charles E. St. Valery Bon "back" implies that he belongs at the Sutpen house, as if originating there.

159:11 **They lead beautiful lives—women. Lives not only divorced from, but irrevocably excommunicated from, all reality.** Mr. Compson's blindness to female agency makes it impossible for him to recognize or incorporate the central roles played by Bon's mother in Haiti, Judith Sutpen, and Rosa Coldfield in these events. At the same time, his assertion that women are "excommunicated" from reality implies that their removal is accomplished by male will.

160:13 **the Irish poet, Wilde** Oscar Wilde (1854–1900). This and the reference at 160:24 to Aubrey Beardsley are not ones we'd expect from Mr. Compson, as Wilde would have been his near contemporary and his references tend to be from the classics. Even so, Mr. Compson's descriptions in chapter IV of Bon's life in New Orleans seem consistent with a worldview Wilde and Beardsley described. Wilde's notorious trial and conviction for homosexuality add to the novel's homoerotic subtext.

160:17 **looking as though they had been cleaned and polished and arranged by scene shifters** Reflects Mr. Compson's sense of history as tragic drama; also signals the novel's consistent emphasis on visual over aural representation.

160:24 **whom the artist Beardsley might have dressed** Aubrey Beardsley (1872–1898) illustrated Oscar Wilde's *Salome* and, like Wilde, was associated with a British homosexual artists' clique. The coupling of Wilde and Beardsley here underlines the novel's homoeroticism. Beardsley became famous outside of artistic circles when his work was accused of indecency. Faulkner's early drawings were heavily influenced by Beardsley and his very early play, *The Marionettes*, combined the influences of both Wilde and Beardsley (Polk "Introduction" xxvi–vii and Hönnighausen *Art*).

160:40 ***(who, not bereaved, did not need to mourn* Quentin thought, thinking *Yes, I have had to listen too long)*** Signals the accumulation of appositions by characters as the narrative ensues; "Sutpen, the demon"; "Judith, who did not mourn"; etc. Quentin realizes that intimate knowledge of these characters emerges as their appositional tags become habitual to the narrative and thus become true to the tale. See entry for 157:37.

161:7 **Then the negress came and handed the octoroon a crystal bottle to smell and helped her to rise** When Charles Bon's octoroon wife or mistress comes to Jefferson to visit Bon's grave, she brings with her their son, Charles Etienne de Saint Valery Bon, accompanied by a Negro servant woman.

161:25 **to receive the trays which Clytie carried up the stairs—Clytie, who did that fetching and carrying as Judith made her** Judith observes the racial hierarchy not of northern Mississippi but of New Orleans, which placed the octoroon in a higher social station than either her Negro female servant or the mulatto Clytie; to Clytie, as noted, she "was another negro whom she served" (161:28).

161:33 **his expensive esoteric Fauntleroy clothing** A complete Little Lord Fauntleroy outfit is a velvet suit with a lace collar; a Little Lord Fauntleroy is a gentle-mannered, elaborately-dressed, sissified boy (OED).

161:38 **duenna** Spanish term for an older woman who acts as governess or companion—a chaperone—for a marriageable female.

162:34 **who would not grow from one metamorphosis—dissolution or adultery—to the next carrying along with her all the old accumulated rubbish-years which we call memory, the recognisable *I*, but changing from phase to phase as the butterfly changes once the cocoon is cleared, carrying nothing** Mr. Compson, relaying his father's sense of Charles Etienne de Saint Valery Bon's mother, articulates a central question in the novel regarding the extent to which memory produces character and perspective. Compson's sense that the octoroon mother has no memory reveals the absence of any information about her which would provide her a recognizable character and perspective on these events. The absence of information, moreover, becomes the substance of what knowledge is passed on about her, so that instead of saying "we do not know" Mr. Compson passes along his father's doubt that the woman had any substance at all, "leaving no bones, no substance, no dust" (163:2)

163:6 **as if he were the delicate and perverse spirit-symbol, immortal page of the ancient immortal Lilith** Typically, Mr. Compson resorts to literary and biblical tropes to explain events and characters for which he has no historical information. Lilith appears frequently in Faulkner to describe or to provide a context for discussing a sexually-problematic woman; Lilith is the essence of female carnality. She appears in the Bible and in other ancient epics and literatures as a demon or a witch, the lover of Satan. In Hebrew myth, she was Adam's first wife who refused to lie under Adam during intercourse because she felt it was an inferior position. She is "immortal" because she escaped from the Garden of Eden and therefore from Original Sin and thus from death. A page is an errand boy or messenger; Mr. Compson thus casts Charles Etienne as Lilith's messenger, presumably bringing news of her existence. If she is Lilith, Mr. Compson may be enforcing Bon's argument later that hers is a position at least of equality with the mythical.

163:11 **that burlesque uniform and regalia of the tragic burlesque of the sons of Ham** Slavery in the American South found biblical justification in the story of Ham, in Genesis 9–10, whose offspring, tradition would have it, are condemned to slavery because he looked upon the naked and drunken body of his father.

164:5 **the child lying there between them unasleep in some hiatus of passive and hopeless despair** Charles Etienne is here nearly will-less, repeatedly placed between Judith and Clytie as if he occupies a kind of medial racial, social, and filial space, which he does. See entry for 164:31

164:15 **Suffer little children come unto Me** In Luke 18:16 Jesus says "Suffer little children to come unto me, and forbid them not: for of such is the kingdom of God." By "suffer" Jesus means "permit" or "allow," but Shreve takes some poetic and dramatic liberties and overlays Jesus's meaning with his own to describe Charles Etienne's position between Clytie and Judith. Clearly both Judith and Clytie add to Charles Etienne's misery and so contribute to his development into the masochist he becomes as an adult.

164:31 **lying there unsleeping in the dark between them, feeling them unasleep too, feeling them thinking about him, projecting about him and filling the thunderous solitude of his despair louder than speech could** Charles Etienne is aware of the way in which he is being defined by the racial hierarchy he has entered in Mississippi which, "*through no fault nor willing of [his] own*" (164:35), places him neither in Judith's nor Clytie's station, but which will compel him to Clytie's by legal and social stricture.

164:38 ***not through any fault or willing of our own who would not what we cannot just as we will and wait for what must be*** we = Judith and Clytie, who would not do or be what they cannot do or be, and who know they cannot overturn the social realities and conventions that determine Charles

Etienne's status any more than can they be held responsible for these conventions, and who therefore have no choice but to yield to them. Instead of taking any action, then, the women's will is to wait; their passivity is their form of action as they wait for *what must be*, just as, in Mr. Compson's and then in Quentin's and Sheve's imaginations, women always do.

165:2 **who could neither have heard yet nor recognised the term 'nigger'** Charles Etienne grew up shielded from the cruelty of American racial hierarchies, the social construction of race to which Thomas Sutpen committed his design.

165:13 **trundle bed** a low bed on wheels that rolls under a larger bed for storing.

165:37 **and then to plow as his strength (his resiliency rather, since he would never be other than light in the bone and almost delicate) increased** The passage is signature Faulkner: the parenthetical statement undermines, contradicts, or otherwise complicates the sentence it interrupts, leaving two mutually exclusive interpretations not only possible but necessary. It's not that one narrator qualifies the statement of another but rather that in Faulkner's epistemology every certainty contains within it if not a contradiction at least a measure of doubt or qualification.

166:1 **Mule** not a particular mule or a mulish, a stubborn and intractable, individual, but one containing all the characteristics associated with mulishness.

166:3 **first father's curse** Ham's vision of his own father, Noah, naked, brought on him and his descendants the curse of blackness, according to tradition.

166:13 **it was neither of them** neither Judith nor Clytie who had sent for or gone to fetch Charles Etienne from New Orleans (see 162:10ff).

166:16 **had interrupted his first contact with a nigger and sent him back to the house** It's not clear whether Clytie is acting under Judith's orders or whether she keeps Charles Etienne segregated from other blacks for her own reasons. Judith seems to want him to grow up as a white person, as his father did.

166:30 **whose presence was not even unaccountable to the town and county since they now believed they knew why Henry had shot Bon** The novel is concerned to a great extent with the way in which gossip and lore produce "common knowledge," which eventually forms the core narrative of history itself. The town apparently believes, on the basis of no evidence beyond hearsay, that Henry shot Bon because of the existence of the octoroon wife and child.

166:33 **believing now that it had been a widow who had buried Bon even though she had no paper to show for it** Local lore would have it, again with no evidence beyond hearsay, that Bon and Judith were married before Henry shot Bon but that Judith possessed no legal evidence of her marriage to Bon. It does not claim to know where or when the marriage took place.

167:01 **to believe that the child might be Clytie's, got by its father on the body of his own daughter** There is no reason for General Compson to believe this other than the fact that here, as in *Go Down, Moses*, it appears to be the substance of a fantasy peculiar to—and often the practice of—white slaver owners.

167:37 **the white man the focal point of it and using a knife which he had produced from somewhere** The "white man" is Charles Etienne, seen as white by those attending the Negro ball whom he taunts until fighting breaks out and he is beaten up. The situation is similar to that created by Joe Christmas in *Light in August*, in which the racially ambiguous Joe seeks punishment at the hands of either race. Christmas's masochism also has sexual pathologies (Polk *Children*), but Charles's seems based completely in his problematic race and in his treatment by Judith and Clytie, at least as Quentin and Shreve and Mr. Compson construct it.

168:9 **with a furious and indomitable desperation which the demon himself might have shown, as if the child and then the youth had acquired it from the walls in which the demon had lived** Mr. Compson is unaware of Charles Etienne's lineage but constructs parallels between Sutpen (the demon) and Charles Etienne (the youth). He suggests that Charles Etienne's adult character, like Rosa Coldfield's, is based in his close affinity to the Sutpen house and his treatment by Judith and Clytie.

169:15 **while your grandfather thought how he could not say 'Miss Judith', since that would postulate the blood more than ever. Then he thought *I dont even know whether he wants to hide it or not*. So he said Miss Sutpen** General Compson refers to Judith as "Miss Judith" when speaking to Charles Etienne, a form of address signifying that Charles Etienne is Judith Sutpen's social and racial inferior. The phrase "would postulate the blood" difference between them more strongly than ever. The more formal "Miss Sutpen," socially neutral, implies that there is no acknowledged racial difference between Charles Etienne and Judith.

169:39 **thinking *Better that he were dead, better that he had never lived:* then thinking what vain and empty recapitulation that would be to her if he** were to say it, who doubtless had already said it, thought it, changing only the person and the number   General Compson thinks that Charles Etienne's racial ambiguity makes his life impossible in the South and that Judith, by changing "he" to "we," the singular to the plural, believes that circumstances have made all of their lives, black and white, impossible to live.

170:11 **spavined**   lame, old, lacking in health or vigor. "lamed by either a bone deposit or an excessive collection of lymph in the hock joint. Since spavins are often caused by work or activities for which the animal is not prepared, and since they yield readily to treatment in the early stages, a spavined animal is likely to be an abused and neglected one" (Calvin Brown 184).

170:14 **flung the wedding license in Judith's face**   Judith has been trying to make it possible for Charles Etienne to live as a white man, but he defiantly thrusts the evidence of his blackness at her.

171:23 **And nobody to know what transpired that evening between him and Judith, in whatever carpetless room furnished with whatever chairs and such**   Another scene behind closed doors creates a gap in factual knowledge which nonetheless does not prevent Mr. Compson from creating the scene as best he can from what he does know of the characters and setting. Throughout the novel, the absence of information opens the door to creative invention.

171:29 **the son of the man who had bereaved her and a hereditary negro concubine**   Charles Etienne, the son of Charles Bon, whose death had bereaved both Judith Sutpen and his New Orleans octoroon wife. The concubine, Charles Etienne's mother, is "hereditary" in the sense that she, like her mother and grandmothers, had been groomed for her life as concubine.

171:34 *Because there was love* **Mr Compson said** *There was that letter she brought and gave to your grandmother to keep* **He (Quentin) could see it, as plainly as he saw the one open upon the open text book on the table before him**   This passage breaks up into fragments with little demarcation of quotation marks to help. Mr. Compson's "*Because there was love*" parenthetically interrupts Shreve's narration as he finishes a sentence—"might have done it"—and Quentin's meditations on the letter Mr. Compson has sent him continues in roman type, apparently as a conscious memory setting the scene on the Compson front porch back in September as they talked about the letter. Then, Quentin's "thinking" turns italic—"*Yes. I have heard too much*" (171:40)—as it turns inward to recall efforts to get Charles Etienne to call Judith "Aunt" Judith, and so to acknowledge a kinship that doesn't exist, rather than to admit to his Negro heritage by calling her "Miss" Judith. Quentin returns to what Shreve is saying at 173:6, at the end of the parenthesis, but without benefit of quotation mark: "Yes, who to know...."

172:2 **Yes, almost exactly like Father: that letter, and who to know what** Quentin affirms that he and Shreve gradually assume his father's voice and tone; they also assume his method when they take the question *"and who to know?"* as license to create.

172:6 **she sitting there beside the lamp in a straight chair, erect, in the same calico save that the sunbonnet would be missing now** The passage indicates Quentin's refusal to be limited by his father's statement—"And nobody to know what transpired that evening" (171:23)—and his effort to create a scene between Judith and Charles Etienne that incorporates his own sense of the actors' and narrators' characters, as when he asserts that Charles Etienne *"would not have sat"* (172:10), and his grandfather's reputation (*"We will have General Compson sell some of the land"* [172:28]); he also re-visions his father's stumbling when he imagines Judith saying, *"Call me Aunt Judith, Charles"* (173:5).

172:30 **I will tell them that you are Henry's son and who could or would dare to dispute** Judith suggests that Charles Etienne claim Henry Sutpen as his father, thus providing him a known white paternity; it is unclear whom Judith has in mind to claim as his mother or how claiming Henry as his father will solve the problems of his racial ambiguity, since from all indications his skin is as white as Charles Bon's. Perhaps Judith's offer to claim him as nephew is simply her gift.

172:36 **No, Miss Sutpen** Quentin and Shreve will have it that Charles refuses her offer at 172:30 by addressing Judith thus: he rejects her gift of whiteness (see entry for 169:15).

172:37 **as if she stood on the outside of the thicket into which she had cajoled the animal which she knew was watching her** The metaphor might suggest that Judith, despite her words, considers Charles Etienne another, nonhuman, species, but it might also mean simply that he represents a threat to her.

173:5 **Call me Aunt Judith, Charles** Judith's final plea for the plan suggested at 172:30, which would make her Charles's aunt and him, therefore, white.

173:6 **Yes, who to know** continues Shreve's oral commentary from earlier. See entry for 171:34.

173:12 **toward the Gethsemane which he had decreed and created for himself, where he had crucified himself and come down from his cross for a moment and now returned to it** Charles Etienne wills his own suffering. The situation created by (or for) him echoes that of Joe Christmas in *Light in August*. Gethsemane is the garden on the Mount of Olives, the scene of Christ's agony before his crucifixion (Matthew 26:36–46); the term refers more generally to any situation of spiritual or mental anguish.

173:31 **in the negro store district on Depot Street** After the Civil War African American residential and business areas were demarcated and segregated by local enforcement.

173:35 **gargoyle** a carved grotesque, often winged and animalistic figure, mostly associated with and used as rain spouts on Gothic cathedrals.

173:40 **yellow fever** an acute infectious disease that targets the liver and kidneys, causing jaundice, fever, hemorrhages, mostly bleeding nose and gum. There was a yellow fever epidemic in Holly Springs, just north of Oxford, in 1878, but Faulkner may or may not have had this epidemic in mind. See Doyle 303ff.

174:1 **and now Judith had the disease too** yellow fever.

174:18 **Judith must have roused herself (from delirium possibly) to write down for Clytie when she knew that she was going to die** Judith writes instructions for the inscription on her gravestone.

174:23 **to finish paying out the stone on which Judith had paid his grandfather** Clytie finishes paying General Compson for Judith's headstone.

174:32 *Judith Coldfield Sutpen, Daughter of Ellen Coldfield . . . Suffered the Indignities and Travails of this World for 42 Years, 4 Months, 9 Days* Judith's inscription directly contradicts Mr. Compson's and then Shreve's contention that women lead beautiful lives (174:40) and so perhaps provides conclusive evidence that she was not "bereaved" (see entry for 152:12) but more likely outraged by the events she witnessed; see also the entry for 159.11, where Judith's voice goes almost completely unheard.

174:40 *because he sounds just like Father* In asserting that women lead beautiful lives, Shreve has incorporated Mr. Compson's ideas into his diction and narrative style. In arguing deductively, from preconception, he is like Mr. Compson.

175:6 *Miss Rosa ordered that one. She decreed that headstone of Judge Benbow*. Rosa Coldfield ordered Charles Etienne's headstone.

175:24 *yet still clung to that delusion, that calm incorrigible insistence that that which all incontrovertible evidence tells her is so does not exist, as women can* a variation on the theme of women's beautiful lives. The male narrators are, in their own way, delusional, even in the face of evidence to the contrary.

175:35 *watching them from behind the curtains of a window* as her father had watched the soldiers marching off to battle.

176:14 *whatever the store had brought* The lack of punctuation at the end of this paragraph indicates an interruption of the thought by what follows immediately in the next paragraph.

176:15 *But you were not listening* The movement here to the second person is arresting. Whom does the speaker address? Who speaks? Quentin? Shreve? Any combination of the two voices as they continue to meld together? The movement here to the second paragraph is equally arresting. Quentin's words return to him in the second person—*"you were not listening"*—as if Quentin now possesses the kind of character tag that will make him a known and recognizable character in this drama, as the demon-Sutpen, the not-listening Quentin, the barracks-filled Quentin, has become by this point equally fixed and ensconced in the narrative. The shift in tense signals that Quentin begins to see himself *in* the drama as much as the maker of the tale, a shift that will culminate in his and Shreve's vision of participation as Quentin-Henry and Shreve-Bon at the end of chapter VIII.

176:15 *But you were not listening, because you knew it all already, had learned, absorbed it already without the medium of speech somehow from having been born and living beside it, with it, as children will and do* The fourth narrative voice (see previous entry and the initial comments at the entry for the title) articulates the novel's sense that consciousness is inherited through nonverbal, environmental (mostly visual) circumstances (such as the way in which Charles Etienne acquired Sutpen's "furious and indomitable desperation" [168:9]); he thus equates knowledge and moments of epiphany with memory *"so that what your father was saying did not tell you anything so much as it struck, word by word, the resonant strings of remembering"* (176:18). This idea recalls Plato's sense that all knowledge is memory, but adds an aspect of social construction to it in that one remembers not "eternal forms" but what is *"absorbed"* by the mind from witnessed circumstances, including preconscious, childhood memory.

176:28 *the wagon full of strangers moving from Arkansas tried to stop and spend the night in it and something happened before they could begin to* *unload the wagon even* To enforce the sense of the house as a formidable, reputedly haunted place, Shreve recounts one of the stories told about the Sutpen house by local Jefferson boys. We do not know whether Shreve is recounting something Quentin has told him or simply making it up for dramatic purposes.

176:36 *set in the middle of the domain which had reverted to the state and had been bought and sold and bought and sold again and again and again* reflects Shreve's knowledge of postbellum land speculation in the South. See Doyle.

177:5 *'Come in out of the rain, Luster,' your father said.* Shreve incorporates and embellishes specific details from Mr. Compson's narrative (see entry for 155:27).

178:2 *snake fence* a fence of interlocking poles that curves zigzagging around the landscape.

178:4 *all right again* The paragraph ends with no punctuation; the narrative's internal movement is interrupted by something oral—Quentin's "Yes"—that begins the next paragraph.

178:16 **who had inherited what he was from his mother and only what he could never have been from his father, and if your father had asked him if he was Charles Bon's son he not only would not have known either, he wouldn't have cared** Jim Bond is wholly unconscious of the significance of his existence in the story of the Sutpen-Bon saga; the story's significance has exhausted itself genetically, and takes on its meanings from the compulsions of present narrators. The characterization of Jim Bond may be racially offensive if taken literally; more likely, his idiocy symbolizes all human design coming to naught. Bond inherits from his father "what he could never have been"—that is, white.

179:10 **wait.")** The parenthesis that closes here opens at 155:23.

CHAPTER VII

180:1 **no snow on Shreve's arm now** Chapter VI begins with Quentin's noting the "snow on Shreve's overcoat sleeve, his ungloved blond square hand red and raw with cold, vanishing" (144:1).

180:2 **smooth cupid-fleshed forearm and hand** Quentin's curious and perhaps revealing comparison. Cupid is the Roman god of eros, usually depicted as a nude young child. Quentin's association of Shreve with Cupid may suggest some homoerotic relationship or bond, whether sexual or not, between them. His "pink bright-haired arms" at 180:11 might simply indicate that they are pink with cold, though Shreve has been inside, naked to the waist, in the "warm and rosy orifice," their room "above the iron quad" (180:7); so it's more likely that his arms' pinkness stresses the comparison with Cupid. There is no hint of any sort of actual sexual activity, but a veiled homoerotic bond between Quentin and Shreve may well project onto their narrative a developing homoerotic bond between Henry Sutpen and Charles Bon, first hinted at by Mr. Compson.

180:5 **So it is zero outside, Quentin thought; soon he will raise the window and do deep-breathing in it, clench-fisted and naked to the waist** Faulkner identifies the source of the narration throughout this chapter by speech tags such as "Quentin thought" and by responses or interjections from the listener or the authorial narrator. Identifying the narrators' sources is as vital to reading the chapter as are identifying and understanding the various levels of narration: speech, thought, contemplation, dialogue, and the authorial narrator's commentary. While these levels are not necessarily or strictly mimetic, their variations are central to the overall narrative method, which signals successive levels of realization and creation by shifts in narrative registers. New England's zero-degree cold will be pointedly contrasted to the South's heat throughout, in ways that contrast and juxtapose differing thought patterns and narrative concerns. This ecological dimension of the novel is cast imagistically at 216:14 in the metaphor of the two pools. Shreve is at home in the cold (note his "deep-breathing" of its air and his appearance "naked to the waist") as Quentin is in the heat.

180:16 **It's better than Ben Hur, isn't it** Shreve refers most probably to the first American stage version of *Ben Hur*, a large, spectacularly popular production in 1899 based on the 1880 novel by Lew Wallace. There were also popular film versions in 1907, 1925, and 1959. *Ben Hur* was so popular that it spawned American fraternal organizations such as the "Supreme Tribes of Ben Hur," which later became an insurance company. Some American towns were named Ben Hur.

180:19 **his hands lying on either side of the open text book on which the letter rested** Quentin's letter from his father, which begins on page 144 and concludes on page 310. Since the beginning and the ending of the letter frames Quentin and Shreve's entire narrative, we may read chapters VI–VIII as Quentin's struggle to read this letter and to understand Rosa Coldfield. See notes at 144 and 310.

180:22 **by the leverage of the old crease in weightless and paradoxical levitation, lying at such an angle that he could not possibly have read it, deciphered it, even without this added distortion. Yet he seemed to be looking at it** Quentin is not reading the letter, but narrating "over" it, as it were, in contemplation of and preparation for reading it. Though it is "weightless" in its physical properties as a sheet of paper, the weight of its content makes the "levitation" of half of it, jutting upward from the crease, "paradoxical": matter so serious should be firmly grounded on a surface.

180:30 **"The demon, hey?" Shreve said. Quentin did not answer him, did not pause** Shreve interjects and Quentin ignores him, here and throughout the chapter (see entry for 181:12). The interjections help identify the source of the narrative as initially Quentin's alone, passed to him through his father, from his grandfather. See entry for 182:20.

180:31 **his voice level, curious, a little dreamy yet still with that overtone of sullen bemusement, of smoldering outrage** Quentin's voice, not Shreve's. This is the first indication we've had that Quentin is "outraged" about anything, though it is not clear where the outrage comes from, whether from Shreve's condescending interjection at 180:30, from the letter's reminding him of his trip to Sutpen's Hundred with Rosa Coldfield, or from the entire galaxy of things the Sutpen story seems to represent to him; but even if it comes from any of these things, it's still not completely clear *why* he is outraged, where his anger comes from. In any case, Quentin is apparently doing his best to control the outrage, keeping his voice "level" and speaking slowly, overlaying his "sullenness" with a layer of "bemusement" that reflects his own confusion and puzzlement. At 181:15 he speaks in a "curious repressed calm voice."

181:4 **and hunted the architect down and made him take earth in a cave under the river bank two days later** The two-day hunt for the architect parallels (or hosts) the two-day narrative in which Sutpen tries to explain—and perhaps understand—his life; see 182:20. Like Sutpen, when he as a boy escapes his humiliation at the planter's door, the architect escapes to a cave.

181:12 **"Maybe he had a girl," Shreve said. "Or maybe he just wanted a girl. You said the demon and the niggers didn't have but two."** Shreve is referring to the architect, not to Sutpen. Quentin does not respond to this either, ignoring Shreve. Quentin's immersion in the story causes Shreve to watch him "with thoughtful and intent curiosity" (181:1).

181:15 **talking in that curious repressed calm voice** The succession of adjectives produces interpretive instability. Quentin's voice may reveal or repress his curiosity; it may be calm, if he's repressing curiosity or agitated, if he's repressing calmness through curiosity. Or, it may be the authorial narrative labeling his voice "curious" for its "repressed calm." See entry for 180:31.

181:29 **Fauntleroy tie** See entry for 161:33.

182:20 **And so he told Grandfather something about it.** The delays in the hunt for the architect and the need to rest in the evenings allow time for Sutpen to engage in a second narrative quest for origins, for an understanding of himself and his drive—not, as he puts it, "what he wanted to do but what he just had to do" (182:23). The two hunts proceed in tandem. Sutpen's self-pursuit, having much to do with his "design," resonates thematically with the parallel hunt for the architect, who designed Sutpen's house.

182:22 **His trouble was innocence** Sutpen is innocent of how history works on people. On the one hand, the innocence gives him an admirable belief that he can overcome the class status that his antecedents have handed him and in that sense he does indeed, as many commentators have noted, represent the American dream, the self-made man; on the other, he seems to believe that because he can erase his own origins he can also erase the history that he himself creates as he lives his life. Critical commentary on this term is extensive. Cleanth Brooks argued "that innocence comes down finally to a trust in rationality—an overweening confidence that plans work out—that life is simpler than it is" (*Absalom* 556). He later refined his understanding, aligning Faulkner's use of Sutpen's innocence with Yeats's "murderous innocence of the sea" (*Yoknapatawpha Country* 37). Millar MacLure defines Faulkner's "innocents" as "those whom the past possesses," those for whom "the past really exists, and for them it exists as a fatality, a doom to be endured" (149). William Sowder equates Sutpen's innocence with Socrates's definition of a bad man in *The Apology*: "A good man, according to Socrates, is one who can think, and a bad man is one who cannot" (497). Richard Sewell equates innocence with amorality: "It was innocence which overlooked the moral relationship of means and ends and with which he could view the collapse of his design, not as retribution, not as 'fated,' not even as bad luck, but as the result of a 'Mistake'" (141).

182:29 **to do it right, fix things right so that he would be able to look in the face not only the old dead ones but all the living ones that would come after him when he would be one of the dead** "To fix" means to repair; but it also means to make rigid. (see "fixed" at 183:31). The question of what Sutpen intends to fix or do right occupies the remainder of his narrative; it concerns fixing his own class relations, fixing his relation to history and to the future: somehow fixing the social structure which abuses him in his childhood. At any rate, he wants to make himself immune to the intolerable shame that his rejection at the plantation owner's front door invested him with. The need to face "the old dead ones" is reflected in the second half of Mr. Compson's letter to Quentin at 310:15. At 188:13 Sutpen says he wants to fix things so future generations won't look down on him.

183:3 **West Virginia wasn't admitted** The geographic area of West Virginia separated itself from Virginia in 1862 and claimed statehood because its population was largely pro-Union. It remained in the Union. Quentin's report that Sutpen was born in West Virginia, part of what he has learned from his father, may indicate a lingering local resentment against Sutpen by placing his birth in a non-slaveholding state, emphasizing his status as an outsider. It's not clear whether Quentin's agitated response to Shreve's insistence that there was no West Virginia in 1833 indicates his irritation at being interrupted or his ignorance of southern history. If the latter, we may have some cause to wonder about how much of Quentin's concern with "history" throughout *Absalom* may be taken as a concern with larger issues of "southern" history.

183:12 **never imagined, a place, a land divided neatly up and actually owned by men** Sutpen's completely chaotic early life gives him no sense that there is actual order in the world and that ownership creates it. Possession, the desire to possess, causes chaos; but it also causes order. At 184:37 Quentin describes Sutpen's early family life as "sliding back down out of the mountains and skating in a kind of accelerating and sloven and inert coherence like a useless collection of flotsam on a flooded river moving by some perverse automotivation such as inanimate objects sometimes show." Sutpen's "design," whatever else it is, whatever other forms it takes, is at base a push to impose some order over his own life. See entry for 182:29 for his desire to "fix" things.

183:16 **he did not even imagine then that there was any such way to live** indicates Sutpen's innocence of class distinctions and property relations, based on his origins in extreme poverty.

183:23 **Because where he lived the land belonged to anybody and everybody** that is, no one owned anything. The language evokes myths of Native American communal property relations but is more accurately understood as a sign of Sutpen's origins in abject poverty, at a considerable remove geographically, psychologically, and economically from the very idea of possessions.

183:31 **So he didn't even know there was a country all divided and fixed and neat with a people living on it all divided and fixed and neat** Sutpen's coming to class consciousness as he descends the mountain with his family is a reification of a classic Western fall from grace; he literally and figuratively falls into history, into the knowledge of class, property, and economic distinctions, as his family travels down the mountain to the coast. At 184:26 Quentin literalizes the image: "That's how it was. They fell into it . . ."

184:5 **Tidewater splendor** The wealthy Virginia planter class tended to live in the Tidewater region, on the Virginia coast and inland from it. See entry for 199:31.

184:28 **when the ship from the Old Bailey reached Jamestown** Old Bailey was a London criminal court; early colonists in North America included inmates released as indentured servants and sent to Virginia; Jamestown was founded in 1607, the first English colony in America.

184:31 **about his mother dying about that time and how his pap said she was a fine wearying woman and that he would miss her; and something about how it was the wife that had got his father even that far West** It's not clear whether the "wife" is a new wife, got after Sutpen's mother died, or whether his mother is the "wife" that got the family so far west. Since the word occurs in a positive context (Brown 212), "wearying" here would seem to mean that his mother was a woman with such energy that she made him tired trying to keep up with her.

184:32 **and how his pap said** The portrait of Sutpen's father, "pap," owes much to Mark Twain's creation of Huck's father in *Adventures of Huckleberry Finn* (1884). See entry for 191:38.

184:38 **a kind of accelerating and sloven and inert coherence like a useless collection of flotsam** The oxymoron built into this phrase ("accelerating" and "inert") separated by the invective, "sloven," and culminating in the final nominative of worthlessness, "flotsam," intensifies the portrait of the Sutpen family as the lowest class of white Americans, commonly known in the South as "white trash." The passage itself is a kind of explosion of the term "trash."

185:20 **("The demon," Shreve said)** Shreve's interruption again reminds us that Quentin is talking, but it responds sarcastically and ironically to Rosa Coldfield's depiction of Sutpen. Quentin describes—perhaps manufactures—the story from what Sutpen told his grandfather who told his father who told him (see entry for 186:7): Sutpen's childhood descent from the mountain and his confusion concerning destination and motive ("He didn't know why they moved, or didn't remember the reason if he ever knew it" [185:4]).

Sutpen's ignorance and his submission to "whatever gods had watched over him this far" (185:19) in Quentin's telling are hardly the qualities of a demon bent upon destruction.

185:29 **he was ten then** Sutpen would be ten in 1817, according to the Chronology; but see the note for 188:10.

185:32 **began the practice of accomplishing that part of the translation devoted to motion flat on his back in the cart** This curious locution shows Quentin's rarely displayed sardonic sense of humor.

186:7 **as he remembered it or as he told Grandfather he did** calls attention to the precarious status of the information with which Quentin and Shreve work. Sutpen told General Compson what he claimed to have remembered, General Compson told his son, who in turn told Quentin. Its accuracy is dubious at best and there is no reason to suspect that either Mr. Compson or General Compson did not amend or attenuate portions of the tale—and likewise no reason to assume that Quentin does not do the same thing.

186:11 **doggeries** A doggery, in American slang since the mid-nineteenth century, is a cheap or disreputable saloon; the term more specifically refers to doglike behavior, including dishonesty, knavery, etc. (OED) (see also "doggery doors" 186:20, and "doggeries and taverns" at 186:38).

186:24 **the nigger's ... mouth loud with laughing and full of teeth like tombstones** This simile very specifically associates slavery with death. That the slave's mouth is "laughing" with "tombstones" suggests Sutpen's awareness—as he tells General Compson of it—of the "balloon faces" as they continue to jeer at him all his life. See 190:38ff.

186:32 **the unusually insensible father who made one stage of the journey accompanied by the raspberry-colored elephants and snakes which he seems to have been hunting for** Sutpen's father suffered from *delirium tremens*, wild and terrifying visions caused by alcoholism and withdrawal.

187:4 **where the old man was not even allowed to come in by the front door** If Sutpen originally supplies this information, it is ironic that he makes so much of his own refusal at the front door of the plantation house (see 192–93) and then refuses Wash Jones entrance into his own mansion (chapter VI). Even so, the novel is marked by a series of barred doors and passageways, literal and figurative, including the central and climactic one of Henry and Bon's confrontation at the gates of Sutpen's Hundred.

187:12 he was learning that there was a difference between white men and white men not to be measured by lifting anvils or gouging eyes marks Sutpen's gradual fall into consciousness of the abstract bases of class and race stratification. In the class structure, men are measured by their control over the means of production and by their possessions, not by their physical strength.

187:20 **lother** more loth. Loth is a variant spelling of loathe, lother of loather.

187:25 **that was the same second when he discovered the innocence** What Sutpen means by his "innocence" is not equivalent to the state he held before his fall into class consciousness, because it outlasts that set of realizations and persists throughout his life. His innocence refers, rather, to the way he processes the knowledge he gathers; it lies at the heart of the design he later envisions. It signals more a worldview than a childlike state. Sutpen's worldview is one in which the moral sense is mechanical, not spiritual, the sense of personal responsibility attenuated nearly to the point of obscurity. Living in a materialist society, Sutpen is innocent of the spiritual animation of human beings, whom he envisions mechanistically, as integers, not as fellow human beings. See entry for 182:22.

188:7 **But that was past now, the moment when he last could have said exactly where he had been born now weeks and months ... behind him** Sutpen's fall into class consciousness is marked by a simultaneous fall out of knowledge of his own place origins. Although he enters consciousness of history and property relations, he does so with the ideologically American sense that he can overcome these relations and reverse the forces which create them to accomplish his own social elevation. Sutpen's sense of his existence is that it takes place outside of the history of which he has only just become conscious. See entry for 188:10.

188:10 **he became confused about his age and was never able to straighten it out again, so that he told Grandfather that he did not know within a year on either side just how old he was** The Genealogy puts Sutpen's date of birth at 1807, but his consciousness, free of an exact date of origins, signals an existence outside of temporal forces; given his origins in a "West Virginia" that was unnamed until 1862, Sutpen thus seems to have originated outside of both time and space. He will, in time, become hyperconscious of the way in which time controls his ambitions. See entry for 229:28.

188:13 **So he knew neither where he had come from nor where he was nor why. He was just there, surrounded by the faces, almost all the faces which** he had ever known. Concomitant with Sutpen's emerging consciousness is an abstract sense of others, attenuated as "faces" and later, "balloon faces" (see entry for 190:37), by which we understand both his sharply curtailed ability to contemplate the subjectivity of others and his oppressive sense of being watched, judged, and mocked.

188:20 **living in a cabin that was almost a replica of the mountain one except that it didn't sit up in the bright wind but sat instead beside a big flat river** Since the two cabins are virtually identical, this passage may suggest that Sutpen's "discovery" of ownership as he and his family came down the mountain was an illusion borne of his ignorance—or "innocence"—of property rights at the top of the mountain; though it's not clear what class relationships exist at the top of the mountain, the existence of poverty there may well posit the existence of wealth.

188:22 **big flat river that sometimes showed no current at all and even sometimes ran backward** The mountain's terrain would have sent the current pretty straightforwardly down, no matter how many twists and turns it took. In the Tidewater, where they now live, the "big flat river," though flowing to the ocean, regularly backs up and flows inland when the ocean's high tide gives it no egress into the sea and actually forces it backward.

188:24 **where his sisters and brothers seemed to take sick after supper and die before the next meal** It's not clear whether the narrator wants to connect the sisters' and brothers' illnesses and deaths with the river or the region or whether they are just a condition of the Sutpens' poverty.

188:27 **the old man did something too** It's not clear what Sutpen's father does for work, though it's clearly work on the plantation. At 189:35 Sutpen still doesn't know "exactly ... what work ... the old man had in relation to the plantation," though apparently he's sharecropping, since Sutpen wears clothes his father gets "from the plantation commissary" (189:33).

188:35 **a barrel stave hammock** a hammock made out of a broken barrel, using the staves, or curved wood, for the wooden stabilizers at either end to attach the bedding rope or webbing to.

189:8 **a broadcloth monkey** an African slave. The identification of American slaves with monkeys is evidence of racial ignorance, a common and derogatory equation based upon skin pigmentation and common origins in Africa. A broadcloth monkey would be a well-dressed slave who worked as a butler or house servant; broadcloth is a cloth of fine twilled woolen or worsted or plain-woven cotton (OED).

189:18 **Because he had not only not lost the innocence yet, he had not yet discovered that he possessed it.** Sutpen discovers his innocence once he concludes that he must act (see entry for 193:32). Subsequent actions will suggest that he never does lose this innocence, his sense of existing outside moral responsibility.

189:21 **He would have coveted the rifle** The rifle analogy which follows indicates Sutpen's struggle to understand how personal status and value can be tied to material possessions. Sutpen originally believes a man's qualities lie in his abilities, not in his possessions; but he discovers after his descent from the mountain that in fact possessions, not performance, mark worth. In his youth, he cannot understand the man who says *"Because I own this rifle, my arms and legs and blood and bones are superior to yours"* (189:26). The ritualistic fighting of his slaves later in his life, for example, marks his insistence that he must perform his superiority rather than base it on his property.

190:13 **Because he was still innocent. He knew it without being aware that he did.** The claim of persistent innocence frames the rifle analogy (189:21) and introduces the pivotal scene in which Sutpen is turned away from the plantation door. That he "knew it without being aware that he did" suggests the novel's successive registers of consciousness. Sutpen is not aware of all that he knows, cannot maintain the full measure of knowledge in conscious awareness. Even so, his actions and his character are influenced by everything he knows, including that of which he is unaware. See entry for 190:17.

190:15 **before the monkey nigger who came to the door had finished saying what he did** Before the house slave had finished telling Thomas Sutpen to go around to the back door with his message.

190:17 **and rush back through the two years they had lived there like when you pass through a room fast and look at all the objects in it and you turn and go back through the room again and look at all the objects from the other side and you find out you had never seen them before** This passage articulates how the experience at the plantation door compels Sutpen to see his own recent past in a new context, with unprecedented and renewed understanding of the true relations between himself and the social world. He sees both new things and old relations in a new way. Compare the abstract statement at 190:14: "He knew it without being aware that he did." He is now aware of that which he has known all along, in some deeper but heretofore inaccessible level of knowing.

190:22 **seeing a dozen things that had happened and he hadn't even seen them before: a certain flat level silent way his older sisters and the other white women of their kind had of looking at niggers** The central content of what Sutpen now sees are the race, sex, and class relations ("white women of their kind") which determine the lives of his family and himself. Sutpen is learning that history is written backward: from the point of view of the present, the past clarifies itself because everything that happens seems to have arrived inevitably and undeviatingly at this present moment; lost are the thousands of options, choices, occlusions, and other interventions that might have changed that history.

190:34 **they were apparently oblivious of it, too oblivious of it** The slaves took little notice of white women of Sutpen's class; either they were *also* oblivious, or they possessed an excess of obliviousness—"too oblivious" possesses both meanings and both meanings combined indicate the encompassing passivity the narrators assume Sutpen senses in them. The narrators are probably wrong in their assumptions; people of an underclass are clearly *always* more aware of the upperclass than vice-versa.

190:37 **that when you hit them you would just be hitting a child's toy balloon with a face painted on it** The image of Negro slaves as balloon faces runs throughout this section of the narrative and forms an important part of Sutpen's growing comprehension and the limits of his knowledge. Balloon faces are abstractions, faces divorced from sentient bodies and subjective lives; they indicate a sense of a gulf of consciousness between the races and a refusal to humanize the slave body. At the same time, the image of "a face slick and smooth and distended and about to burst into laughing" (190:39) may signal Sutpen's simultaneous sense of inferiority and his need to measure his progress relative to his superiority over (and, later, possession of) Negro slaves. James Guetti suggests that the "significance of the 'monkey nigger' for Sutpen is that of an artificial barrier that prevents him from penetrating to what he has assumed is a reality. Ahab would call it a 'pasteboard mask'; for Sutpen it is a 'baboon face'" (82).

191:3 **—of talk at night** first of three prepositional phrases introducing examples in which the Sutpen family responds to perceived humiliations by Negro slaves. In the first, Sutpen recalls how his father or some other man would "break out into harsh recapitulation of his own worth" (191:7) and Sutpen would know that they "were talking about the same thing though it had never once been mentioned by name" (191:11); in the second ("—of one afternoon" [191:14]), Sutpen and his sister are nearly run over by a carriage driven by a Negro; in the third ("—of one night late" [191:31]), Sutpen's father comes home and reports beating or lynching a slave, then has no answer to his son's inquiry into the slave's offense. See entry for 191:38.

191:7 **some man, usually his father in drink, to break out into harsh recapitulation of his own worth, the respect which his own physical prowess commanded from his fellows** Sutpen's assertion of his physical prowess in Jefferson—his shooting exhibition (26:35) and his muddy battles with his slaves (23:19)—doubtless owes a good deal to his father's example here; though he doesn't relate it "harshly," it's easy to understand his autobiography as a "recapitulation" of "his own worth," argued against the circumstances he had to overcome to get where he did.

191:11 **talking about the same thing though it had never once been mentioned by name** same thing = slavery, Negroes. To need to assert their superiority over slaves is simultaneously to admit their own inferiority.

191:20 **all dust and rearing horses and glinting harness buckles and wheel spokes; he saw two parasols in the carriage and the nigger coachman in a plug hat shouting 'Hoo dar, gal! Git outen de way dar!'** Ellen, Judith, and Henry ride to church in a carriage in a way that suggests a source in Sutpen's humiliation on this occasion. See entry for 18:35.

191:23 **a plug hat** a tall silk hat (OED).

191:28 **it had not been the nigger coachman that he threw at at all, . . . it was the actual dust raised by the proud delicate wheels, and just that vain** Even if he does not understand this completely at this point, Sutpen's fury is not aimed at the actual slave but at the abstract quality he represents, which places the slave in the coach and Sutpen and his sister in the road, in the dust, feeling humiliated by this manifestation of class stratification and racial hierarchy. That Sutpen does not *feel* inferior is indicated by the description of his rage as "just that vain": his vanity, like his innocence, impels him toward his design to supplant the slave master.

191:38 **and he asked what the nigger had done and his father said, 'Hell fire, that goddamn son of a bitch Pettibone's nigger.'** Sutpen's father's diction echoes that of Huckleberry Finn's father. See 184:32. His father's response to his question suggests that he is the source of Sutpen's view of slaves as abstractions: "he must have meant the question the same way his father meant the answer: no actual nigger, living creature, living flesh to feel pain and writhe and cry out" (192:1). Advancing this realization is the return of the "balloon face" image to describe the black victim at 192:5, 192:8, and 192:9. The balloon, emitting "roaring waves of mellow laughter" (192:14) when struck, again links Sutpen's projection of the balloon image with his own sense of humiliation and shame. See entry for 190:37.

192:3 **He could even seem to see them: the torch-disturbed darkness among trees, the fierce hysterical faces of the white men** Sutpen could imagine the raiding parties during which the poor whites, including his own father, would beat others' slaves, for what crime Sutpen could never find out, probably because their only crime was being black and better-housed and -fed than these malevolent whites (189:13). But their beating, in Sutpen's memory, is futile, because the slave, the "balloon face," would take the "one single desperate and despairing blow" and watch the whites "fleeing, running," then chase and overtake them, "overwhelm[ing] them again" with "roaring waves of mellow laughter meaningless and terrifying and loud" (192:14).

192:16 **And now he stood there before that white door with the monkey nigger barring it and looking down at him in his patched made-over jeans clothes and no shoes** The shift in subject from Sutpen to the house slave looking down at him indicates Sutpen's awareness that, in the eyes of the slave, Sutpen is also a "balloon face" abstraction. See entry for 194:24.

192:23 **who through no doing of his own** Chance or fate has placed the "monkey nigger," the "balloon face" that laughs at his father and the other white attackers, in a fine Richmond house, albeit it as a slave, with no more of merit on his part than of fault that had made his father a sharecropper.

192:24 **to have had the felicity of being housebred in Richmond maybe, looking—("Or maybe even in Charleston," Shreve breathed.)** Shreve's knowledge of slave hierarchy is apparent here; Charleston and Richmond were among the wealthiest and most aristocratic southern cities.

192:27 **even before he had had time to say what he came for, never to come to that front door again but to go around to the back** We never learn what the message was that the young Sutpen carried to the plantation house.

192:40 **He said he crawled back into the cave** The cave suggests a womb, preparation for a rebirth following the trauma of the scene at the plantation door (see the entry for 193:40); the retreat to the cave also further parallels Sutpen and Huckleberry Finn. It also recalls "the warm and rosy orifice" (180:7) that Quentin and Shreve inhabit. Calvin Brown suggests that the "cave was not

• 121 •

in the earth but in the vegetation. The 'uptorn roots' of the oak would form a disk some 6'–8' in diameter, holding the trunk off the ground at its base, as the branches did farther out. Hence the space under the oak, walled in on both sides by the cane, is in effect a cave" (114).

193:4 **So he was seeking among what little he had to call experience for something to measure it by, and he couldn't find anything.** The scene at the plantation door is an ur-experience for Sutpen: unprecedented, original, and so without established or reliable meaning.

193:32 **because he knew that something would have to be done about it** Sutpen's inability to process his experience at the plantation door produces in him an urge to act out his response. Readers ought thus to make of his subsequent action the meaning of the original experience.

193:36 **which (the innocence, not the man, the tradition) he would have to compete with** In his resolve to act Sutpen competes not with the plantation owner nor even with the plantation system but with his own experience at the plantation door—his realization that he had not expected such treatment and is not able to process its meaning intellectually. His failure to foresee the event and his inability to understand it indicate the innocence against which he will compete throughout his life.

193:38 **the rifle analogy** See entry for 189:21.

193:40 **sitting there with his arms around his knees** Sutpen assumes the prenatal position appropriate to a womb. See entry for 192:40.

194:4 **while both debaters agreed . . . the two of them inside that one body** Sutpen's inner debate echoes Quentin's debate with himself in the novel's opening pages and calls attention to the novel's dialogic structure. Meaning and motivation emerge throughout the text as the product of contending and collaborative voices.

194:12 **The nigger was just another balloon face slick and distended with that mellow loud and terrible laughing** See entry for 190:37.

194:17 **was looking out from within the balloon face just as the man who did not even have to wear the shoes he owned, whom the laughter which the balloon held barricaded and protected from such as he, looked out from whatever invisible place he (the man) happened to be at the moment, at the boy outside the barred door** The image of the "balloon face" becomes a force which holds within itself a disdain (Sutpen senses it as laughter) for Sutpen's class. It is also clear to Sutpen that the balloon face possesses no agency of its own but exists to do the bidding of "the man" who owns the plantation. See entry for 194:24.

194:24 **he himself seeing his own father and sisters and brothers as the owner, the rich man (not the nigger) must have been seeing them all the time—as cattle, creatures heavy and without grace, brutely evacuated into a world without hope or purpose for them** Sutpen's understanding of the balloon face gains him the planter's perspective on himself and his family; part of that perspective is the sense that he and his own family live "in a world without hope or purpose." Purpose, above all, infuses the design that Sutpen will carry away from this experience, the kind of purpose he needs to combat the plantation owner and his ilk.

194:38 *But I can shoot him* Part of Sutpen's mind suggests murder, Henry's solution to his own quandary.

195:11 **he kept on telling himself it was laughing even after he knew better knew that it was weeping.**

195:20 **his sister pumping rhythmic up and down above a washtub in the yard . . . the very labor she was doing brutish and stupidly out of all proportion to its reward: the very primary essence of labor, toil, reduced to its crude absolute which only a beast could and would endure** Sutpen's observations of his sister's labor plants the seeds of what could become a real sense of the injustice of class distinctions; but they only confirm him in his determination to position himself as the owner of labor, not the laborer itself.

196:31 *He never even give me a chance to say it* Sutpen never delivers the message to the plantation owner; its content seems not to matter. Part of what Sutpen learns from the incident is that the maintenance of class order outweighs substance; that is, nothing that he might have had to say is more important than his going to the back, not the front, door. See entries for 192:27 and 196:34.

196:34 *He never gave me a chance to say it and Pap never asked me if I told him or not and so he cant even know that Pap sent him any message and so whether he got it or not cant even matter, not even to Pap* Sutpen's father is complicit in the maintenance of class order and in the plantation owner's command over the social and economic lives of those who work for them; he and the plantation owner share the same valuation of the message's content. The class structure is as much a part of the natural order of things as filial obedience is. The owner expects Sutpen to use the back door just as Sutpen's father expects him to carry out his command. See entry for 196:40.

196:40 **there aint any good or harm either in the living world that I can do to him. It was like that, he said, like an explosion** The explosion evokes the rifle analogy (189:21); the explosive realization is that to Sutpen's class the plantation owner is untouchable.

197:5 **that innocence instructing him as calm as the others had ever spoken, using his own rifle analogy to do it with, and when it said *them* in place of *he* or *him*, it meant more** Sutpen's innocence takes on a voice within his dialogic consciousness (see 194:4) that competes with other voices in an interior, intellectual debate concerning his response to the experience at the plantation door; the phrase "when it said *them*" reminds us that this is a class matter, not a contest between individuals. See 189:21.

197:13 **So to combat them you have got to have what they have that made them do what he did. You have got to have land and niggers and a fine house to combat them with.** Sutpen's dialogic consciousness finally understands that in order to deliver a message to the plantation owner, in order to do "*any good or harm either*" (196:40), he would need to possess what the owner possessed. His use of the term "combat" (rather than "join" or "become") places the source of his ambition in class antagonism rather than in envy or in a desire to emulate. He does not want to supplant the owner; he wants to become one, so that the other owners will take his existence into account.

197:32 **at first they could not understand why the suspenders** "The architect had climbed one tree and then used his sapling pole to vault into another he could not otherwise have reached because of the intervening space. If he had simply done this, his pole would have been left leaning into the tree into which he had gone, or lying on the ground between the two trees, and in either case it would have shown where he had gone. But he tied the top of the pole to the first tree with his suspenders, and they had enough elasticity to let him vault to the second tree and to snap the top of the pole back to the first tree when he released it" (Calvin Brown 193).

198:34 **the bombastic phrases with which Grandfather said he even asked you for a match for his cigar or offered you the cigar** Sutpen reveals his lower-class origins in his unsophisticated use of language and by his transparent attempt to appear learned.

199:3 **how he had put his first wife aside like eleventh and twelfth century kings did** kings who would be permitted to divorce because their wives did not produce male heirs. The gesture invokes Henry Sutpen's later conjuring of the Duke of Lorraine. See entry for 281:37.

199:5 **through no fault of her own** The phrase perplexes. If Sutpen's Haitian wife is faultless, then it is not clear why Sutpen later accuses her of misrepresentation, at 217:13, though to be sure that could be a function of a different narrator. If she is part black, as Quentin and Shreve later posit (chapter VIII), her racial heritage cannot be her fault; but if she withholds this information from Sutpen, he would not consider her faultless. Sutpen never explains why he "put her aside" (199:6), except that whatever it was had been withheld from him until after his son's birth and that the information rendered her antagonistic to his design (see 218:19). The phrase "through no fault" resonates in other complex ways. What happens to Sutpen is nobody's fault, not the "monkey nigger" or the plantation owner or Sutpen's father or mother or Sutpen himself: no complicity among them either, since all are playing assigned roles. Sutpen tries to assert individuality in the face of such predetermined structures, and fails ironically to create an alternative design.

199:5 **adjunctive or incremental to the design which I had in mind** This passage marks the first use of the term "design," the term by which Sutpen encapsulates his sense of the intersection of free will and destiny—his attempt, first, to overcome his origins and, second, to control his future. In one important sense, both are identical: "design" means control, order: he thus wants to overcome the debilitating and humiliating chaos his life has been up to the moment he is telling General Compson about. His commitment to a "design," his preconceived—and unalterable—goal, is so strong that it becomes Faulkner's metaphor for an ideological principle, a sense of how the world *should* be rather than how it *is*, that wants past and future to be tidier than life can ever be. Thus any failure is a failure not of the design itself, but rather of the human beings—himself or others—or of nature to adhere to the design's principle, which alone can insure order and security. The autobiography he tells General Compson is, like Rosa's, a "brief" for himself, an attempt to exonerate himself for any perceived human or moral failings: he did his part, others didn't: failure is their fault, not his. His own total commitment to the design's implementation is thus a perversely "moral" commitment to an ideology and it may be Faulkner's veiled commentary on the major contending ideologies of the 1930s—Capitalism, Fascism, and, especially, Communism; indeed, it is not difficult to imagine Sutpen, as he is depicted by Rosa especially, as a ruthless dictator. For the design to "die still-born" (205:15) would be for it to fail to give birth to "subsequent irrevocable courses of resultant action" (201:4).

199:31 a nest of Tidewater plantations See entry for 184:5.

199:38 his mother was a mountain woman, a Scottish woman who, so he told Grandfather, never did quite learn to speak English The area of West Virginia from which Sutpen originates was first settled by German, Welsh, and Scotch-Irish immigrants in 1726 (Ragan, *Absalom* 162). Sutpen's origins in a bilingual home may account for his occasional misuse of terminology (see entry for 207:1) and for his eventual realization that he would need to learn a new language to advance socially (205:13).

201:2 Perhaps a man builds for his future in more ways than one, builds not only toward the body which will be his tomorrow or next year, but toward actions and the subsequent irrevocable courses of resultant action Sutpen's sense of the need for a "design" emerges from his sense of the accumulation of "irrevocable courses" of events which a man "builds." In this passage, self determination ("a man builds") and predestination ("subsequent irrevocable courses of resultant action") lead him toward the conclusion that his single moment of free will was in the creation of his design. *Requiem for a Nun* voices a similar sentiment at the founding of the town of Jefferson, in which Sutpen was intimately involved, describing "the irrevocable design not only of the courthouse but of the town too," the moment of freedom leading to a future Sutpen's architect tells them "you will never be able to get away from" (499). The idea in both novels accounts for Sutpen's relentless return to origins to locate the error he made which would account for the failure of his design. All that follows from the design may be foreseen in the design, or is contained in the design itself, so that failure marks an error in perception, not action. All errors, in other words, are cognitive, because only in cognition are human beings free. See entry for 204:33.

203:22 ("the demon's," Shreve said) Shreve's interjection comes in the middle of Quentin's claim that Sutpen was controlled by a destiny larger than himself: his "destiny had fitted itself to him" (203:23). Shreve's comment responds ironically, sarcastically, to Rosa Coldfield's sense of Sutpen as a demon. A demon, in other words, is a willful agent of evil, not a being cloaked in a particular destiny beyond his control or influence. Shreve's irony adds to the sympathetic portrait of Sutpen in this chapter.

203:24 his pristine aptitude for platform drama and childlike heroic simplicity Quentin's editorializing seems to contribute to Sutpen's pathos.

A "platform," according to one definition in the OED, is a transitive verb meaning "to plan, outline, sketch, draw up a scheme of"; "a plan or draught to build by." Sutpen's aptitude for it would thus seem to be a projection of how things should be, not of how they actually are.

203:36 **crouching behind a window in the dark and firing the muskets through it which someone else loaded and handed to him** Haiti was colonized by the French and became a major source of sugar in the eighteenth century. The Haitian slave revolution took place in the 1790s and lasted a decade, inspired by both the French and American revolutions. By the early nineteenth century, most whites had left the island and slavery was abolished. Haiti became the first African-ruled nation in the western hemisphere. Godden argues that Faulkner deliberately misdates the Haitian slave revolution to invoke it as an "embodiment" of "that which the plantocracy most fears and must deny—the spirit of revolution" (52). Owada counters that "there must have been many skirmishes even after the Haitian Revolution of 1791 to 1804" (62). See also Donaldson and Ladd.

204:1 **he decided to go to the West Indies and so he went there; ... he not telling how he got there** Unlike the novel's principal narrators, Sutpen feels no need to connect the dots, to show cause and effect and to fill in perceived gaps: he, of course, knows how he got there and deems it to no purpose to retell it.

204:9 **a French sugar planter** The precise lineage of the Haitian planter's family is obscure, as is the actual origin of the captive "French" architect who builds Sutpen's house. "French" may be a term of obscurity itself in the novel: According to *The Hamlet*, in backwoods Mississippi a person whose origins were unknown but whose accent or demeanor marks him or her as foreign would be called a Frenchman "regardless" (731). The origins of the "French sugar planter" are impossible to trace historically.

204:9 **he was barricade in the house** The word "barricade" is one of several in *Absalom* which Faulkner has energized by using it as a part of speech different from what we are accustomed to. In this case he makes a past participle of the noun "barricade," for which usage there is no precedent in the OED. Especially by not using the noun-marking article "a" or "the" Faulkner means that Sutpen was both behind the barricade with the family and also that he himself was the barricade that protected them from the threat outside. In such usage he may be following Shakespeare, as Portia tells Shylock, if in addition to his pound of flesh he takes even one drop of blood from Antonio, "Thou diest and all thy goods are confiscate" (IV.1).

204:33 **he was just telling a story about something a man named Thomas Sutpen had experienced, which would still have been the same story if the man had no name at all** Believing that all actions subsequent to a design are destined by or contained in the design, Sutpen can tell his story in a completely detached manner, as if it were happening to someone else (compare 201:8). The only part of the story he feels responsible for is the design (205:25); the design is the only part he interrogates with a sense of obligation. The detachment is borne also of his sense of "balloon faces" (186:24), including his own, which mark his view of himself and others as abstractions. His "telling a story" also conjoins his efforts with those of the other narrators in the novel and is a further displacement of narrative authority in the novel: the doer of the deed, like the author of the novel, is no more reliable a narrator than any other observer, reader, or teller of the tale.

205:2 **those six or seven years which must have existed somewhere, must have actually occurred** one of many time gaps in the novel, periods of time that pass inexplicably, the most troublesome of which is Sutpen's eight-month delay in returning to Mississippi after the Civil War (see entry for 229:28). It may have taken him six or seven years to learn the local language or to acquire other skills Sutpen had not foreseen the need for, learning which delays the implementation of the design and thus exists outside of what Sutpen needs to narrate.

205:13 **he would have to learn to speak a new language** In much of the novel, language is a complex and invaluable tool used to get at the truth; it is also an unreliable medium which obscures as much as it reveals. Here, language exists in its most utilitarian form, as a definite "foreign" system of discourse he must master before he can act; it recalls as well Sutpen's mother's inability to speak English (199:38). More broadly and metaphorically, in each successive chapter each narrator brings a distinctive use of language to the events of the past, resulting in revisions to our sense of what happened.

205:23 **I was still a virgin . . . that too was a part of the design which I had in my mind** The importance of Sutpen's own virginity lies in his sense that his design represents his own rebirth, a wholly new beginning without antecedent. Sutpen may align himself with variations on American puritanical and ahistorical ideology. The "new beginning" that Sutpen designs for himself is consistent with the moral imperative that his sexuality be reserved for procreation, so that he brings to his marriage a sexuality without history (Polk, "Artist as Cuckold").

206:1 **the thousand secret dark years which has created the hatred and implacability** a millennial reach into the past, beyond Haiti to Africa, that incorporates a history that while hidden to most ("secret dark years") nonetheless fuels the present hostilities.

206:14 **a white slender arm raised** This brief description is Sutpen's unequivocal assertion that he believed that his wife was white. To suggest otherwise, Faulkner would more typically use a term like coffee- or parchment-colored.

206:28 **and he telling it in that pleasant faintly forensic anecdotal manner** The "faintly forensic" manner suggests something deceitful in Sutpen's narrative (in the sense that "faintly" is related to "feigned"), something he is not telling or something he is covering, as if to say that while his design may have arisen from his innocence, his recounting of it is not so innocent. "Faintly" may also mean "feebly" or "indistinctly," in which case the hint of "forensic" content may suggest a defensiveness on Sutpen's part, as if to say that his narrative is told in part to acquit him of an action which one may suspect to have been unjust. "Forensic" means a formal argument such as in a debate or, especially, in a courtroom. Sutpen's autobiography, like Rosa's, is thus his "brief" for himself.

207:1 **he did not mean shrewdness, Grandfather said. What he meant was unscrupulousness only he didn't know that word** Quentin notes his own narrative sources in his grandfather's point of view in the frequent use of the words "Grandfather said." General Compson's patronizing assumption of Sutpen's lack of education may lie in his own class consciousness, nearly all of Jefferson's disdain of Sutpen. He may or may not be right. Having posited Sutpen's "innocence" in one thing—marital and sexual relations—he imposes it on him in everything. On the other hand, Sutpen's occasional misuse of English may be traced to his bilingual home (199:38). In making him "unscrupulous" instead of "shrewd" Grandfather also imposes a moral judgment on Sutpen.

207:14 **the halfway point between what we call the jungle and what we call civilization, halfway between the dark inscrutable continent** Haiti provides a liminal stage between wildness and civilization, halfway between Africa, "the dark inscrutable continent," and the United States (see entry for 207:19). The language used to evoke Africa here and elsewhere owes much to Conrad's *Heart of Darkness*.

207:18 **was ravished** The subject of this sentence is "which" at 207:14; its implied antecedent is Haiti, described but not named in the previous lines (see entry for 207:14).

207:18 **and the cold** completes the compound object of the preposition "between" at 207:14.

207:19 **the civilised land and people which had expelled some of its own blood and thinking and desires that had become too crass to be faced and borne longer** What has been expelled from the European genetic pool may be discrete individuals (in the sense of social ostracism, insane asylums, and prisons) but may as well refer to processes of socialization which breed out of European manners certain forms of behavior that return with the institution of slavery.

207:22 **it** Haiti.

207:26 **an incredible paradox of peaceful greenery and crimson flowers and sugar cane sapling** The paradox is in the juxtaposition between "a soil manured with black blood from two hundred years of oppression" (207:24) and the beauty and tranquility of the landscape.

207:34 **in which the doomed ships had fled in vain** This would appear to describe the infamous "Middle Passage," the horror- and terror-laden slave ships which brought kidnaped Africans to American shores. See 209:33–36.

208:1 **while he learned the language (that meagre and fragile thread, Grandfather said, by which the little surface corners and edges of men's secret and solitary lives may be joined for an instant now and then before sinking back into the darkness** General Compson's idea of language's fragility is also Judith Sutpen's but not Quentin's or Shreve's. The immediate cause of the parenthetical meditation on language is Sutpen's learning French in Haiti [see entry for 205:13], a utilitarian gesture, another link in a recurrent motif (or "thread") in the novel which concerns itself with the ways in which language both reveals and obscures meaning. See Kartiganer.

208:14 **And he not telling that either, how that day happened, the steps leading up to it because Grandfather said he apparently did not know, comprehend, what he must have been seeing every day because of that innocence** The gaps in what Sutpen told General Compson may owe as much to incomprehension and absence of reflection as to an effort to hide anything. According to General Compson, Sutpen's single-minded devotion to his design makes his consciousness of everyday occurrences dim and allows the slaves to carry out a conspiracy right before his eyes (see entries for 207:1 and 208:18). But he might be wrong: he has imposed "innocence" and "unscrupulousness" on Sutpen in all things. As at 204:2, Sutpen may think that the information he does not tell, the gaps, are simply not significant enough to waste time telling, not incremental to his narrative design to justify himself; perhaps he knows very well indeed "how that day happened," and perhaps what happened does not reflect very well on him.

208:18 **a pig's bone with a little rotten flesh still clinging to it, a few chicken feathers, a stained dirty rag with a few pebbles tied up in it** These signals, which evoke but are not necessarily accurate references to voodoo practice, are created by slaves conspiring to rise in rebellion. They may also be attempts to communicate with Sutpen. See entries for 208:39 and 208:19.

208:26 **what he took to be the planter's gallic rage** Sutpen attributes the planter's temperament to what he believes is his French background.

208:27 **and he just curious and quite interested because he still looked upon the planter and the daughter both . . . as foreigners** Our ellipsis contains Sutpen's parenthetical revelation to Grandfather Compson "that the old man's wife had been a Spaniard," as further explanation of why he considered these people "foreigners." However, the slaves in revolt seem to be engrossed in an attempt to warn Sutpen against involvement with the planter. See entry for 208:39.

208:39 **the body of one of the half breeds found at last (he found it, hunted for it for two days without even knowing that what he was meeting was a blank wall of black secret faces, a wall behind which almost anything could be preparing to happen and, as he learned later, almost anything was** The slave conspirators leave the body of the half breed (or mulatto) for Sutpen to find (he "found the body where he could not possibly have missed it" [209:4]); while the "blank wall of black secret faces" appears to provide him with no clues or information whatsoever, they seem to mask an elaborate plan to influence him. During the Haitian revolt, rebellious slaves considered half breeds allies of whites. The body, left for him to find, clearly conveys a message. At 209:23 it becomes clear that Sutpen reads significance into the body, though we don't know what that meaning is. If it's a warning that he will need to subdue the slaves as well as the planter's family if he wants to marry the daughter, it's a message he apparently does receive. The message, in any event, seems specifically for him and is related to the way in which he eventually subdues the uprising. See entries for 209:6 and 210:5.

209:6 telling it, making the gestures to tell it with, whom Grandfather himself had seen fight naked chest to chest with one of his wild niggers That the message of the dead half breed may be a physical challenge to Sutpen is borne out by Grandfather's immediate and subsequent recollection of how Sutpen would engage in physical contests with his slaves in Mississippi. If the dead half breed was a warning to him that he would need to be fierce in order to subdue Africans, it is a message he would carry with him from Haiti to his Mississippi plantation, causing Grandfather to recognize a parallel between the story of the dead half breed and Sutpen's fighting. The fact that the dead body is that of a half breed suggests, however, that this is only part of the message it was meant to contain. Grandfather's recollection does add a new context for Sutpen's fighting, as a continual return to his initial success at subduing the Haitian slave uprising, a sort of ritual reenactment of his founding victory, his first step toward the mastery he seeks.

209:18 or what used to be the half breed Whatever the warning or message, it is sent to Sutpen through the mutilation of the half breed's body.

209:23 he would only say that he found the half breed at last and so began to comprehend that the situation might become serious Immediately after Sutpen finds the half breed's mutilated body, the house comes under siege. Perhaps the revolt has something to do with putting a stop to miscegenation; if so, it is a precursor to the events which will eventually transpire in Mississippi, as Quentin and Shreve imagine them. On Haiti, see Godden, Donaldson, and Ladd.

210:1 the very time of year, the season between hurricanes winter.

210:5 That was how he told it: he went out and subdued them, and when he returned he and the girl became engaged to marry Sutpen does not tell how he quelled the revolt. Perhaps he fought the leader or any number of the rebels in hand-to-hand combat and thereby established himself as the most powerful, creating a pattern of dominance he would continue in his later fights with his slaves. If this is the case, his subduing of the natives involves physical struggle during which he sustains serious injuries from which "it took [him] some time to recover" (210:10), though given the gunfight described in the lines immediately previous to this passage, he could easily have sustained his injuries in more general battle. More likely, Sutpen says something to the rebels, promises something, or comes to some agreement with them, over the course of a physical struggle. Perhaps the agreement they reach has something to do with bodies and with racial identification, since immediately upon returning from the encounter with the rebel slaves, as he tells it, "he and the girl became engaged to marry." The phrase might suggest that the marriage was involved in the negotiations, though what interest the slave rebels would have had in Sutpen's marriage is not clear, nor are the connections between the message contained in the half-breed's mutilated body, the subduing of the rebellion, and the marriage to the planter's daughter. Much more likely is that Sutpen somehow subdued the rebels by sheer force of will and bravado and, in a classic western hero narrative, wins the girl as a result: she is thus a reward, a prize, a mark of gratitude from parents happy to have escaped death.

211:2 **That he got engaged and then he decided he would stop, only one day he found out he hadn't stopped but on the contrary he was married? And all you called him was just a virgin?** Shreve conflates two stoppage points: Sutpen stops his progress in Haiti in order to get married (which, Shreve shrewdly observes, is not stoppage but a furthering of Sutpen's design); he again stops his narrative at the point of the marriage, without explaining how he came to be married. The final joke—"And all you called him was just a virgin?"—is open to multiple readings. Shreve may think that Sutpen, in addition to being a virgin, is a fool for agreeing to the marriage or that he is a super-man for subduing the revolt; or, more simply, that he remains a mystery for the gaps in his narrative. Perhaps, finally, the term "virgin" does not begin to encompass his innocence.

212:20 **took the new hat and looked at it and burst into tears.—a little harried wild-faced man with a two-days' stubble of beard** The hat acknowledges the architect's worthiness, in General Compson's eyes, and elicits from the architect an emotional expression of gratitude or of sudden relief that his ordeal in Mississippi is over and the knowledge that he can now return to the civilization the hat symbolizes. The gift may also be a response to the speech the architect makes upon his capture (see entry for 212:32).

212:32 **making them a speech in French, a long one and so fast that Grandfather said probably another Frenchman could not have understood all of it** Although Grandfather says that the speech is not an apology (212:36) he does not reveal its content. He says that Sutpen, who learned French in Haiti, "turned toward him" (212:37) as he spoke, but apparently did not translate the speech for Grandfather. The speech probably contains an expression of defeat, contained as well in "a gesture" Grandfather described as gathering "all misfortune and defeat that the human race ever suffered into a little pinch in his fingers" (213:11).

213:18 **Brahmin** a member of the highest Hindu caste, a priest; Brahmins do not eat any meat, much less meat considered unclean, as a dog would be.

213:22 **curiously dead voice, the downcast face, the relaxed body not stirring except to breathe** Quentin's demeanor may suggest fatigue; they've been narrating for hours, apparently. Quentin may have stopped narrating because he's simply tired or even bored with the story for the time being, or he may stop, consciously or unconsciously, to repress the conflicting emotions he actually feels, perhaps to protect himself from them as he moves the story toward climax.

213:27 **connected after a fashion in a sort of geographical transubstantiation** A transubstantiation changes one substance into another: Quentin's and Shreve's minds seem interchangeable. The idea of transubstantiation (the transubstantiation of wine and bread into the blood and body of Christ) introduces a passage examining intersubjectivity by way of a detailed ecological metaphor, suggesting its rootedness in shared space, or physical proximity to a shared environment. The passage suggests that "geographical transubstantiation" is accomplished between Quentin and Shreve "by that Continental Trough" (213:28). That is, the river carries out the intellectual interlock—makes interlocutors—of the two boys. It seems a kind of ecotransnationalism. Their minds become interchangeable, sliding one into the other like an ecosystem.

213:28 **that Continental Trough, that River which runs not only through the physical land of which it is the geologic umbilical, not only runs through the spiritual lives of the beings within its scope, but is very Environment itself** As an environmental fact, the Mississippi River affects consciousness, as do climate, landscape, and other factors. This shared environment is what makes it possible for Quentin and Shreve to connect through geographical transubstantiation. They do not share a common environmental origin, and the extreme differences between the climate and landscape of Alberta and Mississippi are made explicit throughout the narrative. The connection between them is thus tenuous, but made entirely plausible (and consequential) through the "geologic umbilical," the "river" that runs from Alberta to Mississippi, that stands as a reification of what they imagine to be, and what the authorial narrator confirms to be, a productive and creative relationship marked by a shared, intersubjective consciousness. The river, moreover, with its intersubjective implications, "is very Environment itself." The intersubjective origins of knowledge presented in the novel are confined not to this particular relationship but is the environment in which all knowledge is produced (see 213:27). See 216:14 for the metaphorical significance of the river conjured by the authorial narrator. The Milk River originates in Montana (U.S.A.), flows into Alberta (Canada), then returns to Montana before eventually joining the Mississippi River and draining into the Gulf of Mexico.

213:33 **though some of these beings, like Shreve, have never seen it—the two of them who four months ago had never laid eyes on one another** The metaphorical effect of the river, the connection it represents, affects all human beings regardless of their level of awareness. The effect of the truth of intersubjectivity—like the effect of any truth in Faulkner—is independent of consciousness: one does not need to know the sources of influence on one's mind or behavior in order for those sources to be real or consequential. The point relates directly to Quentin and Shreve's drive to understand the Sutpen story as one which has affected their lives, but which until this evening they have not known.

214:1 **pandora's box** In Greek mythology, Zeus gave Pandora a box enclosing all human ills, which flew out when she foolishly opened it (or in a later version, containing all the blessings of the gods, which with the exception of hope escaped and were lost when the box was opened); the term is used to name a thing which once activated or broached will give rise to unmanageable and unforeseen problems (OED).

214:2 **filled with violent and unratiocinative djinns and demons this snug monastic coign, this dreamy and heatless alcove of what we call the best of thought** The authorial narrator characterizes Harvard as an institution whose purpose is to produce a particular species of thought and consciousness; the characterization may parallel the way Sutpen's story is passed on to his heirs (176:15). A djinn (or jinnee), in Arabian stories and Muslim mythology, is a supernatural being who appears in human or animal form to exert influence in the world; a coign is a corner of a room, used here to describe the sitting area in Quentin and Shreve's dormitory room; compare Shakespeare's "coign of vantage" (*Macbeth* I:vi:7), a place affording an advantageous view.

214:14 **with a wife and two children—no, three** The third child is Clytie.

214:19 **Nobody ever did know for certain. It was something about a bill of lading, some way he persuaded Mr Coldfield to use his credit** No one ever knows exactly how Sutpen persuades Mr. Coldfield to use his, Coldfield's, credit to start his farm and furnish his house, though it probably has to do with floating credit which could not be backed with assets on demand; apparently, the scheme worked. A "bill of lading" is a receipt for goods to be transported.

214:23 **move to Texas** Economic failure was a primary motivation for migration West, and a "move to Texas"—or, more often, "gone to Texas," or GTT—often served as a shorthand signaling economic ruin, disgrace, or escape from the law.

215:8 **that he would have joined the Yankee army** Mr. Coldfield is not a conscientious objector to war, but a Union sympathizer.

216:1 **he would take that boy in where he would never again need to stand on the outside of a white door and knock at it** Sutpen wants to leave behind a benign legacy as a plantation owner, to welcome into his house whatever nameless stranger came to his front door and thus overturn or correct the treatment he received at the plantation door when he was a child. But Quentin may be sentimentalizing Sutpen in attributing such motives to him. Sutpen seems clearly talking about himself in that situation, not sympathizing with others of his own socio-economic class. If he's sympathizing with them, he is also sentimentalizing: he has no such intention, as far as we can tell from the novel.

216:6 **the still undivulged light rays** This phrase invokes both the light of Jesus Christ and the future as described by Einstein's theory of time and space. In *The Sound and the Fury* Quentin imagines seeing Jesus walking on the "long and lonely light rays" (935); if, as Einstein argued, space and time are curved, and if we could therefore move at the speed of light we might eventually catch up with Jesus.

216:14 *Maybe nothing ever happens once and is finished. Maybe happen is never once but like ripples maybe on water after the pebble sinks, the ripples moving on, spreading, the pool attached by a narrow umbilical water-cord to the next pool which the first pool feeds, has fed, did feed, let this second pool contain a different temperature of water, a different molecularity of having seen, felt, remembered, reflect in a different tone the infinite unchanging sky, it doesn't matter: that pebble's watery echo whose fall it did not even see moves across its surface too at the original ripple-space* The image of the Mississippi river, the "geologic umbilical" (213:30) which unites the spiritual lives of the continent, emerges as a metaphor for understanding the way in which minds influence and are influenced by other minds. Faulkner's thinking is Platonic, with minds forming distinct and idiosyncratic images of *the infinite unchanging sky*, affected by their own experiences and circumstances (*a different molecularity of having seen, felt, remembered*), producing reflections *in a different tone*. The immediate example is the distinction between the ways in which Quentin and Shreve receive the Sutpen story; the larger application is Faulkner's ecological theory of influence. See 216:14. Physicist Tim Johnson writes: "Einstein's relativity implies, roughly, that the way we think of time (everything is right now, the past is gone, the future doesn't exist yet) is wrong. In fact, the past is just as real as the future; all things exist because all time is out there. It just so happens that we experience things as sequential in time. (Why we can't experience past and present is, so far, beyond the reach of physics.) There's a sense in which one might read the opening phrase—that nothing ever happens once and is finished—as echoing that sense in which every event is still out there, existing not somewhere but somewhen.' But Faulkner seems more concerned with the way the effects of an event continue to propagate through time: the event isn't some self-contained happening, but changes everything.

"If you want to draw a connection here, it is with the problem of measurement. It seems obvious that we can measure the size of a desk without changing the desk—just put a ruler up against it. But if you are trying to measure an atom, you have to get something to interact with that atom. And when you interact with that atom, you change it. The desk is so big, and the interaction so small (a little light, say, falling on both desk and ruler so you can read them) that it doesn't change the desk or ruler to make the measurement. But it changes the atom to bump a photon against it. So for modern physicists, measurement is no longer something that can be considered as independent of the thing being measured, but you must consider how your measurement might change the thing measured. Or that you are really looking at a system: the interaction of the measuring probe and thing being measured. There's something vaguely like that going on here—that nothing is isolated; the ripples of events continue to propagate and effect other people—the events can't be understood as isolated things, but influence and are influenced by the 'measurer.' The broader metaphor of the influence of the measurer isn't original to physics (anthropologists have the same problem) but the language of physics used to describe the pools (the 'molecularity' and 'temperature') hints that Faulkner is referring to the physicists' problem."

216:24 **Yes, we are both father. Or maybe Father and I are both Shreve, maybe it took Father and me both to make Shreve or Shreve and me both to make**

Father or maybe Thomas Sutpen to make all of us The theory of influence projected in 216:14 results in an idea of intellectual community which does not accept thought *ex nihilo* as a model for human creation but imagines a series of intellectual and emotional exchanges, something of a creative ecology, resulting in what we conceive of as individual thought: the product of interlocking lives and intersecting consciousness. Intellectual community relies upon the influence of and on outsiders, moreover, as Shreve is produced by Quentin and his father and in turn produces, with Quentin, Quentin's father, while all are produced, or made possible historically, by Thomas Sutpen. Intersubjectivity exists both in and across time periods. Furthermore, by devoting their intellectual energies to creating an image of Thomas Sutpen, the narrators allow themselves to be created by him. The novel thus suggests not only that we are the products of those who have produced us but also that we are somehow constructed by the objects of our intellectual pursuits; we are, in other words, created by the very things we create. Faulkner created the books and so in a real sense the books also created him. Just so, Quentin and Shreve reconstruct the past, but they are also creating the present, forging an ideology and a sensibility through their efforts.

217:2 **he granted that by certain lights there was injustice in what he did but that he had obviated that as much as lay in his power by being aboveboard in the matter** We must read with extreme care the discussion of "what he did" which follows from this admission of possible injustice. We do not know what Sutpen found unacceptable in his wife and child (see entries for 217:15 and 217:17). This information seems deliberately withheld not just to make complete knowledge impossible but to invite speculations such as Shreve's and Quentin's. We may more fruitfully try to understand the narrative effect of the withholding, because that is an aspect of the novel's structure open to and containing various levels of meaning; "what he did," on the other hand, is subject to invention.

217:12 **with no reservations as to his obscure origins and material equipment** One apparent reading of this phrase is that his wife's family agreed to her marriage to Sutpen in full knowledge of Sutpen's lower-class, impoverished origins, which Sutpen presented with complete candor, in the understanding that he would bring nothing to the marriage, no "material equipment" or property.

217:13 **while there had been not only reservation but actual misrepresentation on their part and misrepresentation of such a crass nature** Sutpen's wife's family had not only been less than candid but had misrepresented themselves at the time of the marriage agreement. All we know (from Sutpen through General Compson, Mr. Compson, and Quentin) is Sutpen's claim that the family misrepresented something about the Haitian wife and that the misrepresentation was "crass" (grossly stupid, dull, or insensitive [OED]).

217:15 **as to have not only voided and frustrated without his knowing it the central motivation of his entire design** The nature of the misrepresentation goes to the "central motivation" of Sutpen's design, though the novel never identifies that central motivation. To bring the boy into the house is obviously one central element in the design; another, linked to the rifle analogy (189:21), would place Sutpen in a position to battle the wealthy landowner; yet another is innocence, variously discussed in this chapter. So many possibilities make it impossible to come to a confident, single conclusion regarding the central motivation.

217:17 **but would have made an ironic delusion of all that he had suffered and endured in the past and all that he could ever accomplish in the future toward that design** However his wife's family misrepresented themselves, the misrepresentation seems to give him something that would make of his design a pretense, calling into question the legitimacy of "all that he had suffered and endured in the past" as well as "all that he could ever accomplish in the future toward that design." The implication is that something in the wife's background calls into question or makes ironic not only what Sutpen has defined as his own suffering (which, as we know, is primarily that of humiliation but could also be the physical distress he suffered in quelling the uprising), but what he intends for the future (to be immune from humiliation and, perhaps, to alleviate the humiliation of another boy who comes to the door). There must therefore be a skeleton in the closet of some sort, something that if known would imply that he had not suffered so much as he thought and would also make it impossible for him to be immune to humiliation in the future, should the secret be revealed. What Sutpen may not realize, of course, is that immunity from humiliation requires a large degree of intolerance. The flaw in his design, in other words, may be human nature itself, which cannot, given human imperfection, achieve the immunity he desires. The precise content of the wife's imperfection, therefore, may well be immaterial; what is material is that Sutpen can brook no imperfection, can deal with no humiliation, and as a result cannot forgive or abide faults or deviations from a predetermined "design." Faulkner may deliberately leave ambiguous the nature of the misrepresentation because it is not the fact so much as Sutpen's method of dealing with the fact that is material to the events that unfold—although, as we shall see, the misrepresentation may be filled by whatever personal demons the narrators of this tale must slay.

217:26 **because it was that innocence again, that innocence which believed that the ingredients of morality were like the ingredients of pie or cake and once you had measured them and balanced them and mixed them and put them into the oven it was all finished and nothing but pie or cake could come out** The narrators would have it that Sutpen is innocent of human faulting and inconsistency because he believes that human beings will (or perhaps ought to) behave according to formulae. Recipes for behavior, like ideologies generally, may succeed in corralling behavior, but the recipe will also inevitably change through human faulting and inconsistency. Morality is thus less innocently understood as something in motion, which evolves with experience. Sutpen, for his belief in systems which can wholly order human life and behavior, shares aspects of a totalitarian or fascistic personality, a faith in ideology rather than in human beings. Faulkner's creation of Sutpen may be a veiled response to the ideological battles of the thirties, the growth of Nazism in German and Fascism in Italy and Communism in the Soviet Union.

217:36 **the logical steps by which he had arrived at a result absolutely and forever incredible** The reasoning that led to Sutpen's decision (the "result") to set aside the wife and child in Haiti is judged here as "forever incredible." Its incredibility, however, stops none of the narrators from trying to create believability by forcing a logic on Sutpen's actions.

218:1 **Whether it was a good or a bad design is beside the point; the question is, Where did I make the mistake in it, what did I do or misdo in it, whom or what injure by it to the extent which this would indicate.** We must be alert to what the passage does not say. Sutpen seems deliberately to obfuscate here, as if he cannot or will not say precisely what motivated his action. He begins with the admission that he had made a "mistake in" the execution of his plans, or his design. The "mistake" may be one of commission or omission, and what he seeks to know is (1) where exactly the mistake occurred; (2) what constituted the mistake, and whether it was of commission or omission; (3) whether someone or some aspect of the design was harmed by the mistake; and (4) whether the extent of that injury could have been discovered and repaired. It is not clear how or why he searches for a "mistake" when we have already been told that the wife's family misrepresented something about themselves to him (217:13), unless the mistake is that he believed them.

218:5 **To accomplish it I should require money, a house, a plantation, slaves, a family—incidentally of course, a wife.** The casting of a wife's place in the accomplishment of the design as "incidental" indicates that Sutpen does not incorporate the subjectivity of others into his design. A wife is required to produce a son to preside over his possessions after he is gone and to symbolize his masculinity; she brings nothing to the planning or implementation of the design.

218:13 **as one of my obscure origin** The obscurity of Sutpen's origins are geographic and class-related. By "obscure" Sutpen probably means unimportant, lower class.

218:19 **they deliberately withheld from me the one fact which I have reason to know they were aware would have caused me to decline the entire matter, otherwise they would not have withheld it from me—a fact which I did not learn until after my son was born** Sutpen's suggestion that *he* was approached about this marriage and that the design which he claims he held in his mind may have its origins in whatever offer his wife's father made him. Begged is the question of why a wealthy Haitian planter would curry the favor of Sutpen, a man of "obscure origin" (218:13), to marry his daughter and inherit his plantation (the planter does not appear to have a son), though it may simply be that this father does not have the class pretensions of the planter class in America or, more simply, that the planter does not have a son himself. The planter, however, may also have only "incidentally" required a son-in-law. Sutpen never reveals the "one fact" that they withheld. We know only that he did not know the "fact" until "after [his] son was born." The birth of the son provides the clue to the "one fact," which may be any number of things. Nearly all commentators have followed Quentin and Shreve's dramatic revelation in chapter VIII and taken it for granted that he learns that his son was a Negro, but this is very unlikely, since if Charles Bon is this son he has no trouble passing for white in his youth and young adulthood. The son may have possessed some other feature by which Sutpen surmised that his wife had been unfaithful; Sutpen may have learned from an attending physician or midwife that this birth was not his wife's first, and she was thus not a virgin when she married Sutpen (Polk "Cuckold"). The child may have been born with some physical or mental defect. On the other hand, learning the "one fact" after the birth of the child does not necessarily mean that the fact was revealed by the child itself. Sutpen's language is sequential, but not causal, and he may mean only that it took some time to discover the withheld fact, as if to say that so much time had passed that he already had a son when he finally made the discovery.

218:30 **this new fact rendered it impossible that this woman and child be incorporated in my design** Sutpen seems quite deliberately to refuse to say what this "new fact" was. The reader's lack of certainty about it contributes to the larger meaning of the novel, where interpretive possibilities are constructed upon the absence of information.

218:34 **but which had been given to me by signed testimonials** The marriage has been preceded by prenuptial arrangements that apparently gave Sutpen ownership of some property in advance of his father-in-law's death. The existence of "signed testimonials," whose content we do not know, implies the presence of a lawyer, which may be the origin of Quentin and Shreve's invention of the New Orleans attorney who assists Charles Bon's mother (see chapter VI).

218:37 **providing for the two persons** At first it may seem as if the "two persons" for whom Sutpen provides are his wife and son; however, at 218:40 he notes that his settlement with the family was "agreed to between the two parties." Since an infant cannot make such an agreement, the two parties must be the wife and her father. That is, perhaps Sutpen had to buy his way out of the contract.

219:5 **Conscience? Conscience? Good God, man, what else did you expect?** If the reason for ending the marriage was the discovery that she was part Negro, as Quentin and Shreve will postulate, Quentin's grandfather would hardly disagree or express such shock in his reaction to Sutpen's decision. Faulkner thus continues to suggest and then negate central possibilities and clues to Sutpen's actions.

219:27 **Charles Good** See Godden 4, 69, 72–73, 132.

219:31 **after the siege if he hadn't been sick (or maybe engaged)** Sutpen is injured (although referring to an illness somewhat confuses this point) in the siege and nursed by the woman he would eventually marry; Quentin's conflation of his sickness and betrothal embeds the agreement to marry in an episode of weakness.

219:34 **even though he could have closed his eyes and, if not fooled the rest of the world as they had fooled him, at least have frightened any man out** of speaking the secret aloud Whatever was discovered or revealed after the child was born was not so blatant that it could not have been ignored and overcome by strength of will, so that if the child is Charles Bon, he could easily have passed for white, as indeed Charles Bon has done if in fact he is part black. Nonetheless, to Sutpen such closing of his eyes would have made his design an "ironic delusion" (217:17) because it would be legitimate only in appearance.

219:37 **the same conscience which would not permit the child, since it was a boy, to bear either his name or that of its maternal grandfather, yet which would also forbid him to do the customary and provide a quick husband for the discarded woman and so give his son an authentic name** If the child is assigned the maternal grandfather's name, the social signal is that the child has no father or that its father has abandoned it. Because he does not argue that *he* is abandoning, Sutpen's conscience won't allow such naming to occur. It's as if he is nullifying his paternity entirely. Somehow it is important to Sutpen that the child be fatherless. What Sutpen gains is a clear conscience because he's not passed his mistake to another man, or perhaps it continues the nullification.

220:8 **delayed information** Quentin's present account of Sutpen's story differs from what his father had told him. He now bases the narrative in what he learned on his visit to the Sutpen house with Rosa Coldfield (see 220:15).

220:9 **If he knew all this, what was his reason for telling you that the trouble between Henry and Bon was the octoroon woman?** Given the obscurities and lacunae in pp. 217–20, it is not clear what Shreve means by "all this" that Quentin's father knew or did not know. There's nothing in this about Bon's race, though it may be implied later that that's what Quentin learned on his visit to Sutpen's Hundred with Rosa. But if the octoroon woman is what Henry told Quentin about, why do they make the leap to Bon's putative black blood at the end of chapter VIII?

220:15 **"I did." Quentin did not move.... "The day after we——after that night when we——"** The narrative until this point has as its source what Quentin learned from Henry (and perhaps from Clytie and Rosa) when he went and broke into the Sutpen house with Rosa Coldfield. See entry for 306:24.

220:38 **he stood there at his own door, just as he had imagined, planned, designed, and sure enough and after fifty years the forlorn nameless and homeless lost child came to knock at it and no monkey-dressed nigger anywhere under the sun to come to the door and order the child away**

A good part of Sutpen's motivation (or Quentin's sentimental projection of that motivation) in establishing a plantation was to position himself to offer better treatment toward a child who comes to his door than he got in the same circumstances (216:1). The child who arrives in this case might be the child he abandoned in Haiti. The prospect of allowing him in (and allowing him to marry Judith) may finally make it clear to him why he, as a child, was sent to the back door, make clear the reasons for distinctions that, until this point, he thought he could transcend, and make plain as well the abhorrence the wealthy planter certainly felt for young Thomas Sutpen and all of his class. And so at this juncture Quentin is shrewd to imagine that Sutpen would like to have someone to come to the door for him and dismiss the child, as the Virginia planter had in place to dismiss him.

221:24 **and until he discovered what that mistake had been he did not intend to risk making another one.**

"**So he invited Bon into the house** Quentin's logic is revealing. He asserts that Sutpen does not intend to "risk making another" mistake, and immediately concludes from this that Sutpen "invited Bon into the house." The invitation into the house cannot itself be a mistake because it is in keeping with the original design, which was to allow the child entry. Following the letter of the design is never, in Sutpen's mind, an error. That in this case the child may misrepresent himself to the Sutpens (but see entry for 222:16) parallels his mother's misrepresentation to Thomas Sutpen in Haiti—assuming, as Quentin and Shreve do, that Bon is that same child and that Bon is cognizant of his relationship to Sutpen. If this is the case, Bon's misrepresentation would provide another instance of the design's faulting because of the will of the persons employed in its execution or, more specifically, because of the heritage they bring with them into the design. Sutpen's design, to a great extent, is to achieve some degree of control over events and over the future by eliminating the past as a cause of the present and factoring out human agency.

222:4 **Then Sutpen went to New Orleans.** Quentin presents this trip as a fact but provides no evidence for Sutpen's whereabouts during this absence from Jefferson. Presumably, unless Quentin is inventing it, he learned about it from Henry or Clytie.

222:7 **nobody knows, just as nobody knows whether he ever saw the mother or not while he was there** The purpose and results of Sutpen's extended absence are as obscure as his destination (see 222:4).

222:16 **though nobody ever did know if Bon ever knew Sutpen was his father or not** If Bon is misrepresenting himself to the Sutpen family (see entry for 221:24), he may not realize it himself. Here and elsewhere Quentin makes clear the limits of Bon's factual knowledge about Sutpen. The first example (222:7) is judged to be trivial and thus of little interest to Shreve and Quentin; this second example, concerning what Bon knows, they will reject, and assert unequivocally that Bon does believe that Sutpen is his father. Indeed, this conjecture gives rise to the major thrust of their speculative narrative in chapter VIII and the speculative conclusions they draw there. Paul Rosenzweig suggests that "Such a seemingly incidental remark is a reminder of the hypothetical nature of almost everything that is to follow" (136).

222:30 **and told Henry. And he knew what Henry would say and Henry said it and he took the lie** We never know how the family misrepresents Sutpen's wife or what Sutpen tells Henry about her. If it's news that Bon is Henry's half brother, it's not clear why that should be bad news to Henry, who loves Bon and desires that he be at least his brother-in-law. Apparently, Henry and Ellen wanted to get Bon and Judith married from the start. If Henry already knows that Bon is his brother, there is no reason for him to react angrily here, at this moment. There's no indication that he fears that Bon, as brother, will take his place as heir to Sutpen's Hundred. He may have told his father "it does not matter"—a claim subsequent events reveal to be a lie. On the other hand, the possibility of Bon's fraternity may be secondary to Sutpen's telling Henry that Bon wants to destroy the plantation (something Sutpen may have learned from his first wife if he did go to New Orleans and saw her there), and what Henry lies about may be Bon's reasons for wanting to marry. If so, then what he needs from Bon is assurance concerning his financial intentions. Or perhaps he doesn't want to marry her at all, an argument Shreve will shrewdly advance later in this chapter, but is using Judith and Henry as leverage simply to get from Sutpen an acknowledgment of their relationship.

224:4 **so he put one of the stones on Ellen's grave** The text does not explain why Ellen dies. Her death does underscore the incidental role played by Sutpen's wives.

224:25 **that picayune splitting of abstract hairs** picayune = mean, contemptible, insignificant (OED). The term originated in New Orleans and is taken from the Spanish half-real coin (worth 6.25 cents) of the same name.

225:2 not even to his son by another marriage in order to preserve the status of his life's attainment and desire, except as a last resort Sutpen will not acknowledge or speak to Charles Bon because that would compromise and make a travesty of his design. It would also require him to reveal his first wife's misrepresentation, something that would "malign or traduce the memory of his first wife" (224:38) to Bon and Sutpen's morality will not allow him to do that, not even to save his present status (see entry for 226:17).

225:13 what second choice he was faced with until the very last word he spoke before he got up and put on his hat See entry for 226:17.

225:30 if shrewdness could not extricate him this second time as it had before, he could at least depend on the courage to find him will and strength to make a third start toward that design as it had found him to make the second with Sutpen begins to contemplate his third start as soon as the current manifestation of the design is affected by something from his past.

225:39 hoping maybe (if he hoped at all, if he were doing anything but just thinking out loud at all) Because it causes illusion, Faulkner in *A Fable* casts hope as a sign of weakness; that Sutpen probably does not hope indicates that he is a man of action, not longing; certainly he thinks of himself as without illusion—though just as certainly he is wrong.

226:1 that the legal mind might perceive and clarify that initial mistake which he still insisted on, which he himself had not been able to find Even if Sutpen had been tricked by the Haitian planter, or if the planter had misrepresented the daughter to him, it is still not clear what Sutpen's "initial mistake" is, unless it be his own gullibility—perhaps yielding to sexual desire? Perhaps the mistake is that his design relies upon others for its completion and that he thought he could control all aspects of its execution. Shreve's sense that only a "legal mind" could identify or understand the mistake may foreshadow his invention of the lawyer.

226:6 the absolute and irrevocable negation of the design; or in holding to my original plan for the design It is by no means clear why Judith's marriage to *anyone* would "negate" Sutpen's design. As his daughter, she will not inherit the plantation and further the design with heirs to the Sutpen dynasty; Henry and his progeny will do that. In dynastic terms, if she were to run off or marry someone of dubious heritage she might provide scandal but that would hardly affect what Sutpen has created. Even if it were known that she married Sutpen's son by a previous marriage, who would know (or care), unless Sutpen himself told someone? Judith's role in the design is not clear, and so the nature of the threat posed by her marriage to Charles Bon is uncertain. These concerns indicate the absence of reliable insight into Sutpen's actions, and of reliable comprehension of his mental processes.

226:15 **but that either choice which I might make, either course which I might choose** Choices recur and are central to the action throughout the novel; as concerned as the novel is with destiny and fate, it often depicts characters (and narrators) in situations of clear choices which will have consequences that may be traced quite specifically.

226:17 **either I destroy my design with my own hand, which will happen if I am forced to play my last trump card, or do nothing, let matters take the course which I know they will take and see my design complete itself quite normally and naturally and successfully to the public eye, yet to my own in such fashion as to be a mockery and a betrayal of that little boy who approached that door fifty years ago and was turned away, for whose vindication the whole plan was conceived** If Sutpen allows Charles Bon to marry Judith, the outside world will "normally and naturally" see it as a successful marriage; Sutpen, however, for some reason, will know it as a "mockery" should his son (if Bon is his son), product of the Haitian misrepresentation, marry his daughter Judith, Bon's half-sister. He sees that it will be furthermore a "betrayal of that little boy" who was turned away at the door, to whose "vindication" he has devoted his life. To vindicate that boy would be to prove him correct in his assumption that he could deliver his message to the plantation owner without acknowledging or acting in accord with his place in the social hierarchy. If Bon is his son and he allows him in, Sutpen is not admitting a stranger (as was the boy) but his own son whom he had abandoned. Opening the door would not vindicate the boy Sutpen but would further confirm that outsiders remain outside. As Quentin articulates it, his choice is whether to allow the mockery to stand or to reveal Bon's identity and thus destroy his design by his own hand. General Compson, of course, is not aware of the full implication of what Sutpen is telling him, the "last trump card" being obscure: it arises from the Haitian misrepresentation and would reveal the one unacceptable fact, whatever it is, not discovered until after the birth of Sutpen's child in Haiti.

226:26 **this second choice devolving out of that first one which in its turn was forced on me as the result of an agreement, an arrangement which I had entered in good faith** The choice now facing Sutpen concerning Charles Bon is a repetition of (or it devolves from) the earlier choice, in Haiti, when Sutpen was compelled to abandon his wife and child in order to restart and thus save his design. The first choice was "forced on" Sutpen "as the result of an agreement," the agreement being, presumably, the legal arrangement entered into to make the marriage. The choice would seem to be that between living a life of compromised ideals (or designs) and living one wholly consistent with that design; the novel over and over again proves the latter option to be impossible. Implied here is that the discovered fact suggested or made plain that the agreement had been abrogated, making the marriage, in Sutpen's eyes, null.

226:29 **concealed from me the one very factor which would destroy the entire plan and design which I had been working toward, concealed it so well that it was not until after the child was born that I discovered that this factor existed** Sutpen never reveals the "factor" until Quentin and Shreve's dramatic scene they create at the end of chapter VIII. All we know is that he learned it after the birth of the son, presumably, but not necessarily soon after, and there is no hard evidence that the birth and the revelation are connected, except sequentially, to each other (see entry for 218:19). In any case, they hid something from him which Sutpen adamantly asserts they knew in advance would have kept him from agreeing to the marriage. The term "factor" emphasizes Sutpen's habit of abstracting from human beings their representational value to his design.

226:38 **you wouldn't have known what anybody was talking about if you hadn't been out there and seen Clytie. Is that right?** the information that Quentin apparently gets from Clytie (and from Henry Sutpen) when he breaks into the Sutpen house with Rosa Coldfield.

227:9 **his pink naked almost hairless skin** See entries for 180:2, 5, and Quentin's awareness of Shreve's pinkness and, throughout, his flesh. See entry for 227:10.

227:10 **He chose. He chose lechery. So do I.** Shreve may mean that Sutpen begins at this point to plan the seduction of Wash's granddaughter (See entry for 232:17). Shreve's choice of lechery here, following hard on Quentin's consciousness, at 227:9, of his "pink naked almost hairless skin," may be a dully humorous reflection of the homoerotic element in the narrative they are telling and, perhaps, in their own relationship. Perhaps it's also Shreve's comic and ironic and undergraduate approval of Sutpen's decision to have sex with a young girl. See entry for 227:9.

227:27 **he was still bemused in that state in which he struggled to hold clear and free above a maelstrom of unpredictable and unreasoning human beings** The difficulty with accomplishing his design at every juncture has been Sutpen's inevitable need to involve other human beings, who have wills and designs of their own. As at 226:29, Sutpen's sense of human beings as "parties" is constantly thwarted by a revelation of their agency. The sentiment may refer to Mr. Compson's assertion of "that curious lack of economy between cause and effect which is always a characteristic of fate when reduced to using human beings for tools, material" (98:20).

227:31 **his code of logic and morality, his formula and recipe of fact and deduction whose balanced sum and product declined, refused to swim or even float** Sutpen lives his life according calculations and formulæ that allow no adjustment or redirection as contingency or the unexpected develop.

227:34 **and saw old Mr McCaslin** Theophilus, or Uncle Buck, McCaslin.

228:10 **the parched acorn coffee** During the war, coffee was often cut by or replaced with various ingredients such as chicory and ground nuts.

228:11 **Then it was '65** 1865, near the end of the war, when Union victories forced Confederate armies to retreat.

228:16 **Lee sent Johnston some reinforcements** General Robert E. Lee, the Commander of Confederate forces, sent reinforcements to General Joseph Johnston.

228:17 **the Twenty-third Mississippi** The infantry regiment of which the "University Grays" were a part (see entry for 98:35).

228:21 **as his (Henry's) father had done thirty years ago** Sometime after his arrival in Jefferson, in 1833, Sutpen had somehow coerced Mr. Coldfied's conscience into going into business with him and in allowing him to marry his daughter Ellen.

228:27 **Sutpen had ridden up to Grandfather's old regiment's headquarters and asked and received permission to speak to Henry and did speak to him** At the end of chapter VIII, Quentin and Shreve will revise this episode to have Sutpen send for Henry to come to his, Sutpen's, tent (290).

228:31 **"So he got his choice made after all," Shreve said. "He played that trump after all. And so he came home and found——"** found that Henry had killed Bon; but see entry for 229:4. A "trump" in card games has a particularly and specifically designated higher value than other cards; hence it is an advantage that the holder has over the other players. Here Shreve probably imagines that Sutpen reveals to Henry that Bon is his half-brother; in Shreve and Quentin's revision of the scene at the end of chapter VIII, Sutpen's "trump" is that Bon is part black.

229:4 **—(that** completes the sentence truncated with the dash at 228:33.

229:24 the old imbecile stability of the articulated mud Jones, the "articulated mud," can be counted on, through his "imbecile stability" to continue his stale jokes, his subservience to Sutpen, under any circumstances.

229:28 He was home again where his problem now was haste, passing time, the need to hurry. In two separate places Faulkner sets the date of Sutpen's arrival home in 1866 (see entry for 50:30); the fact that the war ended in April 1865 would seem to contradict assertions of Sutpen's sense of "haste" and "the need to hurry" by the seeming leisure he takes in returning. Even if he were in the Carolinas (see entry for 205:2) when the war ended, it would not have take him eight months to reach Mississippi on horseback; he could even have walked home in that period of time. If Quentin and Shreve are right that he has told Henry to take care of Bon, most likely he was slow to return to give Henry plenty of time to do so, a cowardly delay. He thus corrects his cowardice by a sudden show of haste.

230:14 the one spot vulnerable to assault in Miss Rosa's embattled spinsterhood probably her vanity, and also her lifelong infatuation with Sutpen.

230:16 the Twenty-third Mississippi was in Jackson's corps at one time The Twenty-third Mississippi was W. C. Falkner's, but did not serve in Stonewall Jackson's corps.

230:25 that the problem contained some super-distillation of this lack The problem is not simply that time is running out for Sutpen to restart and complete his design, but is the very essence, or "super-distillation," of the idea of time's lack which he confronts. The language here recalls the novel's opening upon "the quiet September sun impacted distilled and hyperdistilled" and the repeated attempts to distill into essences, so that here Sutpen becomes emblematic of the narrative itself.

230:29 So he suggested what he suggested to her Sutpen apparently suggests, crudely, that he and Rosa have a child together and if that child is male, he will marry her.

231:11 already showing him conclusively that he had been right, just as he knew he had been, and therefore what had happened was just a delusion and did not actually exist The statement is in keeping with the novel's successive examples of imagination and experience as more powerful determinants of perception and knowledge than objective fact or actuality.

231:19 the voice of the faithful grave-digger the grave-digger in *Hamlet* (V.i), here not so much an individual but a prototype who is "faithful" in preparing the graves to which all are destined.

231:28 **the cold room ... dedicated to that best of ratiocination which after all was a good deal like Sutpen's morality and Miss Coldfield's demonising** The authorial narrator draws parallels between formal education and the thought processes of Thomas Sutpen and Rosa Coldfield: all three are constructed systems of thought or abstracted designs, though what's taught at Harvard possesses a privileged position in social and intellectual affairs.

231:33 **could do the least amount of harm;—the two of them back to back** The systems of thought employed by Rosa and Sutpen could (and did) do a good deal of harm, because these human beings took action based on their delusions; the thought system employed by Quentin and Shreve, confined to a place "set aside for it," could not do very much harm because of that confinement. The only harm possible is to Quentin and Shreve's feelings, but "There [is] no harm intended by Shreve and no harm taken" (231:39). Even so, the boys may be polarized now in their collaboration, as Faulkner places them "back to back" instead of facing one another, as Shreve is about to contradict Quentin's views (see entry for 231:35).

231:35 **saying No to Quentin's Mississippi shade** The authorial narrator interrupts Quentin's narrative to point out that Shreve acts as a corrective. Quentin ignores Shreve at this point, but will have his say in chapter VIII.

232:1 **He did not even falter, taking Shreve up in stride without comma or colon or paragraph** Quentin does not allow Shreve to speak at this point, but takes up his point of view, incorporating it into his narration as he turns to the lechery which, according to Shreve, Sutpen chose soon after his (227:10) decision to forbid the marriage between Charles and Judith.

232:9 **And maybe Wash delivered the beads himself, Father said** Apparently Mr. Compson has told Quentin that Wash was complicit in Sutpen's seduction of his granddaughter.

232:17 **that Sutpen let him and the granddaughter (she was about eight then) live in** Sutpen first started giving presents to the granddaughter when she was eight years old, or in 1861, at a time when "Mrs. Sutpen and Judith" (232:27) were still alive.

232:28 **Clytie would not let him come into the kitchen** This scene replicates the causal scene when Sutpen is refused admission to the plantation house's front door, though with a twist, since Clytie won't even let Wash Jones in the kitchen.

233:9 **that this world where he walked always in mocking and jeering echoes of nigger laughter, was just a dream and an illusion and that the actual**

world was the one where his own lonely apotheosis Wash's sense of being mocked by blacks parallels Sutpen's of being oppressed by the laughing balloon faces of Negroes as a boy. Compare 232:30, where Clytie forbids Wash entrance into Sutpen's house, as Sutpen had been turned away in Virginia.

233:13 **how the Book said that all men were created in the image of God** Genesis 1:27: "So God created man in his *own* image, in the image of God created he him; male and female created he them."

233:20 **the next three years while the girl matured fast** From 1866 to 1869, she is thirteen to sixteen. It would seem, then, that Sutpen is having sex with the girl even while he is proposing to Rosa. If so, the action negates the boys' "one shot" theory of Sutpen's need to have the son.

233:31 **not quite cringing and not quite flaunting the ribbons and the beads, but almost; not quite any of them but a little of all: bold sullen and fearful** The tangle of emotions felt by the granddaughter in response to Sutpen's attentions.

233:32 **not quite any of them but a little of all** Wash doesn't know any of the men very well, but has a general knowledge of most of them, perhaps who they are and what they do. But he is not quite friends with any of them.

233:36 **watching her secret defiant frightened face while she told him . . . that Miss Judith had given it to her** The girl appears in public with a new dress and Wash grows concerned and speaks to her about it. When she says that Judith gave her the dress, Wash suspects she is lying in order to keep Sutpen's lechery secret. If Judith did give her the dress, or if she agreed to cover for her father, then Judith is complicit in her father's seduction of the thirteen-year-old girl. See entry for 235:23.

233:40 **when he passed the men on the gallery they would look after him too and that they already knew that which he had just thought they were probably thinking** Wash fears that Sutpen's lechery is becoming obvious; apparently his granddaughter's sexual relations with Sutpen are all right so long as they are secret. Obviously Wash is trading her to Sutpen in hopes of some reward, economic or social, some benefit, that might result from a morganatic marriage.

234:11 **when he heard the voices from the back and he walked on toward them and so he overheard them before he could begin to not listen and before he could make them hear him calling Sutpen's name** Wash's confrontation with Sutpen concerning his granddaughter is not based on a personal morality or protection of the girl but rather stems from his sense of social shame that the men on the gallery are talking about him and about Sutpen's lechery.

234:27 I have knowed you for going on twenty years now. I aint never denied yit to do what you told me to do. And I'm a man past sixty. And she aint nothing but a fifteen-year-old gal. If Millie is fifteen, the incident of the dress occurs in 1867 or 1868.

235:23 Father said Judith actually did this; this was no lie that the girl told Wash Judith seems complicit in Sutpen's attempt to restart his design by seducing Millie.

235:29 telling what that Judith may or may not have tried to shut her eyes to, nobody knew The extent to which Judith is aware of Millie's relationship with her father is unknown.

237:3 That's what Father said Here and at 237:9 the invocation of what "Father said" indicates that Quentin may be weighing information from his father against his own imagination, a procedure that will mark much of the rest of the novel. See also 239:34.

237:23 He is bigger than all them Yankees that killed us and ourn, that killed his wife and widowed his daughter and druv his son from home Wash probably means simply that the stress and deprivation of wartime killed Ellen.

237:29 like the bitter cup in the Book See Matthew 26:39 where Christ asks God to relieve him of the necessity of dying on the cross ("O my father, if it be possible, let this cup pass from me"). A "bitter cup" is a bad fate that cannot be avoided.

238:4 and Father said that for a second Wash must not have felt the very earth under his feet while he watched Sutpen emerge from the house, the riding whip in his hand, thinking quietly, like in a dream Wash's elevation indicates that he achieves a perspective he had not possessed previously, raised above the ground, balloon-like, as if dreaming, or with prescience.

238:21 Only there were two blows with the whip Sutpen slashes Wash with his whip. Perhaps the whip is his only defense, but the passage allows us to read the scene as Sutpen's attempt to get Wash to kill him, as Bon pushes Henry to kill him; if so, they both, in effect, commit suicide.

239:30 the murmuring of tomorrow and tomorrow and tomorrow beyond the immediate fury invokes one of Faulkner's favorite passages, from *Macbeth* (V.v.19), central to *The Sound and the Fury* and recurring in various novels and stories over the course of his career.

239:34 **and then maybe even saying it aloud, shouting it Father said: 'But I never expected that, Kernel! You know I never!' until maybe the granddaughter stirred and spoke querulously again and he went and quieted her** Mr. Compson's speculation on what Wash might have said to Sutpen before killing him ("Father said") is matched by Quentin's corrective speculation ("maybe") about Wash's tenderness towards his granddaughter.

240:5 *in a hand-wrote ticket that he was brave* a handwritten commendation, of the sort that would accompany a medal for bravery in battle.

240:7 **thinking** *Better if his kind and mine too had never drawn the breath of life on this earth. Better that all who remain of us be blasted from the face of it than that another Wash Jones should see his whole life shredded from him and shrivel away* Mr. Compson's extended speculation about the characters' preference for death may be influenced by what he got from his father about Judith and Charles Etienne (at 169:39, Judith is portrayed as "thinking *Better that he were dead, better that he had never lived*"). More likely, the sentiment that a living character would prefer death to life indicates the limits of the narrator's capacity for sympathetic treatment.

240:25 **So they waited in front of the dark house** "Dark House" was Faulkner's working title for the novel. See also 240:31. They just heard him moving inside the dark house.

240:26 **Father said** See introduction to chapter VI commentary.

241:10 **so that now they could see the scythe raised above his head** Wash Jones runs at Major de Spain, the sheriff, knowing they will shoot him. Like Sutpen and Bon, he commits suicide.

CHAPTER VIII

In this chapter Faulkner provides clues and then negates them, either with counter-information or with questions about the clue itself—a process of giving and taking away that results in a readerly experience of unrelieved suspension. Likewise, he increasingly problematizes narrator identification. Quentin and Shreve narrate alternately but their voices meld in to one voice, then in to one voiceless vision as they reach their narrative climax, the confrontation between Sutpen and Henry in Sutpen's tent during which Sutpen reveals the "fact" that Bon has black blood (see 289:28ff). As they narrate, Quentin and Shreve increasingly come to identify with Henry and Bon, becoming "the two" becoming "the four"; at various places, two voices become one voice and then even the "voice" disappears into a single vision.

242:7 **"So the old man sent the nigger for Henry," Shreve said. "And Henry came in and the old man said, 'They cannot marry because he is your brother' and Henry said 'You lie'** Shreve picks up the narrative from 222:26, where Sutpen summons Henry to the parlor; whereas in chapter VII Quentin follows Sutpen from that moment to his death at Wash Jones's hand, Shreve follows Henry and Bon. Quentin does not specify that Sutpen "sent the nigger" for Henry, but merely that he "sent for Henry"; Shreve's assumption that he sent a slave is, in the novel's terms, "probably true enough." Shreve understands this to be what happened because that is what makes sense at this point in the narrative, and is based upon what they now know. But later in the chapter, when he and Quentin have Sutpen summon Henry to his tent on the battleground, they will alter Sutpen's reasons for refusing the marriage from incest to race.

242:31 **now not two of them but four, the two who breathed not individuals now yet something both more and less than twins, the heart and blood of youth** Sympathies begin to shift as Quentin and Shreve move to transcend their general abhorrence of Thomas Sutpen to a more sympathetic (or, as the authorial narrative implies, youthful empathetic) portrayal of him.

242:35 **one of those people whose correct age you never know because they look exactly that and so you tell yourself that he or she cannot possibly be that because he or she looks too exactly that not to take advantage of the appearance: so you never believe implicitly that he or she is** Faulkner's exploration of the nature of evidence is an important subtext to this chapter; we should take nothing at face value, so to speak, especially not appearances. We must assess evidence subjectively as well as objectively, measure what it appears to say against who states or interprets it.

243:6 **Not two of them in a New England college sitting-room but one in a Mississippi library sixty years ago** Quentin and Shreve are already deep into their identification with each other and with Henry and Bon.

243:13 **and they—Quentin and Shreve—thinking how after the father spoke and before what he said stopped being shock and began to make sense, the son would recall later how he had seen through the window beyond his father's head the sister and the lover in the garden, pacing slowly** Quentin and Shreve create this scene, probably from Quentin's memory

• 155 •

of the passage in chapter V in which Rosa depicts herself waking up from the nightmare that her life has become to find domestic bliss at the Sutpen's happy, perfect home: "*Mother and Judith are in the nursery with the children, and Father and Charles are walking in the garden*" (117:2). Their imagined scene dramatizes a moment of domestic perfection—things as they should be—on the verge of destruction.

243:23 **blooms which Shreve possibly had never heard and never seen although the air had blown over him first which became tempered to nourish them** air = probably the jet stream, the powerful flow of air that usually enters North America from the northwest at speeds from 60 to 300 miles per hour, and affects weather across the continent.

243:26 **and it would not matter here that the time had been winter in that garden too and hence no bloom nor leaf** Quentin and Shreve set their created Eden in a garden in full bloom, to dramatize innocence before the fall into history. The authorial narrator's assertion that in fact it was winter—Christmas—when this scene takes place stresses the dramatic superiority of imagination over reality: the setting in a burgeoning, fructive Garden of Eden does serve their dramatic purposes here, before the fall. To be sure, as this chapter develops, the narrators, especially Shreve, indirectly depict Charles Bon as something of a serpent who courts Judith for his own purposes: believing that he knows his history—that Sutpen is his father—he courts Judith not from love but from a desire to force Sutpen to recognize him as his son. In some ways, then, setting this scene in a winter garden might have been equally dramatic and even more apt to the reality and so more ironic, but would have tipped the narrative hand too soon. In narrative, "facts" can be manipulated in numerous ways to create a variety of fictional "meanings," according to the narrators' needs. Nor does it "matter" that the scene really is at night so that Henry could not in any case have actually seen Charles and Judith in the garden (see entries for 243:13, 23).

243:32 **who could without moving** Faulkner supplies a predicate for this sentence at 243:36: "be already clattering over the frozen ruts of that December night."

244:3 **the blood, the immortal brief recent intransient blood which could hold honor above slothy unregret and love above fat and easy shame** That Henry's and Bon's bloods could be "immortal brief recent" *and* "intransient" argues for their youthful pride based in naivete and a hopelessly romantic view of the world that lets them believe that in leaving Sutpen's Hundred they are acting out of honor, whatever their issue with Sutpen is.

244:14 Listen, dont you remember how your father said it, about how not one time did he—the old guy, the demon—ever seem to wonder either how the other wife managed to find him We do not know the extent to which Quentin and Shreve have previously discussed these issues. Their joint narrative purports to take place over the course of one long evening, but such phrases as "So it wasn't her that told Bon" (244:24), "Or maybe she didn't get around to telling him" (244:26), and "Maybe she just never thought" (244:27) pretty certainly point to previous conversations on the subject. The suggestion raises the question of why Quentin would start telling the Sutpen saga to Shreve or anybody else—does the letter trigger his obviously constant confessional mode? To explain? Why does the Sutpen story have such a hold on him? Shreve makes adjustments to details so that they fit the sense of the story toward which he and Quentin are moving. As we noted in the entry for 5:26, there is an obsessive quality about *telling* throughout *Absalom* that we connected with Poe's "The Raven" and Coleridge's "The Ancient Mariner." In both poems the repetitious telling is designed to provoke certain responses from the equally obsessive listener that satisfy the teller in deeply emotional ways, even if it is not always clear what the teller is feeling.

244:30 Or maybe she was already telling it before he was big enough to know words and so by the time he was big enough to understand what was being told him she had told it so much and so hard that the words didn't make sense to her anymore either because they didn't have to make sense to her Shreve draws on Quentin's experience of having to listen before he could understand (176:15) as a way to project and thus produce empathy for Charles Bon's condition. See 231:11 for an instance in which imagination and experience frame understanding and determine the capacity for sympathy. Knowing without being told is a crucial category of Faulknerian knowledge, common throughout his work. By virtue of their being roommates, Quentin and Shreve know things about each other that do not require verbalization. In passages such as this one—"and so she had got to the point where when she thought she was saying it she was quiet, and when she thought she was quiet it was just the hate and the fury" (244:35)—Shreve displays his awareness of this category of knowledge and applies it to his sense of events.

245:25 Jesus, you can almost see him Visualization marks comprehension throughout the novel. At the end of this chapter Quentin and Shreve "see" a dramatic end to all their telling and in chapter 9 Quentin "sees" and describes Rosa's subsequent trip to Sutpen's Hundred with sheriff and ambulance to bring Henry in to Jefferson for medical care.

245:35 **blazing immobility** Shreve depicts Bon's mother as a furious but more or less permanently fixed physical and psychological presence in his life.

245:37 **the face filled with furious and almost unbearable unforgiving almost like fever (not bitterness and despair: just implacable will for revenge)** Bon's mother's face. His mother is the "she" in the paragraph starting on 244, and she is the one whom Quentin and Shreve assume has plotted for revenge. Focusing on the mother's agency, Quentin and Shreve think that Bon was raised by a woman hell-bent on revenge. Shreve attributes Bon's mother's "incomprehensible fury and fierce yearning and vindictiveness and jealous rage" as something "all mothers of children had received in turn from their mothers" (246:27) in turn since the beginning. See entry for 246:37.

246:3 **creating for himself... his own notion of that Porto Rico or Haiti or wherever it was he understood vaguely that he had come from** Perhaps Shreve attributes to Bon his own indifference to the distinction.

246:31 **that Porto Rico or Haiti or wherever it was we all came from but none of us ever lived in** Deliberately or not, Shreve refuses to name Africa as possibly "where we all came from but none of us ever lived in," though he will do so at the end of the novel.

246:37 **no one personal Porto Rico or Haiti, but all mother faces which ever bred swooping down at those almost calculable moments out of some obscure ancient general affronting and outraging which the actual living articulate meat had not even suffered but merely inherited; all boy flesh that walked and breathed stemming from that one ambiguous eluded dark fatherhead and so brothered perennial and ubiquitous everywhere under the sun** Shreve and Quentin, most likely away from their mothers for the first time in their lives, turn the story into one about mothers and mothering. The figure of the "swooping" mother is known to "all boy flesh" and thus known equally well by these roommates and held here against an "ambiguous eluded dark fatherhead" that unites all boys with each other and with Bon. (See 217:12 for similar associations between Bon's father and darkness.) Mothers swoop and oppress while fathers are elusive and dark. That Shreve's assessment of mother hits close to home for both boys is marked by their reaction: "They stared at one another—glared rather" (247:5). Also, beginning with the end of this paragraph, the mother figure will punctuate the end of the next two paragraphs (see 250:8 and 253:10).

247:7 **There was something curious in the way they looked at one another, curious and quiet and profoundly intent, not at all as two young men** might look at each other but almost as a youth and a very young girl might out of virginity itself—a sort of hushed and naked searching** Such passages signal the homoerotic overtones of Quentin and Shreve's relationship; Quentin's constant awareness of Shreve's physical presence, his cherubic pink skin, and their ending the novel in bed, perhaps the same one, suggest a homoerotic relationship, whether it is actively homosexual or not. Their homoerotic intimacy is deeply related to their imaginative depiction of Bon and Henry's developing relationship: it is thus intimately related to the novel's structures and themes (see entry for 250:16). The interruption of the narrative by their glaring and their "hushed and naked searching" seems an emotional response to the suggestion that ends the previous paragraph that fatherlessness and problematic fathers have caused equally problematic relationships between mothers and sons, "hence no man had a father, no one personal Porto Rico or Haiti" to supply pathologies for dysfunctional families but came from "affronts" and "outrages" which mothers and children "had not even suffered but merely inherited" (246:36). See entry for 254:22.

247:25 **and without money there could be no pleasure, and without pleasure it would not even be breathing but mere protoplasmic inhale and collapse of blind unorganism in a darkness where light never began** Shreve borrows from and perhaps parodies Rosa Coldfield's language as he probes thought to its origin in sexuality.

247:30 **coerce and smoothe him into the barrier with when Derby Day came** Derby = the Kentucky Derby. Shreve depicts Bon's scheming mother as an agent of revenge on Sutpen, treating him as a horse being bribed for a contest. A "barrier" apparently is one of the stalls in the starting gate that separate the horses so that they can all get a clean start (see entry for 248:2).

248:2 **like the millionaire horse has only to come in one time with a little extra sweat on him, and tomorrow he will have a new jock** The lawyer worries that if he, the "jock," abuses Bon, the "horse," the horse's owner, the mother, will fire him.

248:4 **Sure, that's who it would be: the lawyer, that lawyer with his private mad female millionaire to farm** Shreve invents the lawyer to explain Bon's mother's capacity to locate Thomas Sutpen and plan her revenge upon him. For his own gain, the lawyer aids and abets the "swooping" mother (246:38) in exacting her vengeance.

248:17 *Today he finished robbing a drunken Indian of a hundred miles of virgin land, val. 25,000. At 2:31 today came up out of swamp with final plank for house. val in conj. with land 40,000. 7:52 p.m. today married. Bigamy threat val. minus nil. unless quick buyer. Not probable. Doubtless conjoined with wife same day. Say 1 year* Shreve concocts a humorous version of the lawyer's reports on Sutpen's activities and his projections of how much he is worth so that he, the lawyer, can calculate how much Bon might be worth to Bon's mother—and therefore to himself. He estimates Sutpen's land and the house together to be worth $40,000. He thinks of blackmailing Sutpen by threatening to expose his bigamy, but concludes that that would get him less than nothing (*"minus nil"*) unless he can find somebody to whom that information would be valuable, a prospect *"not probable"* because Sutpen probably got married the same day he *"came up out of the swamp with final plank for house."* But perhaps he can wait a year, when Bon will be old enough to go to the university at Oxford. See entry for 248:23.

248:23 **Son. Intrinsic val. possible though not probable forced sale of house & land plus val. crop minus child's one quarter. Emotional val. plus 100%... times increase yearly for each child plus intrinsic val. plus liquid assets plus working acquired credit** Son = Sutpen's son, Henry. Beginning here and through the next couple of pages, the lawyer tries to figure how to maximize his income from Bon's mother's obsession with Sutpen and to minimize his risk of getting caught. If he goes ahead and tells her he has found Sutpen, he's likely to lose her as a client, whereas he can count on the income as long as he gives her reports of his whereabouts but never quite catches up with him. He's also worried, apparently, that she might in fact catch on to how he is using her and turn her vengeance on him: hence he worries "whether maybe what he ought to do was to wash his hands of the Sutpen angle and clean up what was left and light out for Texas" (249:19), where she could not catch up with him. He's also concerned about how much of her money Bon is spending in riotous living (248:37ff), money he will not be able to extort from her. Perhaps he thinks that he would do better if he went directly to Sutpen with the information that she has been looking for him, to blackmail him or force him to run after selling Sutpen's Hundred for whatever he can get for it; but he concludes this Sutpen is not likely to run because the land's emotional value to him is more than its intrinsic value. Besides, if he sells the land, he has to give Henry 25 percent, but if he keeps it, he will see its emotional as well as its intrinsic value increase every year. This whole passage could also be Shreve's/Faulkner's satire on lawyers rather than a legitimate or consequential accounting method.

248:30 ***Daughter . . . daughter? daughter? daughter?*** See entry for 248:23. The daughter voids the enterprise. At 248:33, "thinking stopping right still then." The daughter is a fact he cannot pass, cannot assimilate; she will not work in his scheme. But if he wants to prolong the search why does he want to send Bon to the University of Mississippi? Does he know that Henry will go to school there? If he envisions that Henry will invite Bon to Sutpen's Hundred, how does he expect to make money from that, since it would end his enterprise?

249:4 **the octoroon and the left handed marriage** The marriage to the octoroon is not, cannot be, a legal union. A left handed marriage is a morganatic union, by which a man of superior social rank marries a woman of lesser; it's "left handed" because during the ceremony the groom holds the bride's right hand with his left hand. Children of a morganatic marriage may not inherit any of the father's money or property.

249:8 ***He is beginning to ramble. He needs a block. Not a tether: just a light block of some sort, so he cant get inside of anything that might have a fence around it*** The lawyer is worried that Bon is wasting his mother's money, money that she won't be able to give to him, the lawyer, to pay his expenses in tracking down Thomas Sutpen. The "block" he envisions is college, a college deep in rustic north Mississippi, where he won't have much opportunity to spend money on champagne and whores (249:2; see also 253:28).

249:26 **and he would have to deny that he breathed . . . except for that two hundred percent. times the intrinsic value every New Year's** This is the lawyer's calculation of emotional value: "100% times increase yearly for each child." Two children = 200 percent times the number of years he has spent looking.

249:40 **and though you could no more have proved vice or virtue or courage or cowardice to him without showing him the moving people than you could have proved death to him without showing him a corpse, he did believe in misfortune because of that rigorous and arduous dusty eunuch's training which taught him to leave man's good luck and joys to God** Shreve depicts the lawyer as a materialist, whose "rigorous and arduous eunuch's training" in law school recalls the description of Quentin and Shreve's Harvard environment as a "snug monastic coign" (214:3). In this sense, Shreve creates the lawyer out of "what we call the best of thought." Shreve's description of the lawyer's legal education as a "eunuch's training" in a "snug monastic coign" positions him as a chaste mediæval monk cloistered away for his studies precisely to escape the temptations of the flesh. He thus has learned to deny his own emotional needs for intimacy with other human beings, to leave such things as "man's good luck and joys to God." He can thus concentrate on his material needs without being affected by emotion.

250:8 **the old Sabine** Bon's mother. The Sabine people inhabited the central region of ancient Italy; the central event, the myth, of the founding of Rome was the rape of the Sabine women, who then gave birth to the new race of Romans. Shreve again evokes the mother.

250:9 **They stared—glared—at one another** See 247:5 for the same response by Quentin and Shreve when they come close to assessing responsibility to the mother for these events.

250:14 **both thinking as one, the voice which happened to be speaking the thought only the thinking become audible, vocal** Anticipates the "happy marriage of speaking and hearing" (261:7) between Shreve and Quentin, the merging of their consciousnesses into one mind, one organic creative source that gives birth, as it were, to characters and events that will, as they mature, explain or embody the past much as a child embodies the future of its parents.

250:16 **the two of them creating between them, out of the rag-tag and bobends of old tales and talking, people who perhaps had never existed at all anywhere, who, shadows, were shadows not of flesh and blood which had lived and died but shadows in turn of what were (to one of them at least, to Shreve) shades too) quiet as the visible murmur of their vaporising breath** The authorial narrator validates the movement away from documentable facts (they base the narrative on what they have learned from other narrators) toward creative, imaginative projection. Shreve and Quentin are thus cast as idealists—they work from their understanding of how the narrative *must proceed*; that is, of the narrative's necessary end in Henry's killing of Bon. They thus create facts ("people who perhaps had never existed at all anywhere") to accomplish that end. They are, in this sense, diametrically opposed to the lawyer they create, to whom one could not have "proved vice or virtue or courage or cowardice . . . without showing him the moving people."

250:24 **the old Sabine, who couldn't to save her life have told you or the lawyer or Bon anybody else probably what she wanted** In this passage the mother figure changes from a threatening, "swooping" figure to a clueless pawn and Quentin and Shreve soon recast her as the victim of the lawyer's machinations: "—the old Sabine getting the faked reports from the lawyer" (251:9).

250:34 dont bother to shine the brightwork or holystone the decks brightwork = polished metal or varnished wood, perhaps on a boat; holystone = soft sandstone used to scour a ship's deck.

251:15 the report, the communique about how we are not far behind him in Texas or Missouri or maybe California The lawyer is dragging out his search for Sutpen, manufacturing reports from his putative agents in the field who are tracking him down, so as to keep extorting money from Bon's mother.

252:40 he saw that to her he would be little more than so much rich rotting dirt depicts Charles as having had a childhood as lonely as Rosa's, whose emotional needs take second place to his mother's hatred for Thomas Sutpen.

253:7 thinking *I am looking upon my mother naked* since if the hating was nakedness, she had worn it long enough now for it to do the office of clothing like they say that modesty can do, does— She hates Thomas Sutpen as much as Rosa does, is just as pathetic a victim of that hatred. The boys, perhaps revealing a limited knowledge of women, draw on Rosa's demonizing of Sutpen to construct a parallel intense hatred in Bon's mother; they offer the clothing analogy to emphasize its unmistakable quality. Just as nakedness is covered by clothing for modesty's sake, hatred lies beneath the mother's motives and may be plainly seen when we probe those motives.

253:16 and he didn't care enough about what either of them was to try to find out Quentin and Shreve cast Charles Bon as passive throughout, as one manipulated by lawyer and mother, rather than as one who controls or influences events. His passivity continues throughout the chapter, as he waits for events—war, Henry—to decide for him how things will turn out; he's fatalistic, except at last, when he forces Henry to shoot him, though his apparent refusal to take his own life is a form of passivity.

253:28 the light block (not tether) which the lawyer had put on him the lawyer's efforts subtly to control Charles's range of action taken. He uses Bon's mother as a "light block," so that he won't see it as a tether and so resist it. See 249:8 for similar language.

253:31 Maybe the mother found out about the octoroon and the child and the ceremony and discovered more than the lawyer had . . . and sent for him This passage would appear to offer an attitude toward marriage and children with octoroons different from that advanced by Mr. Compson in chapter IV, who described, or had Charles describe, such liaisons as natural in the course of things.

253:36 an expression on his face you might call smiling except it was not that but just something you couldn't see through or past Bon here keeps his own counsel with a face nobody can read. Shreve and Quentin here attribute to Bon the same kind of emotional stoicism that Rosa claims as her sole resource for dealing with her own emotional deprivation as a child. What Quentin and Shreve cannot "see through or past" is Bon's motivation for subsequent actions, his thinking about himself, his identity, and his sense of his relationship to Thomas Sutpen, whatever that is—all of which will form the core of their imaginative creation of events. They repeat the image of a smiling Bon at 254:6: "he looking at her from behind the smiling that wasn't smiling but was just something you were not supposed to see beyond" just as Quentin and Shreve make their first attempt to see what might lie behind it, and again when they imagine him finally abandoning the octoroon (257:14).

254:4 she could not talk about betrayal because she had not told him yet, and now, at this moment, she would not dare risk it It would seem that his mother has not yet told Bon about his father's betrayal of their marriage contract. This may be why at 246:27 Bon finds his mother's fury "incomprehensible" and attributes it to a normal maternal quality.

254:8 Why not? All young men do it. The ceremony too. I didn't set out to get the child, but now that I have . . . . It's not a bad child, either. Bon protests to his mother that "all young men" of his class and stature keep octoroon mistresses, and some even marry them in special ceremonies. Bon regards the child of this union as "not a bad child"—a neutral phrase that expresses more of tolerance than of pride or love or even affection. The child is Charles Etienne de St. Valery Bon.

254:11 not being able to say what she would because she had put off too long now saying what she could: 'But you. This is different' and he (she would not need to say it. He would know because he already knew why she had sent for him Bon's mother fails to tell him that the situation is different between him and his octoroon wife. At the parentheses, the perspective shifts from the mother to Bon. It is he who thinks, "she would not need to say it," because, he thinks, "he already knew." What is left ambiguous is whether what he thinks she does not need to say is in fact what she had "put off for so long now saying." They may be thinking the same thing, but in Bon's subsequent speech, at 254:18, he concentrates more on the marriage than on his own identity.

254:14 because he already knew why she had sent for him, even if he did not know and did not care what she had been up to since before he could remember He knows she is going to reproach him about the octoroon and the child.

254:18 Why not? Men seem to have to marry some day, sooner or later. . . . And as for a little matter like a spot of negro blood Bon may be referring to the "spot of negro blood" which socially defines his octoroon wife. But if so the comment is an odd one, since by his own account "all young men do it" and because without the Negro blood the woman would not be in the social category she occupies and there would be nothing to discuss. The comment is arresting, as is her naivete in thinking that he could participate in New Orleans society as a white man with an octoroon wife, enjoying the privileges of whiteness which his mother desires for him. By the same token, if the "spot of negro blood" is his own, the comment is a cruel one to make to his mother, the extent of the cruelty depending on the extent of Bon's knowledge of her and of his own paternity, about which he doesn't seem to know much. Whatever Bon knows, the matter is not one whose social significance mother and son discuss with ease. See the entry for 265:9 for an extension of Bon's thinking about his mother's bloodlines. The "spot of negro blood" seems clearly the octoroon's, not Bon's. Quentin and Shreve constantly hammer away at incest, not at race, until the final pages of this chapter, when race becomes the only issue that will allow the climax that they are building toward. Bon's mother doesn't want him to "marry" the octoroon because she may fear that doing so will identify him as black and she wants him to live as the white man he is, just as Clytie and Judith want to raise his son as white and to that end refuse him association with blacks. He, passive, seems to accept the fact that he already has a child and is not opposed to a marriage to a woman "with a spot." They do not speculate whether Bon's mother sends him to the University of Mississippi simply to prevent the marriage, not from any desire to avenge herself on Sutpen. Quentin and Shreve really don't insist on race until the end of the chapter (294:36). It's also completely possible, if she exists at all, that she subscribes to her era's racial hierarchies; she is, after all, the daughter of a landholder—and slaveowner—in Haiti, for all of her having been put aside. That she's a racist seems a simpler assumption than that she is even part black. Though of course those categories are not mutually exclusive, and one may argue that her and therefore his blackness might well be a good reason to be even more ferocious in her attempts to keep him as white as possible. Her cosmopolitan son may be more at ease with New Orleans mores than she. She would therefore hate the idea of a black grandchild and the idea of his identifying with black, inferior, life. He would thus indeed be the "father" of Charles Etienne, who makes himself black and marries a black woman despite Clytie and Judith's efforts to keep him "white." If the passage refers to Bon's "spot" of Negro blood, his mother would seem to need him to *not* be white in order to do what she needs him to do, which, if we understand correctly, is to destroy Sutpen through his black marriage to Sutpen's white daughter.

254:21 **And as for a little matter like a spot of negro blood——** it's too late to do anything about that now.

254:22 **not needing to talk much, say much either, not needing to say *I seem to have been born into this world with so few fathers that I have too many brothers to outrage and shame while alive and hence too many descendants to bequeath my little portion of hurt and harm to, dead*** "so few fathers" = none, or perhaps only one, the "ambiguous eluded dark" (247:2), his biological sire, who is preceded by generations of equally dark and unknown grandfathers. At 246:36 Shreve speculates that because of fatherlessness and problematic—"ambiguous eluded dark"—fathers, "no man had a father." Fathers' absences create problematic relationships between frustrated, angry, husbandless mothers, who take their frustrations out on their children, especially their sons. Such fathers and grandfathers, from whom he has inherited, have made him "brothered perennial and ubiquitous everywhere under the sun" to all "boy flesh" (247:3, 1) who share that inheritance. As he joins the list of fathers, he will create descendants to whom he will bequeath his "little portion of hurt and harm," the same "hurt and harm" that all fathers bequeath to their sons, thus perpetuating the family's dysfunction from generation to generation. At 260:8, the authorial narrator gives him, to the contrary but no more simply, not "so few fathers" but rather "so many," and offers another take on Bon's position within his own genealogy.

254:26 **not that, just 'a little spot of negro blood——'** "that" refers to the contents of the preceding italics passage. The speaker suddenly stops and Shreve continues: "and then to watch the face, the desperate urgency and fear, then to depart." He would not need to say "that" which immediately precedes in italics: he would only need to say "a little spot of negro blood" to close off the discussion.

254:31 *she will go to him (the lawyer); if I were to wait five minutes I could see her in the shawl. So probably by tonight I will be able to know—if I cared to know* This dramatic scene closes as Bon's mother leaves him and, Bon believes, heads directly to the lawyer's office to tell him something; Bon is not completely sure what but it would seem to have to do with where Bon will go to college: he will "be able to know" where, if he "cared to know." It could be simpler: maybe he believes he will finally find out what they have been up to. More interesting, however, is the suggested connection between the mother's visit and the lawyer's sudden insertion of Judith—"*daughter? daughter? daughter?*—into his reasons for persuading him and his mother that he should go to the University of Mississippi. Perhaps the mother mentions Judith and the lawyer incorporates her into his own plot (see 255:24f). But note that at 248:32 the narrator says that the lawyer stops thinking after writing the daughter, but the words were never were written on the page, "never had showed" (255:29).

255:9 **paranoiac** Shreve suddenly ratchets up Bon's mother's intensity. Now instead of being merely vengeful, she is paranoiac, though nothing that has preceded or that will follow gives any evidence of paranoid behavior.

255:10 **sit in his office adding and subtracting the money and adding what they would get out of Sutpen** The lawyer apparently plans to blackmail Sutpen.

255:30 *Two children. Say 1860, 20 years. Increase 200% times intrinsic val. yearly plus liquid assets plus credit earned. Approx'te val. 1860, 100,000. Query: bigamy threat, Yes or No. Possible No. Incest threat: Credible Yes* **and the hand going back before it put down the period, lining out the Credible, writing in Certain, underlining it.** More projections of profit from blackmailing Sutpen: two children, vulnerable to scandal, from whom Sutpen would want to keep his secret family (the lawyer obviously doesn't know about Clytie), would, he calculates, double his take. Because Bon's marriage to the New Orleans octoroon woman is illegitimate and may be set aside without consequences (if he is willing to do so), should he wish to marry Judith Sutpen the "*bigamy threat*" is a "*possible*"—that is, not a real issue and so of no legal use to the lawyer and the mother, however useful it may be at an emotional or social level. But Judith is his sister whether he wills it or not, and so marriage to her is "*Certain*" to be an "*Incest threat.*" If vengeful, the lawyer and the mother want to disrupt and potentially destroy his protected world. Shreve casts her as insanely vindictive.

255:36 **And he didn't care about that too, he just said, 'All right.'** he = Bon. He doesn't care where they send him to college. He simply acquiesces.

256:20 **neither of them said 'Bon.' Never at any time did there seem to be any confusion between them as to whom Shreve meant by 'he'** The parenthetical statement indicates that in Shreve and Quentin's hands, the story has now come to be about Charles Bon, and suggests how subtly the two separate narrative consciousnesses are beginning to merge into one.

256:31 **forty miles from——** Quentin starts to say "Jefferson," but Shreve interrupts.

257:8 **Neither did practising with a rapier appeal to me while I was doing it. But I can recall at least one occasion in my life when I was glad I had** Lacking any evidence for such an occasion in the novel, we can only assume that Shreve makes Bon threaten the lawyer slightly, just on general principles.

257:11 **Then by all means let it be the law. Your mother will ag— be pleased.** The lawyer begins to say, "agree," but stops himself, believing that to say "agree" will indicate something of his own manipulation of Bon's mother, and therefore of Bon, for his own purposes. But the manipulable Bon Quentin and Shreve create in these pages is different from the confident, sophisticated Bon Mr. Compson creates in chapter VI and from the "Bon," if Bon it is, who reveals himself in the letter to Judith. If they are to get him to the backwater University of Mississippi, since there appears to be no logical reason for him to go there, they must have him here appear to be manipulable. But they may be preparing to cast him as a victim or at least working toward their conclusion.

257:12 **'All right,' he said, not 'goodbye'; he didn't care; maybe not even goodbye to the octoroon** Bon merely acquiesces; he doesn't care where they are sending him or what they are up to.

257:15 **magnolia-colored arms** chalky white, not pink like Caucasian skin. The phrase "magnolia-colored" nearly racializes *southern* whiteness as distinct from whiteness in other parts of the world.

257:16 **three and a half feet above that boneless steel gyves that expression which was not smiling but just something not to be seen through.** gyves = shackles, especially around the legs; thus the octoroon. As the story centers on Bon, it also centers on sexual desire and, perhaps, on the trap of marriage, of heterosexuality. See entry for 257:22.

257:19 **and thank God you can flee, can escape from that massy five-foot-thick maggot-cheesy solidarity which overlays the earth, in which men and women in couples are ranked and racked like ninepins** Since the general topic of this extended parenthesis is the masculine escape from women, this image would seem to associate women with graves; though men can't escape graves, they can escape women. See entry for 257:22.

257:22 **thanks to whatever Gods for that masculine hipless tapering peg which fits light and glib to move where the cartridge-chambered hips of women hold them fast** peg = penis. Quentin and Shreve recognize heterosexual desire, but emphasize the penis's capacity—"light and glib" to escape the female's trap, her "cartridge-chambered hips."

257:29 **the new extra nigger** The lawyer has no doubt arranged the purchase of a new body servant for Bon, one who does not know him or his past and so cannot reveal his identity to other slaves when he arrives in Oxford. At 256:10 he more or less promises Bon "an extra special body servant."

257:36 **And who knows what thinking, what sober weighing and discarding, who had known for years that his mother was up to something even though he did not (probably believed he never would) know what** Shreve insists not just upon Bon's ignorance but, earlier, upon the fact that he "didn't care" (257:13) and thus leaves him not culpable in the scheme devised by his mother and the lawyer for revenge.

258:6 **which ten years ago did not even exist** The University of Mississippi was established at Oxford in 1848.

258:12 **aware of the jigsaw puzzle picture integers of it waiting, almost lurking, just beyond his reach, inextricable, jumbled, and unrecognisable yet on the point of falling into pattern which would reveal to him at once, like a flash of light, the meaning of his whole life, past—the Haiti, the childhood, the lawyer, the woman who was his mother** Consistent with much of the novel's epistemology, all facts seem to be accessible and in the open; but their significance and relationships remain elusive and subject to change as the "jigsaw puzzle integers" alter, contexts shift, and definitions take on new meaning. What Bon seeks, "the meaning of his whole life," may not be something he can find, moreover, but something either he constructs or permits others to construct for him. In this passage, "the meaning of his whole life" includes "Haiti, the childhood, the lawyer, the woman who was his mother." However, Quentin and Shreve invent the lawyer and perhaps even the mother, and define that "meaning" for themselves, for their own narrative needs.

258:17 **And maybe the letter itself right there under his feet, somewhere in the darkness beneath the deck on which he stood—the letter addressed not to Thomas Sutpen at Sutpen's Hundred but to Henry Sutpen, Esquire, in Residence at the University of Mississippi** The lawyer's letter to Henry, created by Shreve and Quentin, has its parallel in the letter Mr. Compson writes to Quentin, "in Residence" at Harvard. Nearly everything Quentin and Shreve create originates in their present situation and concerns.

258:38 *My brow my skull my jaw my hands* **and the other said** *Wait. Wait. You cant know yet. You cannot know yet whether what you see is what you are looking at or what you are believing. Wait. Wait.* Shreve would have it that Bon recognizes his own physical features in Henry but resists the implications ("Wait. Wait.") of the coincidence, of the odds against discovering in backwoods north Mississippi a brother or cousin. In Quentin and Shreve's construction he has apparently not been coached by either mother or lawyer to be ready to accept what he sees, so that he is confused by and not ready to accept the evidence of his senses. When Henry shows him the lawyer's letter, he experiences a "flash" and "glare" (258:23) of understanding, a "flash of light" that illuminates "the meaning of his whole life" (258:15); that is, gives him a piece that allows him to put together the "jigsaw puzzle," to begin to understand how he has been manipulated.

259:1 **it was not Bon he meant now, yet again Quentin seemed to comprehend without difficulty or effort whom he meant** See entry for 254:14

259:20 **one of whom, a lady and a widowed mother** The lawyer's reference to Bon's mother as a widow is duplicitous; he does not tip his hand about Bon's origins. But her "widowhood" might lend support to an argument that Sutpen had set her aside because she was not a virgin.

260:8 **who had had so many fathers** Compare 254:23, where Bon thinks "*I seem to have been born into this world with so few fathers.*" Now, however, in the presence of the letter from the lawyer, Bon may suspect that his life is not under- but rather overdetermined by those who seek to use him.

260:13 **a little jerkwater college** Early railway stations constructed a large water tank near the railroad that efficiently supplied water to the steam engine. Smaller, remote locations, however, that couldn't afford such tanks supplied water by using buckets on a rope, "jerking" the water to the train's engine using a bucket on a rope. The term "jerkwater" thus means a small, insignificant or hick location.

260:38 **"And now," Shreve said, "we're going to talk about love." But he didn't need to say that either** Quentin and Shreve reach a point in their narrative re-creation at which they must contemplate and project the emotional content of the story. In order to do this, the authorial narrator states that they consider "all that had gone before" to be "just so much that had to be overpassed and none else present to overpass it but them" (261:1). The term "overpass" signals a kind of transcendence, which allows knowledge and insight not strictly on historical fact but on sympathetic (and in some instances empathetic) entry into the emotional condition of the characters whose anguish they project in their narrative. Shreve doesn't "need" to put into words what they are now going to talk about; they don't need to "talk" about what they are going to talk about. The "love" they are going to put into words is that putative love between Bon and Judith; what they are *not* going to put into words may be that between Bon and Henry.

261:1 **all that had gone before** Quentin and Shreve seem to be moving toward their narrative climax, a climax which requires them simply to move beyond all that they have previously narrated in order to get to where they want to go with their story.

261:4 **That was why it did not matter to either of them which one did the talking, since it was not the talking alone which did it, performed and accomplished the overpassing** Released from the need to base knowledge on factual evidence, Quentin and Shreve also release themselves from conventional reliance on individual narrative agency. They achieve transcendence through their interlocked consciousness, not through subjective processes of self-generated vision. The authorial narrator describes the process as one of profound intellectual and emotional trust, "some happy marriage of speaking and hearing wherein each before the demand, the requirement, forgave condoned and forgot the faulting of the other" (261:7). The "marriage" image suggests that the narrative produced between them is one that neither, alone, could accomplish and reflects an emotional state between them, a combined consciousness in which neither is independently responsible for what they produce. The form of their imaginative product is rooted in their intellectual intimacy.

261:10 **faultings both in the creating of this shade whom they discussed (rather, existed in) and in the hearing and sifting and discarding the false** and conserving what seemed true, or fit the preconceived—in order to overpass to love, where there might be paradox and inconsistency but nothing fault nor false** Minor errors (or "faultings") may occur in their narrative (life itself is paradoxical and inconsistent), but because of the level of empathy achieved in their creation of Bon and Henry (or, "rather," whom they "existed in"), the "faultings" may be excused in the name of the more transcendent truth of the situation. At the same time, the authorial narrator indicates that such empathetic narration may also produce a truth that is truth because it "seemed true, or fit the preconceived," which is to say, "fit" into patterns that Quentin and Shreve's experiences allowed them to understand. The truth they reach has a pragmatic nature, which is to say that what is true is what works, or serves the needs of the present. Nonetheless, allowing minor "faultings" lets them "overpass to love," to penetrate to the emotional essence of their story. If they "exist in" their characters, the issue of "fault" or "false" information becomes moot. When they "talk about love" they transcend the realm of fact and enter a realm of knowledge in which "there might be paradox and inconsistency but nothing fault nor false." Unlike facts and material evidence, the emotional content of human life is ephemeral and accounts for the very possibility of understanding. See Matthews 15–16.

261:22 **Henry was learning from him how to lounge about a bedroom in a gown and slippers such as women wore, in a faint though unmistakable effluvium of scent such as women used, smoking a cigar almost as a woman might smoke it, yet withal such an air of indolent and lethal assurance that only the most reckless man would have gratuitously drawn the comparison** Shreve posits Henry's feminising under Bon's influence, then immediately withdraws or qualifies it, attributing to the feminized Henry a quality that would respond viciously to any suggestion that he is not completely masculine.

261:30 **who could know what times he looked at Henry's face and thought, not *there but for the intervening leaven of that blood which we do not have in common is my skull, my brow, sockets, shape and angle of jaw and chin and some of my thinking behind it, and which he could see in my face in his turn if he but knew to look as I know* but *there, just behind a little, obscured a little by that alien blood whose admixing was necessary in order that he exist is the face of the man who shaped us both out of that blind chancy darkness which we call the future*** The passage combines Faulkner's practice in the novel of offering something and taking it away, replacing it

• 172 •

with another idea or perspective or contingency, using the signature sentence construction, "not this but that." The first part of the passage tells us in very precise terms what Charles Bon is *not* thinking, then, just as precisely (with extra spaces that isolate the "but" for emphasis) what he *is* thinking: He's not thinking about fraternity but about paternity, glimpsing his father Thomas Sutpen's face in Henry's.

262:2 *the shadow of whose absence my spirit's posthumeity has never escaped* Bon's emotional essence is inseparable from his father's abandonment.

262:5 **the entire proffering of the spirit of which the unconscious aping of clothes and speech and mannerisms was but the shell** Henry's mimicry of Bon's manner is but the external show of his submission, even unconsciousness, to Bon's personality, his offering of himself emotionally to Bon, if not physically.

262:20 *That young clodhopper bastard. How shall I get rid of him:* **and then the voice, the other voice:** *You dont mean that:* **and he:** *No. But I do mean the clodhopper bastard.* The novel portrays competing motivations, confused wills, and inner conflicts as multiple voices within singular minds, or the presence—almost possession—of other voices within one's mind. Quentin, for example, at times hears the voice of his father in Sheve's narration. The extended dialogue between Quentin and Shreve reifies this process, moreover, and also creates competing voices that tell a single story. Faulkner consistently portrays thought as dialogue, a process of giving and taking away, a process which informs his style syntactically as well as thematically.

263:10 **that instant of indisputable recognition between them and he would know for sure and forever—thinking maybe** *That's all I want. He need not even acknowledge me; I will let him understand* Bon expects steadily less from Sutpen, and will accept even a private, nonverbal understanding, unseen by others: "Because he knew exactly what he wanted; it was just the saying of it—the physical touch even though in secret, hidden" (263:20)

264:4 **and saw face to face the man who might be his father, and nothing happened** Bon expects that during his first visit to Sutpen's Hundred Thomas Sutpen will somehow recognize and acknowledge him as his son, even if not verbally; Bon will even accept a sign rather than the actual words (264:26), but he gets nothing. Quentin and Shreve do not speculate about what Sutpen thinks, whether he recognizes Bon—indeed, how could he be expected to? Sutpen remains throughout as inscrutable to them as he is, in their imagination, to narrators and characters alike.

264:20 **Jesus, who to know what she saw that afternoon when they rode up the drive** Judith's motivation, the extent to which she loved Charles Bon, will become of increasing interest to Shreve and Quentin, as they explore the role of love in this story.

264:23 **the silken and tragic Launcelot nearing thirty** Launcelot is the marriageable knight in the King Arthur tales whose love for the queen brings about the fall of Camelot; his incarnation as Charles Bon is tragic because Bon will not get the "queen" in this version either.

264:26 **And the day came to depart and no sign yet; he and Henry rode away and still no sign, no more sign at parting than when he had seen it first, in that face where he might (he would believe) have seen for himself the truth** The narrative created by Quentin and Shreve hinges on Bon's desire for any sign of recognition from Thomas Sutpen; failure to receive that sign results in Bon's course of self-destruction. He will even settle for not seeing the sign himself—he will even settle for imagining that the sign is given to him—but he fails either to receive it or imagine it.

265:9 *that blood which we both bear before it could have become corrupt and tainted by whatever it was in Mother's that he could not brook* Having Bon speculate on "*whatever it was*" in his mother's blood, instead of acknowledging the issue of race, raises the question both of what Bon knows and does not know and, more importantly, of what Quentin and Shreve want him to know for the sake of the story they are creating, the climax they are beginning to build toward. On the one hand we may understand "*whatever it was*" as an innocent question, given that Quentin and Shreve have insisted that in Bon's view, "a little matter like a spot of negro blood" (254:21) is inconsequential. At this point, Bon may be simply unable to accept the fact that "a spot of negro blood" could be both so important to Thomas Sutpen and so determining of his identity and destiny. On the other hand, by "blood" Quentin and Shreve probably don't, at this point, mean race at all, but whatever of class and character—morality perhaps—that is also often associated with inherited characteristics, carried by "blood," that determine behavior. Bon, Quentin, and Shreve do not necessarily equate "blood" only with race, though given how Quentin and Shreve resolve their plot, having Henry kill Bon because of race, the word here is clearly charged with racial overtones that are hard for the reader to evade, especially upon subsequent readings of the novel. But at 266:40 Shreve at any rate seems far more interested in incest as the operative "problem" for Bon and the Sutpens, the wedge he is going to use to get Thomas Sutpen to acknowledge him.

266:1 **"But it's not love," Quentin said.**

"Because why not? Because listen. Quentin and Shreve begin talking more about sex than about love, but as they talk, they move closer and closer to the emotional content of their story, the factors that would account for actions and events that cannot be accounted for rationally. By locating the place of love in the story, and by empathetic understanding, Quentin and Shreve will reach a level of narration "where there might be paradox and inconsistency but nothing fault nor false" (261:14). Their quest for "love," then, is a quest both to assign motivation to characters and to reach that point where they can believe what they have created.

266:26 **Judas trees** "redbud . . . a shrub or small tree bearing profuse pink flowers in the early spring. The name comes from the botanically impossible legend that this was the tree on which Judas hanged himself" (Calvin Brown 112).

266:39 **There was the knowing what he suspected might be so, or not knowing if it was so or not** Given the next few lines, he almost certainly suspects that Judith is his half sister.

266:40 **And who to say if it wasn't maybe the possibility of incest, because who (without a sister: I dont know about the others) has been in love and not discovered the vain evanescence of the fleshly encounter** According to Shreve, sex is a transient, momentary thing, "vain" because it hopes for what it can never give. Important to Quentin and Shreve's projection of Bon's motivation is the erotic idea of the forbidden; the phrase "without a sister" resonates with Quentin's attack upon Gerald Bland, in *The Sound and the Fury*, as he brags about his sexual conquests: "Did you ever have a sister?" he says (1005).

267:4 **the brief all** sex.

267:7 **and retreat since the gods condone and practise these and the dreamy immeasurable coupling which floats oblivious above the trammelling and harried instant, the:** *was-not: is: was:* **is a perquisite only of balloony and weightless elephants and whales: but maybe if there were sin too maybe you would not be permitted to escape, uncouple, return** As Shreve sees it, a man takes the sex he is offered then retreats from the encounter, gathering up his "rubbish and refuse—the hats and pants and shoes which you drag through the world" (267:5)—since the gods also retreat from such coupling;

sexual encounters are thus a vain momentary escape from "the trammelling and harried instant," a brief moment which before the moment is *"was-not,"* becomes *"is"* during the moment, then *"was"* immediately after. Sex is so common as to be a "perquisite" of animals, including human beings; but if "sin" were attached to it, the sin of incest, the "coupling" might approximate love, might be powerful enough to keep a couple coupled.

267:13 **Aint that right?" He ceased; he could have been interrupted easily now. Quentin could have spoken now, but Quentin did not.** Shreve has answered Quentin's objections about the connection between love and sex, especially in an incestuous relationship. Though Quentin's sister Caddy does not even appear as a hint in *Absalom*, readers of *The Sound and the Fury* can't help but suspect that what stops Quentin from speaking after Shreve's justification of incest is precisely his own thoughts about her, his aborted and abortive attempt at a sexual relationship with her.

267:21 **the cherubic burliness** Again the authorial narrator suggests Quentin's awareness of Shreve's childlike physicality, big as he is; perhaps this too is a function of the homoerotic, a forbidden sexual relationship, that runs parallel with all the discussion of incest, especially through chapter VIII.

267:26 **who had that plumpness once and lost it, sold it (whether with his consent or not) for that state of virginity which is neither boy's nor girl's** Virginity begins at the onset of adolescence, once the characteristics of childhood, such as "plumpness," are "lost" or "sold" for the state of presexuality, or "virginity." The parenthetical "whether with his consent or not" implies that the transition from childhood to adolescence (and the loss of "plumpness," for example) may be as traumatic and unwelcome as the loss of "virginity" can be. The idea is in keeping with Faulkner's often intense empathy for the traumas of childhood. The phrase "neither boy's nor girl's" virginity hints at a bisexuality that may be consistent with the threat that connects incest and homoerotics in chapter VIII. In this state of innocence, sexual attraction is ungendered; it is not limited to heterosexuality but includes homoerotic attraction too.

267:29 **"I dont know," Quentin said.** He finally responds to Shreve's questions at 266:2 and 267:13. He has no answer to Shreve's argument that sex, especially incestuous sex, can also be love.

268:1 **he never had to worry about the love because that would take care of itself** Shreve depicts Bon again as passive in all the manipulations of mother, lawyer, Henry, and Ellen, each of whom seems to have designs on him. If love happens, he has Bon think, that will be fine, but he doesn't have to worry about that himself or take an active role in its development.

268:13 **the old Abraham full of years and weak** See entry for 268:15.

268:15 **and Abraham would say, 'Praise the Lord, I have raised about me sons to bear the burden of mine iniquities and persecutions'** Abraham says no such thing: Shreve is both sarcastic and ironical, speculating upon what Abraham *might* have said. As a younger man, Abraham famously agreed to follow God's instruction to offer his son Isaac "as a burnt offering"; as he was about to slay Isaac, an angel intervened and supplied an actual lamb for the sacrifice. For his faithfulness, God, through the angel, promises Abraham a long life and many children. Shreve ironically imagines Abraham as an old man with many sons to whom he can pass on the legacy, the "iniquities and persecutions," in spite of—perhaps because of—the fact that he was willing to sacrifice one of them. See Genesis 22.

268:27 **after it happened, backfired on him** it happened = they fell in love; backfired = fell in love despite his previous intention merely to seduce her (see p. 266 for Shreve's ruminations that Bon considers Judith to be a plate of sherbet that he finally finds irresistible; see entry for 268:35).

268:35 **maybe that's what it was that came out of the three months of Henry's talking that he heard without listening to:** *I am not hearing about a young girl, a virgin; I am hearing about a narrow delicate fenced virgin field already furrowed and bedded so that all I shall need to do is drop the seeds in, caress it smooth again* Shreve suggests that Henry has apparently talked so much about Judith that Bon has come to believe that Henry and Judith are lovers, so that she becomes not a person but a "field" that he will impregnate, or that he will follow after Henry's preparation of her to receive him. Bon isn't hearing about a virgin whom, as customary, he would have to seduce somehow, but one already prepared and willing to receive him sexually. Bon senses not a call to conquest but an invitation, like the bowl of sherbet. See entry for 268:27.

269:6 **That is, he didn't have anything else but time, because he had to wait. But not for her. That was all fixed. It was the other. Maybe he thought it would be in the mail bag each time the nigger rode over from Sutpen's Hundred and Henry believing it was the letter from her that he was waiting for** Bon is waiting for Thomas Sutpen's acknowledgment that he is his son, and as he waits his anxiety becomes apparent to Henry. However, Henry interprets the level of Bon's anxiety as he awaits his father's recognition as pining for Judith's communication.

269:14 *a sheet a scrap of paper with the one word 'Charles' in his hand, and I would know what he meant and he would not even have to ask me to burn it* Bon's alleged frantic search for some evidence or sign from Thomas Sutpen parallels Quentin and Shreve's quest for logic to support their interpretation of events, since there are precious few documents. In both cases, the mind of the actor seeks validation for what it already believes from the outside world, from actors who may be wholly unaware of the expectations placed upon them.

269:37 *I will not even demand to know of him what it was my mother did that justified his action toward her and me* As Bon reduces his expectations, he searches for "*what it was my mother did,*" what it was in her character or will or action that caused Sutpen to abandon his wife and child. In this Bon exhibits the existential view that action, not essence, reveals character.

270:17 **Decoration Day** established on May 30, 1868 as a day to honor Americans slain in war by decorating their graves. Southern states refused to recognize Decoration Day, instead instituting their own holidays to honor the Confederate dead. It became Memorial Day after World War I.

271:7 **"That's still not love," Quentin said.** Quentin insists that they come up with emotional content that would form a positive motivation for the actions of the principal characters. Shreve still wants to define "love" as "sex," sex intensified by the sin of the forbidden, incest: "I used to think that I would hate the man that I would have to look at every day and whose every move and action and speech would say to me, I have seen and touched parts of your sister's body that you will never see and touch: and now I know that I shall hate him and that's why I want that man to be you" (270:35).

271:18 *I would have done that, gone to him first, who have the blood after it was tainted and corrupt by whatever it was in Mother* Shreve, amending his projection of Bon from 269:35, has him comprehend that there is something in his Mother that is "tainted and corrupt," but he (Shreve) is still unable (or unwilling) to name the sources of the corruption, or to have Bon speak it. It may well be that at this point, Bon cannot accept the social fact which will, of course, result also in his relegation to an inferior caste. Given the significance of blood inheritances in *Absalom*, the reference to his mother's blood at this point raises interesting questions about the narrative resolution that Quentin and Shreve are beginning to work toward. The word probably refers to her fiery temperament but it could also of course refer to that "spot" of Negro blood that they have discussed earlier (see entry for 254:18). In either case, Quentin and Shreve seem to be moving toward a discussion of the mother's essence instead of her acts.

271:33 **Jesus, think of his heart then, during those two days, with the old gal throwing Judith at him every minute now** Shreve displays increasing sympathy for Bon's predicament. Bon is anxiously awaiting some sign from Sutpen, while Ellen (and Henry) interpret his anxiety as an attraction for Judith. Meanwhile, Ellen is doing everything in her power to foster a romance which only Bon knows is impossible because Judith is his half-sister. The phrase, "Think of his heart then" is repeated at 272:23.

272:31 *He knows that I shall never make any claim upon any part of what he now possesses* Bon would have no way of knowing what Sutpen knows; Sutpen has not even indicated that he recognizes Bon, much less what he would do if he did. Quentin and Shreve invent what Bon imagines Sutpen is thinking.

272:33 *gained at the price of what sacrifice and endurance and scorn (so they told me, not he: they) only he knows* Bon knows of Sutpen's heroic efforts to build his Mississippi plantation from his mother and the lawyer, not from Sutpen. By adding "*only he knows*" Bon may express some doubt about the version he has heard, and certainly wants to hear it from Sutpen himself.

272:34 *knows that so well that it would never have occurred to him just as he knows it would never occur to me that this might be his reason, who is not only generous but ruthless* The question of who knows what continues in the passage (see 272:31); "*this might be his reason*" = Sutpen's reason for going to New Orleans or for setting aside Bon's mother in the first place. Bon notes both Sutpen's "*generous*" nature when he "*surrendered everything he and Mother owned*" (272:37) to his mother when he left her and his "*ruthless*" nature in surrendering these things "*as the price of repudiating her*" (272:38). The same combination of generosity and ruthlessness may motivate the putative trip to New Orleans, in Bon's imagination, as he holds out hope for recognition.

273:4 **he had stemmed from the blood after whatever it was his mother had been or done had tainted and corrupted it.—Nearer and nearer, until suspense and puzzlement and haste and all seemed blended into one sublimation of passive surrender** The boys' speculation about what Bon's mother "had been or done" moves a step closer to acknowledging the reason for Sutpen's repudiation of her, a step beyond wondering "*whatever it was in*

Mother" (271:19). Though the passage does not mention race, perhaps Quentin and Shreve are already moving toward race as the resolution of their narrative; if so, Bon's "suspense and puzzlement" might be a refusal to acknowledge (or recognize) the function of race in the social order he occupies. He cannot acknowledge Sutpen's reason for repudiating his mother without simultaneously acknowledging his father's reason for shunning him. That acknowledgment would compel Bon to know that he has no right to ask Sutpen to do otherwise. Bon's refusal parallels his father's refusal to acknowledge him as his son—which could be, as well, an acknowledgment that he had no right to repudiate Bon's mother. By calling Bon his son, he becomes a bigamist; by shunning him he remains consistent with his initial repudiation. In both cases, passivity results, until Sutpen makes his alleged trip to New Orleans. Bon "never learned if Sutpen had been there or not" (273:11).

274:35 **he has sent the nigger for Henry, now Henry is entering the room** Shreve imagines that while Henry is facing his father in the parlor, Bon and Judith are walking in the garden, while awaiting some word that Sutpen has also sent for him, to recognize him as his son.

275:12 **since it did not matter (and possibly neither of them conscious of the distinction) which one had been doing the talking** Narrative identities meld, so that the "source" of the information we read is no longer traceable to a person, but to a collaboration.

275:14 **So that now it was not two but four of them ... four of them and then just two—Charles-Shreve and Quentin-Henry, the two of them both believing that Henry was thinking *He* (meaning his father) has destroyed us all** The heretofore implicit parallels between "Charles-Shreve and Quentin-Henry" are here made explicit: Quentin and Shreve achieve full identification with their historical subjects, not simply narrating but experiencing the events they recreate. "So it was four of them who rode the two horses" (275:33); "So it was four of them still who got off the boat in New Orleans" (276:10). The melding of narrative identities is coupled with the melding of narrator characters, so that Quentin and Shreve come to think of themselves as possessed by, or in possession of, Henry and Charles. The sense of possession results in their capacity (or audacity) to recreate the thoughts of their historical subjects.

275:29 **he must have now understood with complete despair the secret of his whole attitude toward Bon ... he knew, yet he did not, had to refuse to, believe** Perhaps Henry knows but refuses to admit that they are half-brothers; perhaps refuses to admit the homoerotic element in his attraction to Bon.

276:9 **so Shreve and Quentin believed** Behind Shreve and Quentin lies the authorial and omniscient narrator, who, at several times, validates or, in this case, raises doubts about what Quentin and Shreve narrate. In either case, the authorial narrator reminds us that what unfolds is not events but imagination.

276:15 **Henry who knew yet did not believe, and Bon whom Mr Compson had called a fatalist but who, according to Shreve and Quentin, did not resist Henry's dictum and design for the reason that he neither knew nor cared what Henry intended to do because he had long since realised that he did not know yet what he himself was going to do** Henry and Bon go to New Orleans where Henry will meet Bon's mother.

276:22 **which Shreve had invented and which was probably true enough** The authorial narrator employs the phrase "probably true enough" to authorize Shreve and Quentin's imaginative creation of character and events, specifically here of Bon's mother, "whom Shreve and Quentin had likewise invented and which was likewise probably true enough" (276:29). The phrase raises the questions, "true enough" according to what or to whom? true enough for what? The question is answerable only by recourse to another layer of human creation. The literal answer is that what Shreve and Quentin create is "probably true enough" for the narrative they are creating, literal truths or historical accuracy no longer mattering as their story builds toward climax. The problematic word is "probably," which implies that as we approach the source of truth we enter a realm of probability, not fact. It's "probably" true enough to make the narrative complete itself with one result; other narrative "facts" would "probably" be "true enough" to move their narrative in other directions, toward other revelations.

276:26 **the slight dowdy woman ... whom Shreve and Quentin had likewise invented and which was likewise probably true enough** Twice within a few lines, the authorial narrator emphasizes the "created," imagined nature of this entire narrative.

276:27 **with parchment-colored skin** The term signals, throughout Faulkner, a person of (possibly) mixed racial heritage. The term is best known as the descriptive for Joe Christmas, in *Light in August*.

276:32 **who did not say, 'My son is in love with your sister?' but 'So she has fallen in love with him' and then sat laughing harshly and steadily** at Henry who could not have lied to her even if he would have, who did not even have to answer at all either Yes or No. The wicked mother figure returns, having been suppressed. See entry for 246:37. It is not clear what question Henry "did not even have to answer," as she asks no question. See entry for 277:20.

277:1 **though neither Shreve nor Quentin believed that the visit affected Henry as Mr Compson seemed to think** The authorial narrator calls attention to shifts in the story's facts, shifts caused by the change in narrative perspective from Mr. Compson to the next generation of tellers. The novel's drama lies equally in the tale and in the telling. Quentin and Shreve do not find the fact of the octoroon mistress as compelling to the events they now describe as Mr. Compson did; they do not deny its factuality, but it consequences, its truth value in the story. She is now "probably" not "true enough." See entries for 276:22 and 277:9.

277:4 **Perhaps Quentin himself had not been listening when Mr Compson related (recreated?) it that evening at home** In the typescript (p. 411), Faulkner first typed the word "recreated," then later crossed it out and interlined above it the phrase "related (recreated?)" (TS 412) in ink. The editors of the 1936 text not unreasonably assumed that it was not part of the text but rather Faulkner's note to himself to consider revising the typed word "related." The corrected text restores the word as a deliberate interrogatory of the novel's assertion against the assumptions contained in the word "related." The authorial narrator draws a distinction between relating events and recreating them. To relate is to give an account of something; to tell it. To recreate is to create over again, in fact or in imagination. Raising the distinction parenthetically would seem to compromise Mr. Compson's credibility were it not for the fact that the novel's entire thrust is to trust creation over repetition. If Henry's visit to New Orleans were a recreation, it is wholly subject to reinterpretation. If it were related (and the facts as we know them make this impossible: Henry related nothing about the trip to anyone who could have related it to Mr. Compson), then it would fall into something incontrovertible, the slimmest of all truth categories in the novel.

277:9 **and were probably right in this too—that the octoroon and the child would have been to Henry only something else about Bon to be, not envied but aped if that had been possible** The authorial narrator appears to confirm that Shreve and Quentin's interpretation of the octoroon wife is more accurate than that given by Mr. Compson, though the qualifying "probably" throughout the novel indicates the speculative nature of the offered interpretation. That is, here and elsewhere, the authorial narrator assumes no more authority as a narrator than he allows the characters' speculations to have: he becomes one of the several narrators.

277:13 **peace not between men of the same race and nation but between two young embattled spirits and the incontrovertible fact which embattled them** One of the novel's analogies surfaces here, between the Civil War, fought between "men of the same race and nation" over issues related to race and national policy, and the "fact which embattled" Henry and Bon, which, as they construct it, turns out to be racial, the hinge on which their future (like that of the nation) hinges. On the other hand and perhaps more convincing (because Bon's racial identity is not incontrovertible) is that Judith Sutpen is "the incontrovertible fact which embattled" Bon and Henry. There is no question that Judith exists, and that Ellen at least is making a case for her marriage to Bon.

277:15 **the incontrovertible fact which embattled them** Either they are both in love with their sister or, more simply, they are brothers, though Henry doesn't seem to know this yet.

277:18 **wars were sometimes created for the sole aim of settling youth's private difficulties and discontents** At 8:12 Quentin suggests that Rosa believes that God caused the Civil War primarily to destroy and efface Thomas Sutpen.

277:20 **So the old dame asked Henry that one question and then sat there laughing at him, so he knew then, they both knew then.** At 276:33, Bon's mother does not *ask*: "My son is in love with your sister?" but makes the question as a statement. But the question hangs in the air and apparently she finally asks it and he understands why she laughs: he understands that Bon is his brother. For the next several pages the boys want to drive toward a climax based in incest, Bon's being a half brother to Judith and Henry.

278:13 **Do you know that you are a very fortunate young man?** Bon finally forces from the lawyer an explanation of his and his mother's manipulations. The lawyer cynically explains that from his involvement with the Sutpens he, Bon, can emerge wealthy and have a quick and easy pleasure with Judith, whom he calls "a nice little piece," a phrase that angers Bon, who then threatens him for having assaulted Judith's honor. See entry for 279:22.

279:22 *So I cant beat him. I could shoot him. I would shoot him with no more compunction than I would a snake or a man who cuckolded me. But he*

279:25 / VI 271:10

would still beat me. Bon's reasoning about how to deal with the lawyer echoes Thomas Sutpen's efforts to figure out how to deal with the plantation owner's refusal to receive him at the front door.

279:25 **"Listen," Shreve said, cried. "It would be while he would be lying in a bedroom. . . ."** Shreve has a sudden narrative inspiration, a setting for the scene to follow.

279:28 **the letter from the octoroon (maybe even the one that contained the photograph of her and the child) finally overtaking him** This is the photograph that Bon will place in the metal case Judith gave him, to find upon his death. See entry for 295:36.

279:36 **Yes, they knew** Henry and Bon now know they are half brothers.

279:40 **that woman who wouldn't let him play with other children** Shreve suddenly, almost casually, in a flash, creates a childhood for Bon, giving him a mother who isolates him from other children just as Clytie and Judith isolate Bon's son, Charles Etienne, from the black children on the plantation at Sutpen's Hundred.

280:3 **two people neither of whom had taken pleasure or found passion in getting him or suffered pain or travail in borning him** Shreve and Quentin cast the mother and the lawyer (who takes Thomas Sutpen's place as father-figure) as passionless and calculating—"who perhaps if one of the two had only told him the truth, none of what happened would ever have come to pass" (280:5) and whose passionless calculations will cost Bon his life. Bon's innocence and his mother's and the lawyer's culpability are important to Shreve and Quentin's sense of events.

280:7 **while there was Henry who had father and security and contentment and all, yet was told the truth by both of them while he (Bon) was told by neither** Presumably Bon's mother and her lawyer inform Henry of Bon's blood relationship to him, although it is not clear how much of whose "truth" either of them tells. Shreve also posits Bon's mistaken assumption that all has been rosy for Henry—"security and contentment and all"—as Sutpen's son.

280:34 **Alabama convention** The Alabama convention met on January 7, 1861 and voted to secede on January 11 (Mississippi seceded on January 9).

281:27 **University Grays** See entry for 98:35.

281:37 **that Lorraine duke named John something that married his sister** Hawkins reports that he "can find no Duke of Lorraine whose life included any such action. However, John V., Count of Armagnac from 1450 to 1473,

· 184 ·

fathered three children upon his sister Isabella, and, despite a papal excommunication, staged a mock marriage to alleviate her sense of guilt" (22). Hinkle points to the illegitimate son of the elder daughter of Henri II, called "le Bon," who apparently married Anne Elisabeth of Lorraine, his half sister (76–77). See also Ragan, *Absalom* 134.

282:5 **hid somewhere to wait** See entry for 282:9.

282:9 **until the company got through making flags** Henry and Bon, for their own reasons—probably to escape being tracked down by Sutpen—don't go through the ceremonial aspects of making war, "making flags" and "telling girls farewell" (282:10), but wait until their company actually starts toward battle before joining them.

282:39 **because maybe your old man was right here too** Much of Shreve and Quentin's narrative involves testing Mr. Compson's ideas and conclusions about the events they narrate. See entry for 283:34.

283:1 **that since both of the two people who could have given him a father had declined to do it, nothing mattered** The two people may be his mother and Thomas Sutpen or his mother and the lawyer.

283:3 **since he knew now that revenge could not compensate him nor love assuage** Revenge against Sutpen would not compensate for having a father who will not acknowledge him; loving another, Judith or Henry either, cannot assuage what his father denies him.

283:9 **moving toward Shiloh** The Battle of Shiloh took place on April 6, 1962. More than 23,000 died there: 13,000 Union troops and 10,000 Confederate. Shiloh is a Hebrew word meaning "place of peace."

283:15 **Suppose I told you I did not intend to go back to her?** Bon begins taunting Henry in ways that will heighten his conflicted state about the incest and, we shall see, in ways that might push Henry to decide his, Bon's, fate for him. He will ultimately force Henry to kill him, his own form of suicide. Here, the taunt also contains the implicit message that if he doesn't go back to Judith he is also not coming back to Henry.

283:18 **and he would begin to pant, panting and panting while Bon watched him** Faulkner often connected intellectual anxiety to panting, or deep breathing. Quentin will begin to pant at the end of the novel. See 311:18.

283:23 **and who would ever know? You would not even have to know for certain yourself, because who could say but what a Yankee ball might have struck me at the exact second you pulled your trigger, or even before** In Quentin and Shreve's construction at the end of this chapter, he finally does

• 185 •

taunt Henry sufficiently to force Henry to kill him. He may prefer death to the reality of his insignificance in his father's eyes; he may consider the person he thought he was to be dead already.

283:30 **Shiloh . . . Pittsburg Landing** Pittsburg Landing is on the Tennessee River just north of Corinth, Mississippi. The site of Grant's encampment at the Battle of Shiloh, it was itself the scene of fierce fighting during the Battle of Shiloh. See entry for 283:9.

283:34 **"Because your old man was wrong here, too! He said it was Bon who was wounded, but it wasn't. Because who told him?"** At 103:4 Mr. Compson claims that Bon was wounded and that Henry carried him to safety. Here, for his own dramatic purposes, Shreve will have it that the reverse happened.

284:9 **and Henry lay there struggling and panting, with the sweat on his face and his teeth bloody inside his chewed lip, and Bon said, 'Say you do want me to go back to her. Maybe then I wont do it. Say it' and Henry lay there struggling** More of Bon's taunting of Henry as Quentin and Shreve build toward their scene at the gates of Sutpen's Hundred. While Shreve and Quentin cast Bon as passive and almost innocent, they cast Henry as "struggling" with the need to act, decide, and judge. They seem to assume that Bon's actions are determined by what Henry does or does not do.

284:40 **massed cautious accretionary battles** battles involving vast numbers of soldiers led by cautious generals who avoided direct massive confrontations in favor of a continuous series of smaller, less immediately decisive battles.

285:1 **as obsolete as Richard or Roland or du Guesclin** Probably King Richard I, the "Lion-Hearted" (1157–1199); Bertrand du Guesclin (1320–1380), French commander in the Hundred Year war. Though battle heroes in their own times, they would be mystified and completely useless in modern warfare (Ragan, *Absalom* 136).

285:9 **and on the next night be discovered by a neighbor in bed with his wife and be shot to death** A soldier who performs heroically in battle one day and survives may die the next in a situation where he is far less likely to be killed. Often in Faulkner's war narratives situations degenerate to farce.

285:29 **(—the winter of '64 now, the army retreated across Alabama, into Georgia** The italics signal the beginning of Quentin and Shreve's imaginative dual recreation of events. The projection goes through the end of the chapter except for an interruption at 288:23.

285:31 *We will either be caught and annihilated or Old Joe will extricate us* Confederate General Joseph E. Johnston, well-known for his defensive postures, a lack of aggression, throughout the War. Bon's faith in Johnston's ability to help them is thus misplaced—or perhaps a high irony.

286:25 *but we, the three—no: four of us* The three are Henry, Bon, and Judith; the fourth would be Thomas Sutpen.

286:27 *since the three of us are just illusions that he begot, and your illusions are a part of you like your bones and flesh and memory* Henry, Bon, and Judith are sired by Thomas Sutpen both as fleshly creatures and as ideas, or illusions, according to Henry. As illusions that he created, all three are as inseparable from him as are his own body and mind.

287:13 *Then for the second time he looked at the expressionless and rocklike face, at the pale boring eyes in which there was no flicker, nothing, the face in which he saw his own features, in which he saw recognition, and that was all.* The first time Bon faced Sutpen was at Sutpen's Hundred at Christmas. This time he "saw recognition" in Sutpen's face; or he saw both his own features *and also* that his father recognized him. The grammar of the sentence allows both readings.

288:9 *and Bon: 'No. He has never acknowledged me. He just warned me.'* Given what "happens" in the novel, the only time and place Sutpen could have "warned" Bon would have been in the parlor on the night that Henry and Bon leave Sutpen's Hundred. Shreve thus supplies some content to that meeting that may or may not have been part of the blow-up on that Christmas Eve.

288:32 **And she didn't tell you in so many words because she was still keeping that secret for the sake of the man who had been her father too as well as for the sake of the family which no longer existed** On the one hand, Clytie has kept the secret of her half brother Henry's existence in the house in order to keep peace in what was left of her family. In this context, the word "secret" is highly charged: it could have to do with Bon's race and the novel's gothic surround may suggest incest as the family "secret."

288:39 **when they brought Bon's body in and Judith took from his pocket the metal case she had given him with her picture in it** That is, when she gave him the metal case, she gave it to him with her picture in it. According to 295:24, Bon replaces her picture with that of his octoroon wife and child. We do not need to decide which version is the correct one: they are both correct according to the different narrators' needs.

289:13 **it was not about herself but was about whatever it was that was upstairs, that she had kept hidden up there for almost four years** Clytie has kept Henry in the house, hiding him and the secrets that will explain the Sutpen saga.

289:15 **and she didn't tell you in the actual words because even in the terror she kept the secret; nevertheless she told you, or at least all of a sudden you knew** To the very end Clytie attempts to protect Henry; she does not tell Quentin that he is upstairs, but Quentin divines the fact based on her reaction to his presence.

289:26 **compounded each of both yet either neither** language derived from Shakespeare's "The Phoenix and the Turtle."

289:28 ***bivouac fires burning in a pine grove*** Quentin and Shreve's voices here finally meld into one unvoiced imaginative vision, creating a dramatic scene during which they imagine that Sutpen supplies Henry with the information that Bon is part Negro, a new piece of "information" that he has somehow, for some reason, mysteriously withheld from Henry until this moment, all else (the war) having failed to stop Bon's apparent attempt to marry Judith. The "fact" of Bon's black blood is thus no more factual than any other "fact" in the novel, but rather a dramatic device, a clincher, which will finally supply a satisfactory motive to explain why Henry kills Bon. All other explanations the various narrators have offered, in Mr. Compson's words, "just [do] not explain" (83:21). Bon's putative mixed blood lets Quentin and Shreve move immediately to their climax at the gates of Sutpen's Hundred—no more wrangling or parsing out of possibility and projection: race explains what nothing else will. A consistent but critically marginal line of commentary has noted the absence of any factual basis for Bon's racial identity. Lind calls it Quentin and Shreve's "conjuring" (897). Adams says that there is "nothing even as concrete as hearsay" to justify the boys' claim that Bon is part Negro: "The authority for the 'fact' of Bon's Negro blood is therefore the whole tissue of hypothetical reasoning which Quentin and Shreve have woven and which Shreve in particular has pieced out with purely fanciful fabrications" (199). Kartiganer calls the conjecture that race explains everything the novel's "great imaginative leap" (98). See also Schoenberg (81), Steinberg (61), Levin (137), Parr (160), Hagin (215), and Aswell (69).

Quentin and Shreve's italicized, imagined confrontation between father and son takes the form of a film script, a "treatment" for a film, perhaps; we may even imagine that for this scene Faulkner adopted James Joyce's use of the dash instead of quotation marks to designate speech precisely in order to "silence" the text as much as possible, even more than the italics seem to, to remove all traces of spoken language from Quentin and Shreve's narration (Urgo). Lurie notes that throughout the book Faulkner describes Quentin as "seeing," "watching," or "seeming to see" as he listens to Rosa (10, 17), the narrator (109), his father (157), and himself (308). This passage, building toward the dramatic climax at the gates of Sutpen's Hundred, finally melds narration with wordless vision.

291:1 *moved by what of close blood which in the reflex instant arrogates and reconciles even though it does not yet (perhaps never will) forgive, who stands now while his father holds his face between both hands, looking at it* The narrators imagine an almost tender moment between father and son, Henry reconciled to his father's will, even though he "*does not yet (perhaps never will) forgive*" his father for his treatment of Charles Bon. Sutpen holds Henry's face in his hands, "*looking at it*", issuing the very recognition he denies Bon.

292:17 —*He must not marry her, Henry. His mother's father told me that her mother had been a Spanish woman. I believed him; it was not until after he was born that I found out that his mother was part negro* These events would have occurred on Haiti, on Sutpen's first attempt to fulfill his design. The "fact" of Bon's Negro heritage negates Henry's sympathy for the marriage between him and their sister. Neither Mr. Compson nor Rosa Coldfield nor General Compson knew this: all of this "information" is a fabrication, a fabulation created by Quentin and Shreve—there is no possible source for the *fact* that Bon is part Negro. However, Bon's Negro blood is the one fact that can explain the fratricide. Henry, for his part, is surprised to find out that "*it's the miscegenation, not the incest, which you cant bear*" (293:32), as in Bon's experience mixed racial backgrounds are common and not objectionable.

294:35 —*You are my brother.*
—*No I'm not. I'm the nigger that's going to sleep with your sister. Unless you stop me, Henry.* Bon provokes Henry to kill him, as Thomas Sutpen provokes Wash to kill him. The exchange encapsulates the drama created by Quentin and Shreve to explain the murder: black men and white men do not recognize themselves as brothers.

295:10 **"And he never slipped away," Shreve said.** The return to roman type signals the end of the projected scene and the return to the Harvard dialogue.

295:12 maybe he even went to Henry and said, 'I'm going, Henry' and maybe they left together and rode side by side dodging Yankee patrols all the way back to Mississippi Bon and Henry are AWOL. Not clear is why Thomas Sutpen gives this task to Henry—the task of killing his own brother. Given the power Sutpen has as commander and as father, it seems unnecessary. But Quentin and Shreve elide this question in fealty to what is perhaps the one incontrovertible "fact" of the entire novel, the event toward which all the narration has been moving, Henry's killing of Bon at the gates of Sutpen's Hundred.

295:24 holding the metal case she had given him with her picture in it but that didn't have her picture in it now but that of the octoroon and the kid For their slightly sentimental purposes and in line with their new-found sympathy for Bon as a tragic hero, Quentin and Shreve propose that, contra Rosa, it's not Judith's picture but that of Bon's New Orleans octoroon wife and child, put there to explain to Judith that he, Bon, is not worth her love. See entry for 288:39.

295:26 And your old man wouldn't know about that too: why the black son of a bitch should have taken her picture out and put the octoroon's picture in, so he invented a reason for it A curious, even shocking passage, for Shreve's obscenity: almost immediately after inventing Bon's blackness in the previous scene in Sutpen's tent, and in spite of Quentin and Shreve's growing sympathy for Bon (see entry for 295:24), Shreve calls Bon a "black son of a bitch." It's not clear whether the phrase comes from his own latent racism, from his mordant sense of humor, or from his imitation of what he thinks a Southerner—Mr. Compson—might say under the circumstances. Perhaps it's Shreve's adolescent distancing from emotional attachment, a characteristic he displays throughout his narration. In any case, what he describes— Bon's replacing Judith's picture in the locket with one of the octoroon and child—harsh as it seems, might well be Bon's act of kindness to ease Judith's pain at his loss by making himself seem unworthy of her love and therefore more easily forgotten, and so would certainly seem to belie his being a son of a bitch. As important to Quentin and Shreve as the invention of this "better" reason is the fact that it revises what Mr. Compson thought about the matter.

295:36 *I was no good; do not grieve for me* By placing the photograph of his octoroon wife and their child in Judith's metal case, Bon makes certain that if Henry kills him, Judith will get his final message. The detail raises Bon to the level of a tragic figure in a sentimental novel, in Shreve and Quentin's imagination, and locates, finally, the love they have been looking for in this chapter.

CHAPTER IX

296:1 **At first, in bed in the dark** It is not at all clear what Quentin and Shreve's sleeping arrangements are; perhaps, doubtless even likely, Quentin and Shreve share a room with two single beds. But the text's failure to specify allows some speculation that they are in the same bed. At 296:22 Quentin begins "to jerk all over, violently and uncontrollably until he could even hear the bed, until even Shreve felt it." It might be possible for Shreve to "hear" Quentin's shaking in bed, but hardly likely for him to "feel" it if they are sleeping across the room from one another. The setting for the final chapter thus provides more suggestive evidence for a homoerotic reading of *Absalom*.

296:11 **Bayard attenuated forty miles (it was forty miles, wasn't it?); out of the wilderness proud honor semestrial regurgitant** Bayard is a spirited and fabulous horse in the French *Chansons de Geste*; Faulkner used the name for members of the Sartoris family in *Flags in the Dust* and *The Unvanquished*. Apparently, though, here Shreve means Bon. His language vaguely parodies the chivalric romance from which "Bayard" derives, and he seems to be commenting on Bon's *geste* or romantic *gesture* of exchanging Judith's picture for one of the octoroon and her son, the gesture which ended chapter VIII. He has stretched himself away from the university in the wilderness (attenuated forty miles), a proud man full of honor, doing a valiant thing. "Semestrial" is at best Faulkner's coinage or Shreve's mistake or parody of the language; at worst it is Faulkner's typescript mistake (on the holograph he wrote "semesterial"), though the Corrected Text concluded that the typescript word was his intention. In any case it's not clear what "semestrial (or even semesterial) regurgitant" means, though it would appear to suggest that Bon—and perhaps implying even the doomed University Grays—got their ideas of heroism and chivalry from a university, not from life; and that a university, structured on semesters, regurgitated (vomited) such romantic "heroes" in to the world, where they cause more harm than the heroes of their books do.

296:31 **what are you doing that for?** Quentin is shaking.

297:15 **you wont be anything but a descendant of a long line of colonels killed in Pickett's charge at Manassas** Shreve perhaps deliberately confuses the battles of Manassas with the Battle of Gettysburg. Quentin corrects him in the next line.

297:34 **Do you?** Shreve repeats his statement that ended two paragraphs before: "You dont even know about [Rosa]." Quentin admits he doesn't, for all his insistence, at 297:26 and throughout, that she is Miss Rosa, not Aunt Rosa.

298:37 **the girl who had been a child when he saw her last** Milly Jones, Wash's granddaughter.

299:34 **That's what I have got to find out** Rosa seems to indicate here that she doesn't actually know who or what is hidden at Sutpen's Hundred. If she is telling the truth, it's conceivable that since she never saw Bon's body and Henry disappeared immediately after the shooting she might believe either Henry or Bon, or both of them, could be hiding out there. Her statement, at 301:39, that she is Ellen's "sister, her only living heir," suggests that she thinks that Henry is dead and that it might be Bon hiding there, and that because she is therefore the "only living heir," she has a right to enter her own property. See entry for 301:40.

301:31 **Why, she's not afraid at all. It's something. But she's not afraid.** We might have gotten the impression from Rosa's "whimpering pants" (300:15) and her "steady whimpering, almost a moaning, sound" (301:20) that accompany them toward Sutpen's Hundred that Rosa is indeed afraid of something. The fact that Quentin doesn't read her that way allows us to wonder what else might cause the panting. If she believes that Charles Bon might be "hiding" there, perhaps her response is sexual, since Bon was the animating figure of her budding but thwarted adolescence.

301:40 **her only living heir** She is one heir; Henry is another. The question here is whether Rosa knows that it's Henry in the house; if she does, she's lying. See entry for 299:34.

302:26 **the room was empty; the echo of his voice** At Sutpen's Hundred, Quentin fulfills the narrator's description of him at the novel's beginning: "his very body was an empty hall echoing with sonorous defeated names; he was not a being, an entity, he was a commonwealth. He was "a barracks filled with stubborn back-looking ghosts" (9:16).

303:3 **he** Unless he knows or suspects that somebody else lives in the house, Quentin probably means Jim Bond, the Negro known to live there with Clytie.

303:10 **square-ended saw chunk** a contrivance for a lathe or saw. It would be a steadying piece of wood large and clunky enough to serve as a table stand.

303:27 **"Dont you go up there, Rosie" and Miss Coldfield struck the hand away and went on** This scene reflects almost precisely the earlier scene when Rosa tried to storm up those stairs to see the unfolding of the tragedy in Judith's room (see entry for 114:31 and Raper 22).

304:7 **Whatever he done, me and Judith and him have paid it out** It's still not clear to Quentin who is in the room; nor is it clear precisely what Clytie means, if she means anything coherent, since Judith has long since been dead, Henry has been gone, and she has lived at Sutpen's Hundred as a recluse, with only Jim Bond as companion. Perhaps she simply means that they've "paid" for Henry's or even Sutpen's sin by being out of sight and out of mind.

304:14 **a hulking young light-colored negro man in clean faded overalls and shirt** Jim Bond.

304:26 **It's not shock. And it never has been fear. Can it be triumph?** After seeing Henry for himself, Quentin understands (at 304:33) that what he sees in Rosa's face is anything but triumph, no matter what either of them thought she hoped to gain from the trip to Sutpen's Hundred.

305:14 **"Help me up! You aint any Sutpen!"** Rosa puts Jim Bond in what she considers his "place." If Charles Bon is Thomas Sutpen's son, Jim Bond is Thomas Sutpen's great-grandson. If Rosa knows this lineage to be a fact, she here displays more knowledge of the family than she has heretofore given any evidence of. More likely, she is simply asserting that even though he lives at Sutpen's Hundred he is still of the serving class, and therefore must obey an order from a white person.

305:16 **When he stopped the buggy at her gate** After the almost interminable trip out to Sutpen's Hundred and what must have been a lot of talk about the Sutpen family, Quentin and Rosa, incredibly, seem to be silent on the way home. Afterwards, they clearly hurry home, to get away from each other and from the Sutpens.

306:11 **he said 'I have been asleep' it was all the same, there was no difference: waking or sleeping he walked down that upper hall between the scaling walls and beneath the cracked ceiling** Quentin, in bed in his Harvard dormitory room, recalls the night when he lay in bed in his Mississippi home reliving his encounter with Henry Sutpen. The encounter is so integral a part of his consciousness now that "waking or sleeping it was the same" (306:18 and 22).

306:24 ***And you are——?*** This insubstantial account of Henry and Quentin's conversation is a circular, dreamlike representation of what, given what Quentin learned that evening, must have been a longer conversation. The conversation as Quentin represents it moves into and then out of Henry's reasons for coming home with the precision and balance of a ritual. The confrontation with Henry clearly has unmoored Quentin emotionally, perhaps psychologically. The text almost certainly does not pretend to represent this "dialogue" as exactly what Quentin and Henry said to each other but rather as the distilled essence of the encounter's effect on Quentin. The scene presents itself as the emotional center of *Absalom*, the novel's dramatic climax. But, as throughout, it actually tells us nothing but what we can tease out from the formalized, ritualized, visual form in which the authorial narrator presents it. It's pretty much a conversation with a skeleton, at the center of which is the question, "To die?" and the answer, "Yes. To die."

307:4 **Nevermore of peace. Nevermore of peace. Nevermore. Nevermore. Nevermore.** The allusion to Poe's "The Raven" invokes a gothic literary context that reflects Quentin's education and takes us back to the novel's opening pages. See entry for 5:26.

307:8 **that hating is like drink or drugs and she had used it so long that she did not dare risk cutting off the supply, destroying the source, the very poppy's root and seed?** Coming on the heels on the allusion in the previous lines to Poe's "The Raven," this passage may help us understand the narrator's sense, on the novel's first page, that Sutpen appears to Rosa, "as though by outraged recapitulation evoked, quiet, attentive and harmless" (5:25), as a function of her need to keep the hatred alive, just as the narrator of "The Raven" asks the dark bird questions which the one word the raven can speak, "nevermore," will respond to adequately, to help him feed his grief, to keep it alive.

307:33 **he, Quentin, could see that too, though he had not been there** Here and throughout the remainder of the novel, Quentin manufactures the scene of Rosa's final assault on Sutpen's Hundred. We have no way of judging the accuracy of his depiction, but we may well believe what he says, if we believe Quentin and Shreve's depictions of her throughout the novel.

308:11 **something human since the bellowing was in human speech, even though the reason for it would not have seemed to be** Jim Bond's wail is not for the burning house or for any material, articulate reason, but for something profound and ineffable.

309:38 **It was becoming quite distinct; he would be able to decipher the words soon, in a moment; even almost now** Quentin has reached a level of comprehension where he may attend to the words his father has written to him on the occasion of Rosa Coldfield's death. His father's letter, which began at 144:13, resumes at 310:7.

310:14 ***the one*** Thomas Sutpen.

310:15 ***the other*** Rosa Coldfield.

310:22 **Charles Bon and his mother to get rid of old Tom** by her manipulating Charles to the contact with Sutpen through Henry.

310:23 **Charles Bon and the octoroon to get rid of Judith** by putting obstacles in the way of Bon and Judith's marriage.

310:24 **Charles Bon's mother and Charles Bon's grandmother got rid of Charles Bon** Shreve is a bit more enigmatic here than in the previous two entries, since Bon's maternal grandmother makes no appearance in the novel. If he is referring to his earlier discussion of what harridans mothers become when they have to raise their sons without fathers, he can only mean the genealogical inheritance from generations of harridan mothers and grandmothers who made Bon into the kind of man that would commit the sort of suicide Bon committed. If, on the other hand, Shreve is convinced that Bon is Sutpen's son, then perhaps he is referring to the heritage of white trash that Sutpen's mother lived in. The grammatical structure implies that it is his mother's mother to whom he refers. If there was something in Bon's mother that tainted Bon (i.e., black blood) she would have gotten it from *her* mother, possibly. This has thus become a tale not of action and merit but of inheritance and, we might say, fantasies of essence.

310:33 **You've got one nigger left. One nigger Sutpen left. Of course you cant catch him and you dont even always see him and you never will be able to use him.** Shreve speaks of Jim Bond both as historical character and as emblematic of what to whites is the elusive mind of the African American. In fact Quentin and Shreve have played a game of "catch the nigger" when they use Bon's supposed black blood to explain the actions which, absent the black blood, were otherwise incomprehensible.

311:7 **I think that in time the Jim Bonds are going to conquer the western hemisphere. Of course it wont quite be in our time and of course as they spread toward the poles they will bleach out again like the rabbits and the birds do, so they wont show up so sharp against the snow. But it will still be Jim Bond; and so in a few thousand years, I who regard you will**

• 195 •

also have sprung from the loins of African kings. One of the most enigmatical and perplexing passages in all of Faulkner. As the races intermingle, the offspring inevitably will "bleach out" until there are no longer visible differences between the races, but there will always be ("it will still be") a Jim Bond lurking genetically under all the whiteness. Thus "difference" will disappear—"I who regard you will also have sprung from the loins of African kings." One would be tempted to think that that would be a good thing; but that's precisely what white people fear, the disappearance of that difference, that blackness, that defines whiteness as good; whites can thus never overcome the fear that that one genetic drop of black blood will someday assert itself in the birth of a child. If Quentin and Shreve have "used" race to explain the Sutpen history, then what Shreve asserts is that one day we'll see that race differentiation cannot continue as a viable social system, not because races have intermingled but rather because they've been falsely differentiated. Genetically, then, "African kings" are at the top of our genealogies. Shreve here thus defends the invention of "black blood" to explain Henry's murder of Bon. Jim Bond is thus the one drop of black blood that will never disappear: "Of course you cant catch him and you dont even always see him and you never will be able to use him. But you've got him there still. You still hear him at night sometimes. Dont you?" (310:34).

311:14 **Why do you hate the South?**
"**I dont hate it,**" Quentin said, quickly, at once, immediately; "**I dont hate it,**" he said. *I dont hate it* **he thought, panting in the cold air** Like others of Faulkner's novels, *Absalom* ends not with a narrative resolution of the complications that the plot has generated, a tying up of loose ends, but with an emotional resolution that compounds, complicates, and even regenerates the novel's tensions. Given what has been for the most part a fragmented family history *nearly all* of which has been a fabrication and a good deal of which Quentin and Shreve have probably rehearsed on previous occasions—likely from the moment Quentin arrived at Harvard—Shreve's question is almost a non-sequitur which fairly explosively raises the narrative's stakes from that family history into a history somehow emblematic of the South. Scholars have of course debated the extent to which *Absalom* is "about" the South, Cleanth Brooks famously arguing that because Sutpen is from poor white stock in *West* Virginia he is not one of the Southern aristocrats who imported the slaves and caused all the trouble. Shreve's question seems curiously aggressive,

perhaps even meanspirited, and it's not completely clear what motivates either its aggression or its content; but it seems to emerge from the previous several paragraphs' emphasis on the racial content of their mutual discovery of the "real" reason Henry killed Charles Bon, and of Shreve's rather flip but dead serious reduction of the entire Sutpen family chronicle, Jim Bond, to that one inescapable drop of black blood that white people fear infects their own purity. Is the problem of racial purity what Quentin, so clearly in denial, doesn't hate about the South? Does Shreve's portrait of a miscegenous world a thousand years from now, in which all visible racial differences have disappeared, terrify Quentin? Do he and Shreve postpone considering race as Henry's motive because they simply do not think of it or because it is so powerful they cannot face it until the end? These are questions the form of the novel's ending insists upon asking but refuses to answer.

CHRONOLOGY AND GENEALOGY

The question of the Chronology's and the Genealogy's relationship to the novel "proper" is a very interesting one, perhaps essential to the novel's meaning, since they contain information that both does not appear in the novel proper and that contradicts the information in the novel proper. Are these "appendices" in fact appendicular material designed to help readers work their way through a very complex novel or are they rather integral parts of the novel itself and to be read as such? That is, in a novel full of contending narrative voices that create and discard "fact" according to the needs of their narrative, do the Chronology and the Genealogy provide yet another voice, a putatively factual one (because in a form, a list, that at least presents itself as factual because it seems to have no crosses to bear, no interpretive agenda to advance) against which readers can and should measure the complications of the preceding pages? Are they an integral part of the novel? Should we read them as we read the newspaper reports of the "mutiny" and its consequences at the end of Melville's *Billy Budd*? Except for Ragan's extended and very useful discussion (*Absalom* 163–78) the Chronology and Genealogy have garnered very little critical commentary. Duncan Aswell, for example, suggests that the chronology "should make us question whether we have any of the facts straight about Sutpen's legends" (81–82) and proposes that "The effect of the Genealogy is to evoke the capriciousness of human experience and the arbitrariness of structuring it in ordered works of art" (82).

The Corrected Text treats these materials as guides to, but not parts of, the novel proper. As published in the 1936 first edition, the Chronology contains several discrepancies from the novel proper: for example, Ellen, according to the Chronology, was born in 1818, but the tombstone in the novel gives her birth as 1817; in the Chronology Charles Bon was born in 1829, the evidence of the novel suggests 1831. There is an early manuscript and an early typescript version of the Chronology; nothing remains of the Genealogy but the published version, and neither Chronology nor Genealogy is connected to the novel's extant manuscript, typescript, or galley proofs. Given Faulkner's many experiments with novelistic structure, it is certainly possible that discrepancies between these chronologies and the narrative proper are deliberate. Yet the editor of the Corrected Text was persuaded to make the Chronology's "facts" agree with the "facts" of the novel, when it was possible to do so, believing that the evidence suggests that these pieces should be treated as aids to the reader of a very complex novel. Two pieces of information are crucial. First is the outright error in the Chronology which lists the fall of 1910 as the date on which Quentin and Rosa Coldfield go out to the Sutpen house and find Henry there: this is unquestionably an error. Perhaps more telling is that according to the novel proper, Judith Sutpen and Charles E. St. Valery Bon die, in 1884, of yellow fever; according to the 1936 published Chronology, they die of smallpox. The holograph version of the Chronology says simply that they "died." In the holograph manuscript of the novel, they die of smallpox, as in the published Chronology. Page 258 of the typescript setting copy, however, shows that Faulkner, following the manuscript, originally typed "smallpox" and at least the next word, then went back, x-ed out "smallpox" and typed in "yellow fever" above. He did *not*, however, go back and change the manuscript or the Chronology to agree with his revised thinking (Polk, "Where the Comma Goes" 17–18).

The evidence, then, suggests, though of course does not prove, that Faulkner manufactured the Chronology for himself—he put *Absalom* aside and wrote *Pylon* because, he said, it had gotten too "inchoate"—to help him keep straight all the dates and relationships; then he discarded it, for his own purposes, as he wrote past a particular date. Someone, perhaps at Random House, suggested that it be appended to the book and Faulkner allowed it to be printed without correcting or updating it; and apparently none of the original editors, for all their wholesale revision, had read it or the novel closely enough to be aware of the discrepancies. See Polk ("Where the Comma Goes" 16–18), Parker, and Dalziel.

312:11 **Charles Bon born, Haiti. Sutpen learns his wife has negro blood, repudiates her and child** Much hinges on this assertion since the only thing resembling evidence in the novel proper, the inscription on Bon's tombstone, claims that he was born in New Orleans. If the tombstone is correct, then Bon clearly cannot be Sutpen's son from Haiti. On the other hand, Judith, who installed the tombstone and wrote the epitaph, might have assumed that he was born in New Orleans *or* she might well have had her own reasons, not supplied in the novel, for wanting posterity to think that he was from New Orleans rather than Haiti, though the novel proper supplies no evidence that she knows much more about him than that he met Henry at the University of Mississippi and lived in New Orleans.

314:4 **Married (I) Eulalia Bon** Here and 314:8 are the only places Faulkner or any of the narrators supply Sutpen's Haitian wife—and possibly Bon's mother—with a name. Connolly notes that the name Eulalia, derived from Greek, means "fair of speed" or "sweetly spoken" and wonders whether, under the circumstances Quentin and Shreve create in their narrative, this is a "Faulknerian irony" (261).

314:13 **became engaged to Judith** The novel proper supplies no real evidence that they were actually engaged.

314:29 **Became engaged to Charles Bon** The novel proper does not confirm this as a fact or as anything but Ellen's and Rosa's fantasy.

315:25 **SHREVLIN McCANNON** In *The Sound and the Fury* Mrs. Bland calls him Mr. MacKenzie (989).

WORKS CITED

Adams, Richard P. *Faulkner: Myth and Motion*. Princeton: Princeton UP, 1968.
Aswell, Duncan. "The Puzzling Design of *Absalom, Absalom!*" *Kenyon Review* 30 (1968): 67–84.
Bible, The. King James version.
Blotner, Joseph. *Faulkner: A Biography*. New York: Random House, 1984.
Brewer, Karen S. Email communication with the authors, September 3, 2008.
Brooks, Cleanth. "*Absalom, Absalom!*: The Definition of Innocence." *Sewanee Review* 59 (Autumn 1951): 543–58.
———. *William Faulkner: The Yoknapatawpha Country*. New Haven: Yale UP, 1963.
Brown, Calvin. *A Glossary of Faulkner's South*. New Haven: Yale UP, 1976.
Brown, William R. "Mr. Stark on Mr. Strawson on Referring." *Language and Style: An International Journal* 7:3 (Summer 1974): 219–24.
Campbell, Harry Modean. "Faulkner's *Absalom, Absalom!*" *Explicator* 7 (December 1948), Item 24.
Connolly, Thomas E. "Point of View in Faulkner's *Absalom, Absalom!*" *Modern Fiction Studies* 27 (Summer 1981): 266–72.
Dalziel, Pamela. "*Absalom, Absalom!*: The Extension of Dialogic Form." *Mississippi Quarterly* 45.3 (1992): 277–94.
Davis, Robert Con, ed. *The Fictional Father: Lacanian Readings of the Text*. Amherst: U of Massachusetts P, 1981.
———. "The Symbolic Father in Yoknapatawpha County." *Journal of Narrative Technique*, 10 (Winter 1980): 39–55.
Davis, Thadious. *Faulkner's "Negro": Art and the Southern Context*. Baton Rouge: Louisiana State UP, 1983.
Donaldson, Susan V. "Visibility, Haitian Hauntings, and Southern Borders." *Global Contexts, Local Literatures: The New Southern Studies*. Ed. Kathryn McKee and Annette Trefzer. Special Issue. *American Literature*. 78 (2006): 714–16.
Doyle, Don H. *Faulkner's County: The Historical Roots of Yoknapatawpha*. Chapel Hill: U of North Carolina P, 2001.
Duvall, John N. *Faulkner's Marginal Couple: Invisible, Outlaw, and Unspeakable Communities*. Austin: U of Texas P, 1990.
Faulkner, William. *Absalom, Absalom!* 1936. *Faulkner: Novels 1936–1940*. New York: Library of America, 1990. 1–315.
———. *Absalom, Absalom! Typescript Setting Copy. William Faulkner Manuscripts 13:* ed. Noel Polk. New York: Garland, 1987.

———. *Faulkner in the University.* Ed. Frederick L. Gwynn and Joseph L. Blotner. Charlottesville: UP of Virginia, 1959.

———. *Flags in the Dust* (1973; as *Sartoris* 1929). *Faulkner: Novels 1926–1929.* New York: Library of America, 2006. 541–875.

———. *The Hamlet.* (1940). *Faulkner: Novels 1936–1940.* New York: Library of America, 1990. 729–1075.

———. *The Marionettes.* 1922. With Introduction and Textual Apparatus by Noel Polk. Charlottesville: The Bibliographical Society of the University of Virginia by the University Press of Virginia, 1977.

———. *Requiem for a Nun* (1951). *Faulkner: Novels 1942–1954.* New York: Library of America, 1994. 471–664.

———. *The Sound and the Fury.* (1929). *Faulkner: Novels 1926–1929.* New York: Library of America, 2006. 877–1124.

Fowler, Doreen. *Faulkner: The Return of the Repressed.* Charlottesville: UP of Virginia, 1997.

Godden, Richard. *Fictions of Labor: William Faulkner and the South's Long Revolution.* Cambridge: Cambridge UP, 1997.

Guetti, James. *The Limits of Metaphor: A Study of Melville, Conrad, and Faulkner.* Ithaca: Cornell UP, 1967.

Gwin, Minrose C. *The Feminine and Faulkner: Reading (Beyond) Sexual Difference.* Knoxville: U of Tennessee P, 1990.

Hagin, John. "Fact and Fancy in *Absalom, Absalom!*" *College English* 24 (December 1962), 215–18.

Hawkins, E. O., "Faulkner's 'Duke John of Lorraine.'" *American Notes and Queries* 4 (October 1965): 22.

Hinkle, James. "Answers to some of Calvin Brown's Questions." *The Faulkner Journal* 1 (Spring 1986): 75–77.

Hodgson, John A. "'Logical Sequence and Continuity': Some Observations on the Typographical and Structural Consistency of *Absalom, Absalom!*" *American Literature* 43 (March 1971): 97–107.

Holder, Alan. "The Doomed Design: William Faulkner's *Absalom, Absalom!*" *The Imagined Past: Portrayals of Our History in Modern American Literature.* Lewisburg, PA: Bucknell UP, 1980. 53–72.

Hönnighausen, Lothar. *William Faulkner: The Art of Stylization in His Early Graphic and Literary Work.* Cambridge: Cambridge UP, 1987.

———. *Faulkner: Masks and Metaphors.* Jackson: UP of Mississippi, 1997.

Irwin, John T. *Doubling and Incest/Repetition and Revenge: A Speculative Reading of Faulkner.* Baltimore: Johns Hopkins UP, 1975.

Johnson, Tim. Email to the authors, October 2007.

Jones, Norman W. "Coming Out through History's Hidden Love Letters in *Absalom, Absalom!*" *American Literature.* 76:2 (June 2004): 339–66.

Kartiganer, Donald M. *The Fragile Thread: The Meaning of Form in Faulkner's Novels.* Amherst: U of Massachusetts P, 1979.

Kinnet, John. *Cabaret101: A History of Cabaret* (2003). http://www.musicals101.com/cabaret.htm (accessed February 3, 2007).

Kinney, Arthur. *Faulkner's Narrative Poetics: Style as Vision.* Amherst: U of Massachusetts P, 1975.

Ladd, Barbara. *Nationalism and the Color Line in George W. Cable, Mark Twain, and William Faulkner*. Baton Rouge: Louisiana State UP, 1996.

Langford, Gerald. *Faulkner's Revision of* Absalom, Absalom!: *A Collation of the Manuscript and the Published Book*. Austin: U of Texas P, 1971.

Levin, David. "*Absalom, Absalom!: The Problem of Re-Creating History*." In *Defense of Historical Literature: Essays on American History, Autobiography, Drama, and Fiction*. New York: Hill and Wang, 1967. 118–39.

Levin, Lynn Gartrell. "The Heroic Design." *Faulkner's Heroic Design: The Yoknapatawpha Novels*. Athens: U of Georgia P, 1976. 7–54.

Lind, Ilse Dusoir. "The Design and Meaning of *Absalom, Absalom!*" *PMLA* 70 (December 1955): 887–912.

Lockyer, Judith. *Ordered by Words: Language and Narration in the Novels of William Faulkner*. Carbondale: Southern Illinois UP, 1991.

Lurie, Peter. *Vision's Immanence: Faulkner, Film, and the Popular Imagination*. Baltimore: Johns Hopkins UP, 2004.

McDaniel, Linda Elkins. *Flags in the Dust* (Annotations). New York: Garland, 1991.

Matthews, John T. *The Play of Faulkner's Language*. Ithaca: Cornell UP, 1982.

MacLure, Millar. "Allegories of Innocence." *Dalhousie Review* 40:2 (Summer 1960): 145–55.

Muhlenfeld, Elisabeth, ed. *William Faulkner's* Absalom, Absalom!: *A Critical Casebook*. New York: Garland, 1984.

———. "'We have waited long enough.'" 1978. Muhlenfeld 173–88.

Owada, Eiko. *Faulkner, Haiti, and Questions of Imperialism*. Tokyo: Sairyusha, 2002.

Parker, Robert Dale. *Faulkner and the Novelistic Imagination*. Urbana: U of Illinois P, 1985.

Parr, Susan Resnick. "The Fourteenth Image of the Blackbird: Another Look at Truth in *Absalom, Absalom!*" *Arizona Quarterly* 35 (1979): 153–64.

Pitavy, François. "The Narrative Voice and Function of Shreve." Muhlenfeld 189–205.

Poirier, Richard. "'Strange Gods' in Jefferson, Mississippi." 1951. Muhlenfeld 1–22.

Polk, Noel. "The Artist as Cuckold." *Children of the Dark House: Text and Context in Faulkner*. Jackson: UP of Mississippi, 1997. 137–65.

———. "Introduction." *William Faulkner's The Marionettes*. Charlottesville: Published for The Bibliographical Society of the U of Virginia by the UP of Virginia, 1977. ix–xxii.

———. "Where the Comma Goes: Editing William Faulkner." *Children*, 3–21.

Ragan, David Paul. *William Faulkner's* Absalom, Absalom! *A Critical Study*. Ann Arbor: UMI Research P, 1987.

———. *Absalom, Absalom!* New York: Garland, 1991.

Raper, J. R. "Meaning Called to Life: Alogical Structure in *Absalom, Absalom!*" *Southern Humanities Review* 5 (Winter 1971): 9–23.

Ringold, Francine. "The Metaphysics of Yoknapatawpha County: 'Airy Space for Your Delirium.'" *Hartford Studies in Literature* 8 (1977): 223–40.

Roudiez, Leon S. "*Absalom, Absalom!*: The Significance of Contradictions." *Minnesota Review* 17 (Fall 1981): 58–78.

Rosenzweig, Paul. "The Narrative Frames in *Absalom, Absalom!*: Faulkner's involuted Commentary on Art." *Arizona Quarterly* xx (1979): 135–52.

Ross, Stephen M. *Fiction's Inexhaustible Voice: Speech and Writing in Faulkner*. Athens: U of Georgia P, 1989.

Schoenberg, Estella. *Old Tales and Talking: Quentin Compson in William Faulkner's* Absalom, Absalom!. Jackson: UP of Mississippi, 1977.

Schrank, Bernice. "Patterns of Reversal in *Absalom, Absalom!*" *The Dalhousie Review* 54 (Winter 1975): 648–66.

Scott, Arthur L. "The Myriad Perspectives of *Absalom, Absalom!*" *American Quarterly* 6:3 (Fall 1954): 210–20.

Sewell, Richard. *The Vision of Tragedy*. New Haven: Yale UP, 1959.

Sowder, William. "Colonel Thomas Sutpen as Existential Hero." *American Literature* 33 (January 1962): 485–99.

Singleton, Marvin K. "Personae at Law and in Equity: The Unity of Faulkner's *Absalom, Absalom!*" *Papers on English Language and Literature* 3(Fall 1967): 354–70.

Steinberg, Aaron. "*Absalom, Absalom!: The Irretrievable Bon*." *College Language Association Journal* 9 (September 1965): 61–67.

Trelease, Allen W. *White Terror: The Ku Klux Klan Conspiracy and Southern Reconstruction*. New York: Harper & Row, 1971.

Urgo, Joseph. "*Absalom, Absalom!: The Movie*." *American Literature* 62.1 (Fall 1992): 354–70.

Whan, Edgar. "*Absalom, Absalom*! as Gothic Myth." *Perspective* 3 (Autumn 1952), 192–201. www.sonofthesouth.net

Zoellner, Robert H. "Faulkner's Prose Style in *Absalom, Absalom!*" *American Literature* 30 (January 1959): 486–502.

INDEX

Abraham, 177
Absalom, 3
Adams, Richard P., 188
Aegisthus, 14, 89
Agamemnon, 14, 89, 90
Alabama convention, 184
American dream, 112
Anne Elizabeth of Lorraine, 185
Apollo, 14, 89
Apology, The, 112
Artist figure, 20, 21
Aswell, Duncan, 197–98

Bayard, Pierre du Terrail, 85
Beardsley, Aubrey, 100
Beelzebub, 91
Biblical references: Absalom, 3; Abraham, 177; I Corinthians, 70; Genesis, 7, 102, 152; Ham, 102, 103; Isaac, 177; King David, 3; Luke, 102; Mark, 54; Matthew, 107, 153; Moloch, 59; 2 Samuel, 3
Brewer, Karen, 87
Brooks, Cleanth, 112, 196
Brown, Calvin, 22, 34, 121–22
Bull Run, Battle of, 49–50

Cadmus, 30
Campbell, Harry Modean, 36
Capitalism, 125
"Carcassonne," 74
Cassandra, 14, 30, 89, 90, 97
Chansons de Geste, 191
"Chronology," 197–99
Civil War, the, 10, 51–54, 55, 81

Class consciousness, 17–18, 24, 37, 91, 112–14, 116, 117, 119, 120–22, 123–24, 138, 174, 193
Clytemnestra, 14, 30, 89, 90, 97
Coleridge, Samuel Taylor, "The Rime of the Ancient Mariner," 5, 157
Communism, 125, 140
Connolly, Thomas E., 199
Conrad, Joseph, *Heart of Darkness*, 129

Davis, Jefferson, 89
Davis, Robert Con, 62
Davis, Thadious, 12, 63
Decoration Day, 178
Domination theme, 17
Du Guesclin, Betrand, 186

Ecological themes, 7, 110, 134, 137–38
Eleventh Mississippi infantry, 50

Fable, A, 146
Fascism, 125, 140
Fatalism, 14, 15, 16, 19–20, 33, 41, 46, 50–51, 60, 66, 69, 73, 77, 83, 90, 112, 163
Flags in the Dust, 82, 191
Fort Sumpter, 37
Fowler, Doreen, 83

"Genealogy," 197–99
Geographical transubstantiation, 134–35
Gettysburg, Battle of, 98, 192
Go Down Moses, 104
Godden, Richard, 127
Goethe, Wolfgang von, 66, 91
Guetti, James, 56, 119

• 205 •

INDEX

Guinevere, 86
Gwin, Minrose, 56, 89

Haiti, 127, 129, 131
Hamlet, The (Faulkner), 32, 127
Hawkins, E. O., 184
Henri II, 185
Hercules, 30
Hinkle, James, 185
Hodgson, John A., 26
Holder, Alan, 8
Homoeroticism, 100, 191; Henry and Bon, 40, 41, 42, 43, 46, 50, 109–10, 159, 171, 181; Quentin and Shreve, 94–95, 109–10, 148, 159, 171, 176
Hönnighausen, Lothar, 69

Imagery: balloon face, 62, 115, 117, 119, 121, 122–23, 128, 152; barred doors/passages, 115, 122; cocoon, 32, 58, 68, 101; light/dark, 3, 29–30, 69, 70, 80, 136; wistaria, 3, 4, 5, 40, 67
Imagination, as insight, 4–5, 8, 9, 39–40, 98, 99, 108, 110, 150, 156, 171, 181, 182, 188–89
Incest, 38, 43, 45, 86, 165, 167, 174–75, 176, 178, 179, 183, 185, 187, 189
Italics, use of, 8–9, 19, 26–27, 56, 86, 95, 96, 98, 105, 186, 188–89

Jamestown, 114
John V (Count of Armagnac), 184–85
Johnson, Tim, 137
Johnston, Joseph E., 149, 187
Jones, Norman, 72
Joyce, James, 188

Kartiganer, Donald M., 188
King Arthur, 86
Kinney, Arthur, 4, 8, 9
Ku Klux Klan, 74, 78

Lancelot, 86
Le Chat Noir, 36
Lee, Robert E., 12, 34, 89, 149

Light in August, 4, 104, 107, 181
Lilith, 101–2
Lind, Ilse Dusoir, 188
Listening/hearing, 4–5, 7–8, 11, 27, 36, 57, 157
Lurie, Peter, 57, 189

MacLure, Millar, 112
Manassas, Battle of, 192
Marionettes, The, 100
Marlowe, Christopher, 91
Marriage, nature of, 48–49
Melville, Herman, *Billy Budd*, 198
Menelaus, 31
Middle Passage, 130
Milk River, 135
Milton, John, *Paradise Lost*, 7, 91
Mississippi, State of, 38
Mississippi River, 134, 135, 136
Morganatic marriage, 44, 152, 161

Narrative method: collaborative nature of, 95, 154–55, 180; dialogic structure of, 8, 122; instability of, 9, 83, 154–55; speculative nature of, 9–10, 22, 39–40, 56, 84–85, 169–70, 172, 180; speech tags in, 26–27, 56–57, 108, 110; syntactical ambiguity in, 6
Nazism, 140

Odyssey, The, 114
Old Bailey, 14
Original Sin, 14
Ovid, *Metamorphoses*, 89
Owada, Eiko, 127

Pandora, 135
parental relations, 4, 63, 71, 72, 94, 166
Penelope, 97
Pittsburg Landing, Battle of, 52–53, 186
Poe, Edgar Allan: "The Fall of the House of Usher," 39; "The Raven," 5, 157, 194
Poirier, Richard, 10
Priapus, 51

INDEX

Proust, Marcel, *À la Recherche du Temps Perdu*, 67
Pylon, 198
Pyramus, 89–90

Race, 25, 40, 47, 60, 61, 62, 90, 92, 101, 102–3, 104–6, 119–21, 125, 131–32, 143, 165–66, 174, 178–79, 180, 183, 188, 189, 190, 195–96, 197
Ragan, David Paul, 39, 47, 62, 197
Random House, 198–99
Requiem for a Nun, 126
Richard I, 186
Ringold, Francine, 8
"Rose for Emily, A," 4
Rosenzweig, Paul, 145
Rowe, Nicholas, *Fair Penitent*, 43

Sans Souci, 36
Saxon, Lyle, *Fabulous New Orleans*, 47
Schrank, Bernice, 3
Scott, Sir Walter, 38
Scythia, 42
Sewell, Richard, 112
Sexuality, 3–4, 12, 23, 28, 33, 45, 48, 56, 67, 69–70, 76, 79–80, 82, 90, 92–93, 96, 101–2, 152–53, 168, 175–76, 177. *See also* Homoeroticism; Incest; Virginity
Shakespeare, William, 127–28; *Hamlet*, 66, 87, 150; *Macbeth*, 35, 82, 135, 153; "The Phoenix and the Turtle," 188
Sherman, William Tecumseh, 55
Shiloh, Battle of, 52–53, 185, 186
Singleton, Marvin K., 57
Slaves/slavery, 10, 12–13, 17–18, 21, 38, 39, 47, 60, 61, 62–63, 102, 115, 117–18, 119–21, 130, 132, 169
Socrates, 112
Sound and the Fury, The, 4, 23, 35, 45, 48, 49, 82, 86, 97–98, 136, 153, 175, 176, 199
South Carolina, 38
Sowder, William, 112
Stevens, Wallace, "Thirteen Ways of Looking at a Blackbird," 40

Strophe and antistrophe, 8, 19
Sullivan, John L., 22
Sutpen's design, 113, 125, 136, 128, 139–41, 142, 144, 146–49

Thisbe, 89–90
Thousand and One Arabian Nights, A, 43
Title, 3, 154
Truth, nature of, 9, 40, 98, 128, 135, 172, 181, 182
Twain, Mark, *Adventures of Huckleberry Finn*, 114, 120, 121
Tyndareus, 30–31

University Grays, 50, 52, 191
University of Mississippi, 42
Unvanquished, The, 191

Virginity, 6, 23, 43, 45, 52, 70–71, 128–29, 176

Wallace, Lew, *Ben Hur*, 110
Wedgwood, Josiah, 91
West Virginia, 113
Whan, Edgar, 79
Wilde, Oscar, *Salome*, 100

Zeus, 135
Zoellner, Robert, 6